PLATO'S CRAFT OF JUSTICE

SUNY Series in Ancient Greek Philosophy
Anthony Preus, Editor

PLATO'S CRAFT OF JUSTICE

Richard D. Parry

STATE UNIVERSITY
OF NEW YORK
PRESS

Published by
State University of New York Press, Albany

© 1996 State University of New York

Production by Susan Geraghty
Marketing by Bernadette LaManna

Printed in the United States of America

For information, address State University of New York Press,
State University Plaza, Albany, N.Y., 12246

Library of Congress Cataloging-in-Publication Data

Parry, Richard D., 1939–.
    Plato's craft of justice / Richard D. Parry.
        p.   cm.—(SUNY series in ancient Greek Philosophy)
    Includes bibliographical references and index.
    ISBN 0–7914–2731–5 (HC : alk. paper). — ISBN 0–7914–2732–3 (PB :
alk. paper)
    1. Plato—Ethics.   2. Justice (Virtue)   3. Justice (Philosophy)
I. Title. II. Series.
B398.J87P37   1996
172'.2—dc20   95-3471
                                                                            CIP

10 9 8 7 6 5 4 3 2 1

To

Sara Dicey Parry and Lloyd George Parry

CONTENTS

INTRODUCTION

There has been much interest lately in virtue ethics. Part of the reason for this interest is the notion that modern ethical theories concentrate too much on actions, the rules that govern actions, and the consequences of actions. By contrast, virtue ethics concentrates on the person who performs the actions; the focus of its moral assessment is the agent of the action and the dispositions of that agent. In turn, the moral assessment of the agent and her dispositions allows us to make the vital connection between morality and the question of the sort of person the agent is. Virtue ethics makes a clearer link between the issue of morality and the issue of leading a successful human life. In what has turned out to be a long career of teaching bright and inquiring undergraduate students, I have noticed that these students become fascinated with philosophy when it does what it was originally intended to do. In the case of the *Republic,* they appreciate this text at the point where Plato says something important about how to lead a life that one would want to call "worthwhile." Unlike philosophers who seem to be taken up by intellectual puzzles, remote from the trials of negotiating a good life from one end to the other, Plato seems to be taken up with the most important question: what sort of person should I be or become? As I attempted to explicate this aspect of his moral theory, it became increasingly clear to me that the analogy between craft and virtue was the key to understanding what Plato was trying to tell us. The moral life was, just as Socrates had said, a kind of craft performance. The craftsman of the moral life knows the materials with which he works; he knows how to put these materials together so that the result—his life—is not only useful but even elegant. Such a life is happy—prosperous, fortunate, flourishing—because it is the conscious construct of someone with a craftlike knowledge.

However, the use of the notion of craft is not only of historical interest; I believe it also holds much insight for our own understanding of virtue. Perhaps another way of putting the last point

1

is to say that, since Plato found the notion of craft fruitful in his investigations of virtue, it is likely that we also will find it so. Virtue ethics is peculiarly able to locate morality within the context of the project of leading one's life; it makes morality part of the question of what kind of person I want to be—and it does so in a way that seems better than the way in which utilitarian and deontological moral theories do. The superiority of virtue ethics is in the way it can combine other-regarding and self-regarding concerns. Virtue consists of dispositions that are valuable for an individual to have and valuable for others when that individual has them. In turn, if the virtuous life is something like the project of discovering and establishing dispositions that are both self-regarding, in some sense, and other-regarding, in some sense, we might well find some interesting parallels in craft. After all, the latter in some ways seems to be both other-regarding and self-regarding. A horse trainer finds something intrinsically valuable for herself as a horse trainer in exercising her craft, and by doing so she trains a fine horse. Of course, Plato himself subjects the craft analogy in the early dialogues to criticisms. To me the criticisms are only preparatory to Plato's presentation of a refined craft analogy, the one so beautifully set forth in Books IV–VII of the *Republic*. However, some commentators take these early criticisms to be fatal; most other commentators ignore the craft analogy in Plato's mature moral theory. In spite of clear textual evidence to the contrary, these commentators, in effect, miss one of Plato's most fruitful moral insights. Morally successful people are craftlike in arranging their lives; they seem often inspired by ideals beyond the ordinary. They value their lives not because they are pleasant but because they embody these ideals. The ideals have an intrinsic value, which the morally successful person tries to recreate in a craftlike way.

This book differs from contemporary scholarship in that it seeks to bring to light the central role of the craft analogy in Plato's mature moral theory. We see the way in which the craft analogy ties the project of the *Euthydemus, Gorgias, Republic,* and *Symposium* together into a coherent whole. In attempting this reading I am not maintaining that Plato's entire project can be reduced to an explication of the craft analogy. Indeed, as I say, the craft analogy does not even occur in an explicit form in the latter dialogue. What I do maintain is that the craft analogy can be found and consistently traced, and that it is essential to understanding Plato's mature moral theory. Another way to put this project is to say that the craft analogy is one of the keys that Plato left for his intended audience in these dialogues. Our approach to Plato's theory of virtue is through the craft analogy then. As we shall see, Plato develops this theory in three stages or levels. In the first level, Plato elaborates and refines the analogy between craft and virtue. In order to understand the craft analogy, however, we begin, in the earlier dialogues, with the craft of ruling and distinguish that craft from the analogy between craft and virtue. After distinguishing the craft of ruling from the craft analogy we are ready to see the way in which, in *Republic* IV, Plato transforms the craft analogy into a refined version. He does this latter task by incorporating elements of the craft of ruling into the analogy. On this level—our chapters 1 and 2—we see that virtue is a craft of ruling practiced by reason in the soul. However, this account is not complete until Forms are brought into the picture. The introduction of Forms takes us to an entirely different level of Plato's moral theory. On the second level, then, Plato develops the craft of ruling as an imitative craft in which the Forms serve as paradigms or models. Thus, in chapter 3, we see how Forms function as paradigms for the craft of reason's ruling in the soul. However, Plato is still not finished. Not only are Forms paradigms for imitation, they are also the inspiration. This is the third and highest level of Plato's account and the subject of chapter 4. Here we look at the role of the highest Forms—the beautiful itself and the good itself—and the way in which they inspire one to lead a life of virtue.

Thus, while we will approach Plato's theory of virtue through the analogy between craft and virtue, chapter 1 begins with a type of craft, not the craft analogy. Much attention has been devoted to the analogy between craft and virtue; but there is another use of the notion of craft—one that is often confused with the analogy between craft and virtue—the craft of ruling. In the early dialogues there are many significant references to the craft of ruling. For example, ruling is a kind of craft that, according to the first book of the *Republic,* looks out for the welfare of the ruled. It is a central thesis of this book that in order to understand Plato's moral theory, we must start with, and carefully distinguish, the craft of ruling from the craft analogy. Put another way, some of the failure to understand the analogy between craft and virtue rests on the confusion between the craft of ruling and the craft analogy in the earlier dialogues. However, the distinction between the two notions of craft is preparatory to showing that, while they are distinct in the earlier dialogues, in the *Republic* they are combined into a new and powerful craft analogy—an analogy between virtue and the craft of ruling. In our consideration of this craft of ruling, we will concentrate our attention on *Republic* I and *Gorgias*. In these dialogues, Socrates has in mind the craft whereby a ruler manages a city. It is a hallmark of this craft—unlike the craft analogy—that it manages the lives of others. The ruler can be a tyrant, an aristocratic ruler, an elected official in a democracy, or even someone who can sway the crowd in the assembly. Each has a measure of political power; each is a ruler of some sort. Exercising that power successfully is a craft. The issue is what practicing that craft actually means. To some, being a craftsman of political power means using others for one's own welfare. To Socrates, being a craftsman of political power means looking after the welfare of others. As a way of explicating the Socratic notion of the craft of ruling, we will try to present as sympathetically as possible the case for Socrates' somewhat puzzling claim in *Republic* I that ruling is a craft that looks after the welfare of the ruled. What we will find is that the *Gorgias* attempts to address that very claim. However, the defense rests on some other strange claims. In this latter dialogue, the craft of ruling is said to be a craft like medicine; it is therapeutic. While medicine looks after the body, ruling tends the souls of those who are ruled. The craft seeks the welfare of the ruled by establishing or tending to an order and harmony within the souls of those who are ruled; the welfare of these souls turns out to be this order and harmony. Further, in a move fraught with significance, the desires are said to be that in the soul that is ordered and harmonized by the therapeutic craft of soul tending. It can already be seen that the Socratic craft of ruling has many counterintuitive features. We will spend much of chapter 1 explicating those features and testing them.

In the first section of the second chapter, we will look at the craft analogy properly speaking—the analogy between craft and virtue. We will look at its first appearance in the earlier dialogues, especially in the *Euthydemus*. In this dialogue, the analogy is presented in its fullest form; virtue is said to be a craft that manages one's own physical and spiritual assets. For instance, if one has wisdom, then he knows how to manage his beauty, good birth, and wealth so that he is benefited, that is, happy. One's spiritual assets turn out to be such qualities as memory or even types of virtue—for example, courage. As we are told in the *Meno*—in a passage closely paralleling that of the *Euthydemus*—courage, if it is not managed by wisdom, is just a kind of overconfidence. In the *Euthydemus*, the comparison between craft and virtue uses the craft of carpentry as the analogue for virtue. The virtuous person knows his assets in the way that a carpenter knows his tools and materials. The craft analogy differs in two respects from the ruling craft. First, it does not manage the lives of others but one's own life; second, it does not manage one's soul and its desires but one's physical and spiritual assets—beauty, good birth, and wealth or temperance, justice, and courage. Here we have a very suggestive notion. Someone who leads a successful human life must know how to manage her assets so that they actually serve her happiness. Even if one is wealthy or beautiful, it is well known that wealth and beauty can destroy as easily as they can benefit. A successful human being uses these assets in an artful way rather than letting the assets use *her*. She uses her assets well the way a carpenter uses his materials and tools well. The result in the first case is a well-made life; in the second case, the result is a well-made table. As suggestive as it is, however, the notion of virtue as a craft is problematic. Again we will consider some of the problems the analogy presents in this dialogue.

After distinguishing and considering the two notions of craft—the craft of ruling and the analogy between craft and virtue—we are ready to approach the heart of this interpretation. It is a central claim of this interpretation that the theory of virtue given in *Republic* II–IV combines aspects of the craft of ruling and the craft analogy at the same time that it remedies some of the defects our investigation will have turned up. This refinement of the craft analogy is so important a departure from what went before that we will call it "the craft of justice"—the leading virtue in *Republic* IV. As we shall see in chapter 2, Plato's mature doctrine about virtue holds that the craft of justice is a craft of ruling, rather than a manual craft like carpentry (441c ff.). But more important than the shift from carpentry to ruling is the shift from what exercises the craft. In the craft of justice, reason is the practitioner of the craft; reason rules. Thus the craft of justice will have some of the features of the craft of ruling found in *Republic* I and the *Gorgias*. However, this new ruling craft is different from the ruling craft in these latter dialogues; it does not tend to the souls of others but tends to oneself. In that respect, it is like the craft analogy found in the *Euthydemus*. However, it is somewhat different from the craft analogy, which manages one's physical and spiritual assets; the craft of justice manages not one's assets but the nonrational parts of one's soul. The craft of justice is a ruling craft practiced by the reason over the rest of the soul. By tending to one's own soul, the craft of justice provides for one's own benefit and happiness. In order to present justice as a craft of ruling, Plato must give an account of the soul and its parts or subdivisions. We do not need to elaborate that account here. An example of a part—appetites—should suffice to illustrate what Plato means by parts of the soul. In the well-governed soul, then, reason rules over the appetites rather than the appetites ruling over reason. In the well-governed soul, it is reason that makes choices about, for example, one's career or life partner. Such a government is better than one in which the appetite for fancy pastry makes such decisions. Thus, given that there are different parts of one's soul, the craft of justice fits them together so that they do have an order, with one part dominant and the others subordinate. However, the order is not just for the benefit of the dominant part; there is also a harmony of the parts so that each can be said to express itself within the order. Thus one achieves a craftlike blending of the parts.

At this point we have finished the first level of Plato's moral theory. However, the theory of virtue in Book IV of the *Republic* is not complete, as Plato himself notes. Establishing order in the parts of the soul, under the guidance of reason, entails knowledge of the Forms. In introducing the Forms into his account, Plato enters the second level of his moral theory. The craft of reason's ruling in the soul requires knowledge of the Forms as does the craft of ruling in the city. In adding the Forms to the account of virtue, Plato is extending the craft analogy. The craft of justice is not only a therapeutic craft; it is also imitative. The *Cratylus* gives a picture of the way in which craft uses a paradigm—a model to which the craftsman looks for guidance in his production of, for example, a weaver's shuttle. The same notion comes out in *Republic* VI, where the philosophical ruler looks at the Forms of justice, temperance, and beauty to establish virtue in his own soul and in the city; the ruler is explicitly compared to a painter who looks at a model in his production of an image (500c ff.). This second level of Plato's theory is also the focus of the third chapter.

This chapter takes the notion of Forms as paradigms in a literal sense. Forms exhibit, in some way, the property the philosophical ruler is to imitate; thus Forms are paradigms of which particulars are copies. However, it is the thesis of this chapter that we must understand the relation between paradigm and copy in terms of the rather different relation between reality and appearance. Plato combines these two different kinds of relation in Book VI where, in order to imitate the Form paradigms, the philosopher must be able to distinguish between reality and appearance (484c–d). While the combination of these two relations presents notorious difficulties, we get at least some new light on those difficulties in the treatment of chapter 3, where Forms are not only the object of an epistemological quest but also the objects of craftlike imitation. Up to this point, the craft of justice has been presented as imitative. So far, the Forms are paradigms in the sense that they are patterns we imitate; Forms are something like elaborate instructions about how to build a life. However, at this point, Plato's craft of justice enters another level. Besides being patterns we imitate, Forms also inspire imitation; they are the objects that motivate one's becoming virtuous. Unlike blueprints or instructions, the Forms not only describe what is to be instantiated; in a way they prescribe it as well. The Forms do not model a psychic state of affairs that we otherwise desire; they tell us what to desire. How Forms can be the objects that motivate becoming virtuous takes us to the third level of Plato's account.

In chapter 4, we explicate the way in which the highest Forms inspire the acquisition of virtue. Beginning with the central books of the *Republic*, we give an account of the notion that the Form of goodness is the final cause for imitating the Form of justice. The Form of goodness is the final cause in the sense that it is the object of desire, love, or admiration. This desire, love, or admiration, in turn, motivates imitation or propagation. In *Republic* VI, Plato touches on this issue very quickly. At 490b–c, he casts the philosopher as a lover of reality whose desire is fulfilled when he attains the Forms and thus begets (*gennēsas*) intelligence and truth. Later Socrates says, in reference to the philosopher's contemplation of the Forms of temperance and justice, that one cannot help imitating what one admires (*agamenos*), thereby becoming virtuous (500c–d). Another key passage at the end of Book VII shows that the Form of good, whose preeminent role is introduced in Book VI, becomes the inspiration for the philosopher's pursuit of justice in the city (540a–b). Thus the third level of Plato's account shows that one does not understand how the Form of justice is a paradigm until one sees it in its proper relation to the Form of good. In the sequel we explicate this important relation. Nevertheless, even from the present limited perspective, one can better understand the importance of the craft of justice as an imitative craft. The craft of justice imitates, in one's soul and in the city, the Form of justice. In turn, the latter is valuable to imitate because of its necessary relation to the Form of good. Thus, in this interpretation, the Form of good itself is the ultimate justification for imitation. There is a sense in which imitating the just itself is done for the sake of the good itself; imitating the just itself is a way of disseminating goodness and goodness deserves, even requires, dissemination. We use this account to address the problem of the reluctant philosophical ruler—the philosopher who is tempted to withdraw from public life in order to contemplate the Form of goodness; imitation, inspired by the Form of goodness, is motivation enough for the philosopher to assume rule in the city. In these passages the Form of goodness has become the object of admiration and thereby exerts a quickening effect on the philosopher.

However, this aspect of Plato's moral theory receives its fullest treatment in the *Symposium*. In this dialogue, we leave the public and practical context of the *Republic* for the deeper concerns of personal motivation. In this dialogue, it is the Form of the beautiful that is the inspiration for true virtue; this account in the *Symposium* is almost breathtaking in its novelty. We find out that within the soul the true motive force for acquiring virtue is *erōs*; that is, the consuming and possessing passion, whose chief effect usually is the abandonment of virtue, is actually to become the force that moves one to acquire virtue. Obviously, to fulfill this unaccustomed and unexpected role, the concept of *erōs* must undergo a transformation. In the *Symposium* Diotima transforms the concept of *erōs* from that of a consuming and possessing drive to a creative one. The object of love is to "bring forth in the beautiful"; the physical lover begets children with a woman and the spiritual lover begets virtue in the soul of the beautiful boy. However, it is not enough to have transformed the concept of *erōs*, Diotima also proposes a discipline that will perfect the practice of this new concept of *erōs*. In her narrative of the mysteries of *erōs*, she tells Socrates that one must give up humanly beautiful objects of love—women and beautiful boys—in order to love the perfect object, the Form of the beautiful. Finally the lover of the Form brings forth not physical children nor the mere image of virtue but true virtue. In this way Diotima perfects *erōs* into a kind of love whose highest expression is love of the Form of beauty; by inspiring this love, the Form is the object that motivates the lover's becoming virtuous.

In this account there is contained a claim that is the burden of the third level of Plato's account. In order to explain this somewhat fantastic transformation and perfection of *erōs*, Diotima uses a problematic argument based on immortality. Later, we will analyze the problems of the argument closely. Here suffice it to say that we resolve the problems by interpreting the argument as making a profound point about the motivation of the perfected lover of the Form of beauty. Analyzed, the argument makes a point similar to one made in the account of the good itself as final cause, found in the *Republic*. The true lover brings forth virtue under the inspiration of the Form of beauty; he propagates beauty—in this case the beauty of virtue—out of love for the beautiful itself. The beautiful itself becomes the final cause of his actions because it is the object—but not the aim—of his desire. In this way, the philosophical lover of the *Symposium* is analogous to the philosophical ruler of the *Republic*. In both, the final cause is the Form—in one case beauty and in the other goodness. Imagine two seekers after virtue. The first believes having virtue in the soul is the highest good that one can have and values the Form as a means to having virtue. She has a lofty sense of what constitutes her own welfare but, still, it is her own welfare that is the supreme good. The Form is a means to gaining that good because it is a pattern—like a blueprint—that shows her how to obtain what she already desires. She already knows what the supreme good is, she just wants to know how to achieve it. She does not love the Form in itself; she values it as a means to her goal. The second believes that the Form of beauty is the highest object of love, the supreme good. In loving the Form, she becomes virtuous. Virtue is a great good for her; it is after all happiness. However, virtue is a great good because of its relation to the Form of beauty; it is the effect of loving the Form. The Form, as it were, is the ultimate source of the value of virtue. Virtue may be valuable in many other ways. It may be pleasant. It may constitute one's happiness. It may be the foundation of goodness in the city. None of those values is inconsiderable. Ultimately, however, virtue is valuable because of its relation to the Form of beauty. The motivation of the second aspirant is different from that of the first; for the second aspirant, the Form of beauty is the final cause for her acquiring virtue in her soul.

I first studied closely the moral theory of the *Republic* with Professor David Falk, at the University of North Carolina at Chapel Hill, in 1965. Through his detailed analysis, I came to appreciate that the text, though brief and compact, was rich with much wisdom about the moral life. Later, in 1975, I was able to consider the same material under the patient guidance of Professor Gregory Vlastos in his Summer Seminar for College Teachers, sponsored by the National Endowment for the Humanities. I was fascinated by what we, in both seminars, read together. It seemed to me that there was a treasure trove contained in the few pages. But, in those days, most people seemed to read them very quickly and dismissed them as quickly. Since then I have taught many undergraduate courses, two graduate courses, and four Summer Seminars for School Teachers, sponsored by the National Endowment for the Humanities, all of which featured Plato's moral theory. In each I have found new insights into the depth and extent of the role of the craft analogy in that theory. This book is an attempt to articulate those insights. In this long *agōn*, there are several people whose kind help has been greatly prized and much appreciated. First of all, my bright and hard-working students at Agnes Scott College have kept me attentive to the important questions. The Professional Development Committee at Agnes Scott College, and its predecessors, have funded various aspects of this project over the years. The stipend from the President's Award for Excellence in Teaching afforded one particularly delightful summer of writing. Professor Gerard Elfstrom, Department of Philosophy at Auburn University, generously read and critiqued a earlier version of this manuscript. Professor Anthony Preus also provided valuable criticisms of an earlier manuscript. Early on Professor Louis Dupré of Yale University offered crucial encouragement for this project. I wish to thank Jean McDowell, who fixed the bibliography and notes, with her usual efficiency and acuity. Last of all, Susan McConnell Parry—not only in this project but in the larger and infinitely more important project—has been both inspiration and companion.

CHAPTER 1

Craft of Ruling
in Republic I and Gorgias

One of the most intriguing themes in the early dialogues is that of craft (*technē*).[1] Plato easily uses craft as a way of explicating several kinds of endeavor, especially virtue. For instance, in Book I of the *Republic* Socrates introduces, in his conversation with Polemarchus, the notion of craft to explicate the way in which justice—in Polemarchus' sense of the latter term—is useful (332e). Although he invokes the notion without any explanation, neither Polemarchus nor the other listeners finds anything strange about explicating justice by citing ship's pilots, farmers, and cobblers. In turn, when Thrasymachus enters into the dialogue it is Thrasymachus himself who uses craft to explicate his notion of justice, although his use is significantly different from Socrates' (340d). Again, the interlocutors find it natural to compare the ruler to the physician, the calculator, and the schoolmaster, even when Thrasymachus characterizes these occupations with the general term *craftsman* (*dēmiourgos*).

Plato's use of craft to illustrate various aspects of virtue is frequently called the "craft analogy." Usually an analogy compares two things—in this case activities—on some points of similarity, even though the two are actually different kinds of activities—for example, an analogy between stock trading and football. We turn to the craft analogy properly speaking in the next chapter when we will consider Plato's craft of justice. As preparation, in this chapter, we investigate a use of the notion of craft that is clearly not an analogy.

At the beginning of this chapter we referred to two instances in *Republic* I where craft was used to explicate justice—Socrates' conversation with Polemarchus and then his conversation with Thrasymachus. In fact, only the former is the craft analogy in the sense in which commentators usually use the phrase. The latter is not an analogy at all but the investigation of the concept of ruling as a craft. This distinction between the craft of ruling and the craft analogy is central to our major thesis. It depends on some obvious differences between the way Socrates talks about the craft analogy and the craft of ruling. The most important difference is in the objects of the two crafts—that is, what they work on. As we shall see, when virtue is compared to craft its object is the person who practices the craft. The craft analogy depends on one's management of one's assets in order to become happy. However, in *Republic* I—and in the *Gorgias*—Socrates holds that the ruling craft looks after others, not the one who practices the craft. Indeed, that difference is the bone of contention with Thrasymachus—as it is with Callicles in the *Gorgias*. This craft of ruling is built upon the notion of a craft that takes care of the souls or virtue of others. In the *Apology* (20a) Socrates presents Evenus of Paros as making such claims about virtue. In the *Crito*, Socrates, assuming there to be expert knowledge of the just and unjust, the honorable and dishonorable, and the good and the bad, says that he and Crito should listen to that expert rather than the multitude lest they harm their souls (47d). In the *Laches* Socrates hypothesizes a craft knowledge that looks after the souls of the young (185e).[2]

We will begin our consideration of Plato's moral theory, therefore, by investigating the craft of ruling. In this chapter, first of all, we will explore Socrates' account of the craft of ruling in *Republic* I and *Gorgias*, as well as some of the problems generated by this account, especially the claim that ruling seeks the welfare of the ruled. Then part of our goal in the next chapter will be to investigate the craft analogy as that phrase is usually understood, that is, the way that, in the early dialogues, Socrates uses craft to explicate virtues—for example, wisdom in the *Euthydemus* and justice in his conversation with Polemarchus in *Republic* I. We call this use of craft the "craft of virtue." As with the craft of ruling, we will consider some of the problems with the craft of virtue. This investigation of the craft of ruling and the craft of virtue will set the stage for our consideration of Plato's theory of justice in *Republic* II–IV. Finally, we will be in the position to see that in the latter books Plato brings together these two uses of the notion of craft into his mature theory of justice and in so doing addresses some of the problems our investigation will have uncovered. What we find in this chapter is that there is in *Republic* I and in the *Gorgias* a craft of ruling, although its nature is not uncontroversial.[3]

Using *Republic* I and *Gorgias* we will outline Plato's account of this craft; it is a rich account with many interesting details. The salient feature of this account is the claim that the ruling craft seeks the welfare of the ruled. In our exposition we first consider it in *Republic* I. In the *Gorgias* the claim is more elaborate; there we find that the welfare sought for the ruled is the perfection of their souls.[4] More significant still, Socrates says that perfection is defined as order and harmony among the desires.

Since this order and harmony is also said to be virtue, what we see here is the extremely important notion that virtue is an order among the desires of the soul. Of course, in Greek the word that we translate as "virtue" also means "excellence." Socrates is introducing the fruitful idea that excellence for a human being is a certain order within the soul, an order that includes the desires. Of course, that order is also connected, in unspecified ways, to what we call "moral virtue." But the idea that excellence—human perfection—is, or at least includes, some sort of order among the desires is intrinsically interesting. It is a psychological account of the good for human beings. Instead of the good being the possession of certain goods, or a certain standing within the city, or the ability to accomplish certain goals, it is shown to be fundamentally a state of the soul. Plato's account of this order and harmony among the desires is somewhat elusive. Using recent scholarship we attempt to reconstruct it. Although this reconstructed account is necessarily somewhat speculative, it does give us an idea of the kind of thing Plato had in mind when he talked about order and harmony among the desires of the soul. Order and harmony in the soul is a notion that will be seen again in *Republic* IV, although there Plato's moral psychology will have become more complex. Nevertheless, the notion of order and harmony in the soul will remain paramount. It is important then to attempt to understand this psychic harmony, and the way the ruling craft promotes it, in its first appearance in the *Gorgias*. We will then be better able to understand how the craft of ruling becomes the craft of justice.

I

In the early dialogues Socrates talks about all kinds of crafts (*technai*). He uses them, of course, to illustrate various philosophical points.[5] What I wish to do here is to dwell on the notion of craft as it occurs in these illustrations without concentrating on the philosophical points for which these occurrences are illustrations. In the early dialogues, then, Socrates mentions, among others, horse training, medicine, physical training, huntsmanship, farming, shepherding, building, geometry, calculation, and even shoemaking, working in brass, wood and wool.[6] In fact, once we see this profusion, we might be tempted to think that not all of these activities are crafts. Part of our problem has to do with translation. The Greek word *technē* can be translated as craft, or skill, or art; each word shows a different emphasis. To us, contemporary English speakers, craft seems to mean largely handicraft—a practice that has a material product. In this sense of craft we would include building, shoemaking, and working in brass, wood, and wool. On the other hand, we might call geometry and calculation "skills," hoping to mark the distinction that these have no material product. Of course, we should recall that building and shoemaking, working in brass, wood, and wool can also be called "skills." Again, we might call medicine and horse training "arts," perhaps in an attempt to distinguish their greater finesse. In doing so, perhaps we would be trading on a notion of fine art in which finesse is most often seen. However, fine art is not a notion held by the ancient Greeks. It is not that they lacked painting, music, and poetry; rather, they did not have a separate word, or phrase, to distinguish them from the other *technai*. In what follows we will continue to translate *technē* as "craft"; but we will stipulate that craft has the following features, found in Plato's early and middle dialogues.

First of all, there is the end of the craft, what the craft provides. The Greek word *ergon* is used to indicate the end of the craft; literally meaning "work," *ergon* harbors the ambiguity between function and result. In the *Euthydemus* (291e), medicine provides health and farming provides food from the earth. Health is the *ergon* of medicine in the sense that providing health is its function; of course, the health of the patient is the *ergon* in the sense of result. Food is the *ergon* of farming in the sense that producing food is its function while the food is its product. In the *Charmides*, Critias denies that computation has an *ergon* in the way in which a house is the product of the activity of building. But the transitional dialogue *Gorgias* shows that computation has an *ergon* in some other sense (453e). Indeed, it would be impossible to conceive of a craft without some goal since craft is a systematic and reasoned way of achieving a goal.

In contrast to crafts like calculation, the crafts Plato most frequently used are ones that have objects on which they work, on which they carry out their function. The objects can be either inanimate or animate (*Gor.* 503e1–504b10). This distinction among objects allows a distinction among crafts and their functions and goals. When objects are inanimate, the function of the craft is to produce them and its goal is a separate material object (cf. *Charm.* 165e5–166a1, 170b12–c4; *Prot. 319b5–c1*; *Euthyd.* 281a1–4). When the objects are animate, the function of the craft is not to produce them but to improve or perfect them; the goal, then, is the improved state of the object (cf. *Apo.* 20a6–b2; *Gor.* 464b3 ff.). Thus, while the goal of farming is food, the goal of medicine is health; food, as a material object, is clearly a different kind of result from health. We shall call the former crafts "productive" and the latter "therapeutic." The therapeutic crafts care for or tend an object; they provide *therapeia*, as the following examples illustrate. The physician, of course, provides care for the body *(Rep.* 341c). The shepherd tends the sheep (*Rep.* 345c). The horseman tends the horses and the huntsman tends the dogs (*Euthyphro* 13a). *Epi*—a preposition meaning "over," "for," or "having to do with"—is used to indicate the objects of such crafts. In the *Gorgias* (464b), the four crafts of legislating, judging, physical training, and medicine, are divided into pairs, "the first pair has to do with (is *epi*) the soul . . . the other pair has to do with (is *epi*) the body." In the *Republic* (345d) reference is made to shepherding, whose job is to provide the best for that over (*epi*) which it is set.

In the early dialogues, Plato tends to use craft (*technē*) interchangeably with knowledge (*epistēmē*).[7] The interchangeability implies that craft, like all knowledge, reliably produces results. Moreover, knowledge in the context of craft does not mean just knowing how to accomplish the goal of the craft, but includes a theoretical component as well. In the *Apology* (22d), craftsmen are said to know what they do because they can explain their craft; presumably they can explain why they do what they do. In the *Gorgias* (465a; 501a), Socrates says that craft can give a rational account of the nature of what it prescribes. We get an insight into this explanation in the *Charmides* (165c4–e1), where it is said that each craft has knowledge (*epistēmē*) of the goal of the craft. Craft can explain its procedure because it knows what its goal is

and how to go about accomplishing it. This theoretical component may explain what, for Plato, is perhaps the most significant
feature of craft—its ability to produce results with a high degree
of reliability. Indeed, in *Republic* I, Socrates' argument at 342a
seems to imply that craft never fails, only the craftsman. This
infallibility of craft is echoed in other dialogues. Craft knowledge
has such a high degree of reliability presumably because it has
established a theoretical connection between its goal and its procedure.[8] Of course, even Plato knew that a craft does not always
produce the expected results. Physicians do not always obtain a
cure. However, one way to explain this failure is to say that the
theory of the craft is correct and that its failure is due to the vicissitudes of applying the theory to cases.[9] To the usual crafts of
medicine, horse training, shepherding, farming, and building,
Socrates adds that of ruling. In some ways this addition seems to
be surprising. It is not clear that ruling has the characteristics of a
craft. In *Republic* I, Socrates and Thrasymachus are at odds precisely over what the goal of ruling is, for instance. Indeed, it is not
obvious who the practitioners of the craft of ruling might be or
where one might go to learn the craft. Nevertheless, Socrates, in
Republic I and in *Gorgias*, treats ruling as a craft, not just as an
analogue for craft.

When Thrasymachus introduces the precise notion of a ruler
(*Rep.* 340e) he uses the general concept of a craftsman and
deduces from that general concept a conclusion about the ruler. In
this case ruling seems to be at least a species of craft. However, in
a subsequent passage, craft seems to be a species of ruling. When
Socrates argues that the ruler, precisely speaking, does not seek his
own advantage but the advantage of the ruled, he uses an elaborate and rather full argument in which he makes the generalization
that all crafts rule (*archousi*) and are stronger than that over
which they rule. Then he says that no craft seeks the advantage of
the stronger but that of the weaker over which it exercises rule
(342c). He then applies that generalization successively to a series
of craftsmen, ending with the ruler (341c–342e). Finally, the general account of craft in the *Gorgias* does not treat ruling—that is,
judging and legislating—as analogous to craft but as a craft (*Gor.*
464b–465e).

The claim in *Republic* that all crafts rule is a little puzzling.
Indeed, in the *Euthydemus* (291e), Socrates says that the physician
is a ruler; but he also says that the farmer is a ruler. Such an odd

statement seems to presuppose that all crafts rule. Of course, the Greek word for ruling, *archein*, means to begin something; Aristotle says that rulers are origins of movement and change (*Metaphysics* Book V, 1013a10). But Plato seems to be using a sense of ruler that includes more than being the origin of change. Of course, since, in the *Republic*, all of his examples are of therapeutic crafts, perhaps his meaning there is that all therapeutic crafts rule; that certainly is all that is needed for his argument to work. Now, it seems natural to think of therapeutic crafts as exercising rule over their objects. After all, physicians, horse trainers, and sea captains issue orders and commands, as do kings, aristocrats, and oligarchs. Moreover, the objects of these crafts are animate beings over whose lives the craftsmen exercise some control. His use of therapeutic crafts in this context does show a preoccupation of Plato's. He wishes to assimilate the craft of ruling to therapeutic craft, in order to make what he takes to be a vital point about ruling—that it, like therapeutic craft, cares for its object. He wishes to make the claim that ruling, like therapeutic craft, looks out after the welfare of its object.

II

Having said this much by way of introduction, we can turn to the second part of our task. We can begin investigating what appears to be a highly implausible claim about the ruling craft. In *Republic* I Socrates argues that craft, because of its perfection, never seeks its own advantage but always the advantage (*sympheron*) of that over which it is set (342b). In the terminology of the previous section, we could say that, according to Socrates, ruling has as its object the ruled—those over whom it is set—and as its end, their welfare. The argument depends on the assumption that a craft never seeks its own advantage because it does not have any defect (342a). To contemporary ears, the assumption sounds strange, especially when Plato illustrates it with the example of medicine—the craft of the physician. To us, medicine is always in need of improvement; indeed, scientific experimentation is the established method for medicine to improve its principles and practice. For Plato, however, it is as though the craft of medicine were perfect and all fault lies with the practitioner (cf. *Euthyd.* 280a). As we have just seen, the reason for this view is that, at this point, Plato takes craft to be a knowledge (*epistēmē*); as knowledge it cannot be mistaken. Thus, as a craft, medicine's theory is correct; any failure comes in the application of the theory. In any event, it is not necessary for our purposes to go into the intricacies of this somewhat obscure argument.[10] Rather, we will concentrate on the claim, made in the argument, that craft seeks always the advantage of that over which it is set. It is this claim to which Thrasymachus objects in his answer to Socrates, while he ignores the argument that leads to it. This claim is, of course, at the very heart of Socrates' disagreement with Thrasymachus; with this conclusion, Socrates will maintain that Thrasymachus is wrong when he asserts that justice is the advantage of the stronger.[11] And yet, it seems like such a slender reed.

Thrasymachus has just offered a view that holds that the craft of ruling is completely self-serving. It is a view that can be compared to views of our own contemporaries—for example, the Marxist thesis that class rule is simply the rule that works only for the advantage of the class in power. In dividing up scarce resources the ruling class always gets more than its share; moreover, it contrives to write the laws and promulgate the morality that sanction and mystify this advantageous position.[12] Some feminists, using Marxist categories, have substituted gender rule for class rule; in their analysis, men have created the laws and morality to mask, as legal and right, what is really nothing more than male domination. Thrasymachus' position is just a generalization: whoever is in power—men, women, capitalists, or proletarians—defines justice in terms of its own advantage. Unlike Marxists, who see the proletarian revolution as the prelude to a classless (and repressionless) society, Thrasymachus seems to see no end to repression and exploitation.[13]

One may share Socrates' abhorrence for Thrasymachus' idea of justice as a moral and legal system that aims only at the advantage of those in power; but one tends to sympathize with Thrasymachus' impatient objection to Socrates' counterclaim that the craft of ruling always looks out after the advantage of the ruled:

> . . . you think that the shepherds and the cattle herders look out
> after the good of the sheep and cattle and fatten them and care
> for them with any other good in view than their own good and
> their masters'. (343b)

Here, Thrasymachus is making the welfare of the rulers the end of the craft, while the object of the craft seems to remain the ruled. While this view of the craft of ruling goes counter to the way craft has so far been presented in the dialogues, it does have the ring of empirical truth to it. On the other hand, Socrates seems to be using a somewhat sentimental definition of the craft of ruling in order to read out of court Thrasymachus' realistic, perhaps even empirical, claim that rulers are self-seeking and venal. One is sympathetic with Thrasymachus because Socrates seems oblivious to all of the political chicanery surrounding him. Socrates sounds like a civics teacher who has no grasp of the reality of democratic politics; he might be on the verge even of claiming that those people who hold power in order to aggrandize themselves and their cohorts are not really rulers at all.[14] To Thrasymachus, such a claim would sound hopelessly naive.

The trouble with Thrasymachus' objection, however, is that it seems not to get to the heart of the disagreement between himself and Socrates. And it is Socrates' answer to this objection that gives us this impression:

> . . . but you think that one who shepherds the sheep, insofar as he is a shepherd, does not look out after what is best for the sheep; but it is as though he were a banqueter and was looking forward to a good feast; or again to selling them, as though he were a businessman and not a shepherd. But there belongs to the shepherding craft no other concern than the way in which it can provide the best for that over which it is set. (345c–d)

As an answer to Thrasymachus' objection, this argument might seem to be only a reiteration of Socrates' original position, as though he were trying to get Thrasymachus to see what he had failed to see before. Yet Socrates' answer is not a reiteration. There has occurred a shift between Socrates' original claim and this one. The original claim said that a craft seeks the advantage (*to sympheron*) of that over which it is set; the present claim says that a craft seeks what is best (*to beltiston*) for the thing over which it is set. Although there is a clear shift in the text from *to sympheron* to *to beltiston*, that fact alone does not mean that Plato recognized a shift in meaning. However, intended or not, the shift does strengthen Socrates' argument with Thrasymachus, as we shall see. Moreover, as we shall see, in the *Gorgias* where these matters are taken up again, *to beltiston* plays an important role in the argument. For now, let us see what difference the shift makes in this argument. I will show that there can be a distinction between to *sympheron*—which is translated in these passages as "advantage"—and to *beltiston*—which is translated in these passages as "what is best."[15]

Socrates might be referring to something like the following when he introduces to *beltiston* in place of to *sympheron*. The shepherd who sought the advantage or the welfare of the sheep could do so by seeking their contentment. He would see that they led long and languid lives, in pastures with plenty of clover bordered by clear cool water. The goal for this shepherd would be to raise fat sheep who mated with whomever they desired and when they desired. For whatever reason, these sheep would become something like outdoor house pets. On the other hand, the shepherd who sought what is best for the sheep would seek to make the sheep the best sheep according to standards for sheep raising. And, as we all know, what makes them content will not always be what is best for the sheep. Put another way, the shepherd would be seeking the perfection of the sheep as agricultural specimens. Accordingly, these sheep would be subject to a certain regimen. There might be some kinds of greenery they should not eat if their fleece is to shine in the preferred way; certainly their breeding habits would have to be controlled so the lambs would have certain bodily characteristics the judges would find outstanding.

In using this notion of perfection, Socrates seems to be pointing out an important aspect of craftsmanship. There is among craftsmen a kind of liking for the perfection of their objects that is a part of their attitude toward their craft. Craftsmen take satisfaction in and admire a job well done; they take satisfaction, then, in the object of the craft being put in its best possible shape by the craft.[16] This attitude is sometimes called the "pride of craftsmanship." This pride is personal since it is pride over one's own performance. But there is a nonpersonal element in the craft. This nonpersonal element is seen in a craftsman's admiration of another craftsman's job well done. There is a love of the well-wrought work. This love of the well-wrought work determines the goal of the craft since it is by seeking the perfection of the object that the object becomes the well-wrought work. Perhaps the limiting case of this seeking the perfection of the object is given in the account of Hephaestus' making Achilles' armor at *Iliad* XVIII, line 462 ff. One of the important consequences of seeking the perfection of the object is a disinterested attitude towards the personal gain of the craftsman; it precludes the craftsman from turning out an inferior product just because doing so, for instance, would speed-up his work and bring in more money from an unsuspecting public. The love of the well-wrought work is not disinterested, of course, when it comes to the success of the craft itself. But the craftsman's pursuing the success of the craft, or even pursuing his own success as a craftsman, just is his pursuing the perfection of the object. Moreover, the person who does not have this pride of craftsmanship is said not to have that craft at all: "He's not a surgeon; he's a butcher."

In the passage from *Republic* I (346e) we have been considering, Socrates gives a negative characterization of this attitude of disinterestedness. Socrates says that the craft of ruling is so disinterested that people have to be paid to do it:

> For these reasons, beloved Thrasymachus, as I was just now saying, no one willingly chooses to rule and to take into hand others' problems to set them aright. Rather he demands a reward, because the one intending to practice a craft well never does so for his own improvement (*to beltiston*); nor when taking charge by means of the craft, does he take charge for his own improvement but for that of the one who is ruled. (346 e)

In fact, it is this disinterested attitude that makes it necessary to have another craft to deal with the welfare of the craftsman, that is, the wage-earning craft. The ruler is so intent on what is best (*to beltiston*) for his subjects that he would get no reward for himself if he did not get paid.

While Socrates does not in this passage invoke the positive sense of the pride of craftsmanship, I believe that notion sheds light on the attitude of self-disinterest that he does invoke. If we see the self-disinterest as a result of the craftsman's seeking the perfection of his object, we can understand the motivation of the craftsman much better. He is motivated by a desire to see the object of his craft put in the best possible shape as defined by his craft. This account makes the self-disinterested ruler seem less like a saint who sacrifices himself for the welfare of his subjects and more like a carpenter or horse-trainer. Thus, it makes Socrates' claim somewhat more plausible.

Moreover, if this disinterested pursuit of perfection is a defining feature of craft, it is harder for Thrasymachus to argue that ruling is self-seeking in the way he means for it to be. Even if ruling were a craft of looking out for one's own welfare, the welfare would have to be understood to be one's own perfection according to some standard of the craft. Given Thrasymachus' ideas of the value of ruling for the ruler, it hardly seems likely that that value would include anything that might be thought of as perfection of oneself.[17] Still, using this notion of craft it might not be impossible for Thrasymachus to argue that the ruling craft is self-seeking, even in his sense—for example, that perfection of self entails having power and wealth— but it would be a good deal more difficult than his previous argument. As well, understood according to the present interpretation, the second claim—that the craftsman seeks the perfection of his object—stands up to Thrasymachus' objection in a way that the first does not. Using an analogy with shepherds, Thrasymachus objected that the shepherds and neatherds had *only* their own good and that of their masters in view. But if a craft seeks the perfection of an object, the shepherd, as a practitioner of the craft of the shepherd, does not seek *only* his own good and that of his master. He seeks the perfection of the sheep according to the rules of shepherding. That is a craft and talent all its own. The motivation to pursue it is his pride in the quality of his sheep; and a shepherd imbued with the love of his craft would seek this quality in his sheep at considerable sacrifice to himself, if necessary. Such a craftsman does not seek *only* his own good but the goals of his craft, which can be different from his own in some important cases. For instance, such a craftsman would find immobilizing sheep in feed pens abhorrent, even if it maximized profits.[18] Similarly, rulers who seek only their own welfare ignore the dynamic of the craft of ruling, which seeks to make the subjects better in some sense.

Perhaps we can see this latter point if we use the contemporary notion of legitimacy. When self-seeking is seen to be the only goal of a group of rulers, they lose legitimacy. To lose legitimacy is to lose the position of being a ruler in anything but name only; such rulers are not *really* rulers. Indeed, the point of much Marxist and Marxist-inspired analysis is to show that the entire goal of class or gender rule is simple self-aggrandizement for the class or gender in power. Such an exposé automatically robs that form of rule of legitimacy—at least in the eyes of those who are not in power. Legitimate rule must seek more than the advantage of the rulers; it must improve—in some sense—those who are ruled. In contemporary parlance, we might say that Socrates is raising the issue of the legitimacy of a ruler. While Thrasymachus is saying that the only goal of a ruler is self-advantage, if he had had the concept, Socrates could have said that the legitimacy of a ruler is based on his ability to exercise the craft of ruling. In turn, the craft of ruling is based on the ability to improve the objects of the craft, that is, those who are ruled. Of course, the contemporary notion of legitimacy implies something about the obligation of the ruled to accept rule—and the loss of obligation with loss of legitimacy; such a notion seems foreign to Socrates. Nevertheless, with his account of the craft of ruling, he does seem to be raising the possibility that some people who call themselves rulers are not *really* rulers. Like our contemporaries, Socrates is saying that if the rulers do not seek to improve the ruled in some way, they are not *really* rulers—not so much because the ruled no longer have an obligation to accept their rule but because the rulers are no longer true practitioners of the craft of ruling.

However, having argued that there is a shift in Socrates' argument from saying that the ruling craft seeks welfare to saying that it seeks perfection, we should not be taken to mean that the shift is total. Socrates means only a shift in emphasis because he does not mean to abandon the claim that the ruling craft seeks the welfare of the ruled. Surely, Socrates means that ruling seeks the welfare of the ruled by seeking their perfection, that the perfection sought is also the welfare of the ruled. In fact, whether Socrates has made such a shift in his argument, and what is the nature of the relation between perfection and welfare, is unclear, in part, because we do not have any sense of what the perfection (*to beltiston*) sought by craft means in *Republic* I. If we turn to the *Gorgias,* we get a better picture of that perfection brought about by craft, especially if the craft is therapeutic. In the *Gorgias* the craft of ruling is presented in greater detail.[19] Of importance for our project in this chapter, the presentation adds content to the notion of *to beltiston* because it develops a full account of the way in which a craft seeks to improve its object and thereby provide for its welfare. At this point, we will leave aside the dispute between Socrates and Thrasymachus. We do not have to decide whether Socrates is correct in his claim that the ruling craft seeks the welfare of the ruled for our purposes. In the following sections we will concentrate on the way, in Socrates' account, the craft of ruling provides for that welfare by perfecting the ruled. In particular, we will develop the account of the improvement or perfection that the ruling craft confers on the ruled. What we will see is how this perfection is aimed at the soul and its desires. It is at this point that Plato's account begins to be a moral theory—an explanation of that perfection conferred by the ruling craft, both as the good for human beings and the source of moral action.

III

In the *Gorgias*, Socrates holds conversations with the sophist Gorgias and two of his pupils, Polus and Callicles. One of the overarching themes of the dialogue is the contrast between the rhetoric of Gorgias and the philosophy of Socrates. Plato wishes to convey how deleterious the first is and how salutary the second. In his conversation with Polus, Socrates argues that rhetoric is deleterious because it is not a craft (*technē*). In this argument, he presents an elaborate taxonomy of therapeutic crafts designed to show why rhetoric is not a craft.

At 464c in the *Gorgias*, Socrates gives his first account in the dialogue of these therapeutic crafts, an account that he will repeat in his conversation with Callicles later in the dialogue. First there are crafts that care for the body and crafts that care for the soul. Each of these divisions is subdivided into a craft that cares for the healthy and one that cares for the diseased. Thus, we obtain the four therapeutic crafts—physical training, medicine, law making, and judging. Just as physical training has as its object the healthy body and medicine the sick body, law making has as its object the healthy soul and judging as its object the sick soul. These four are characterized as "always providing the best (*aei pros to beltiston therapeuousōn* [464c4]) for the body, on the one hand, and the soul, on the other." It is this seeking *to beltiston* of its objects that sets craft apart from routine (*empeiria*). The latter is a practical technique for achieving an end, without thought for the good of the object. There are four routines—cookery, cosmetic, sophistry, and rhetoric—which are parallel to the four crafts of medicine, gymnastic, judging, and law making. These routines seek after pleasure, always without any thought for *to beltiston* of their objects. As an example, cookery provides pleasantly tasty dishes that can actually ruin the health, while medicine can prescribe a strict diet to make the body healthy. So seeking *to beltiston* is a very important characteristic; it distinguishes craft from routine. The second contrast between craft and routine is that the former has an account (*logon*) to give of the nature of what it prescribes and thus the reasons for prescribing it (465a). This account presumably includes the goal of the craft as well as the means to achieve it—that is, it includes a notion of what the perfection of the object is.

The division of crafts into those directed toward the body and those directed toward the soul is Socrates' way of introducing the issue of the ruling craft, since the crafts directed toward the soul are identified with the ruling craft—or at least the ruling craft as it is found in a democracy—law making and judging. Clearly Socrates has in mind the political functions of his contemporary Athenian citizens. The background of these distinctions is Socrates' concern about the way that sophists and their pupils use rhetoric in the assembly and law courts. He is contrasting their use of rhetoric with the true craft of statesmanship. Sophistic rhetoricians do not seek *to beltiston* for the citizens but only what pleases them—what they want to hear. In the sequel we will trace the development of this account of the craft of ruling through the dialogue, concentrating (for reasons soon to be apparent) on the conversation with Callicles. Obviously, the dialogue is, like all the dialogues of this period, a complex tapestry of themes; the theme of craft is only one strand of the fabric. However, this particular strand can be followed consistently throughout the dialogue. As we shall see, this somewhat theoretical account (at 464a ff. and repeated in an abbreviated form at 501a) is applied and illustrated at important junctures in the dialogue. This account of therapeutic craft is especially illuminating in Socrates' and Callicles' discourse on the role of desires in what we would call "moral psychology."

So first of all we can note that Socrates connects *to beltiston* with the soul. By contrast with the usual rhetorician, the true statesman who speaks in the assembly seeks *to beltiston* of his hearers; the way of accomplishing this goal is to seek to make the souls of his fellow citizens the best they can be. The introduction of the soul as the object of the ruling craft is an important difference between this account of ruling in the *Gorgias* and that in *Republic* I. In the latter dialogue, Socrates said that rulers seek the perfection of those over whom they rule, but that which was to be perfected about the ruled was passed over in silence. Presumably, they were to be perfected as citizens, but what that kind of perfection entailed was not further disclosed. In the *Gorgias*, this lacuna is filled in; it is the soul that is the focus of the political craft. However if making the soul the focus of ruling is an important development in Socrates' account, it also raises to a new level the conflict between him and his opponents. We have already noted, in considering *Republic* I, that Thrasymachus' view of ruling seems overly cynical while Socrates' view seems overly idealistic. In the *Gorgias* the contrast between Polus and Callicles, on the one hand, and Socrates, on the other, seems even greater. Although they do not explicitly articulate it, Polus and Callicles seem to agree with Thrasymachus' view of politics as a highly "realistic" game of power. In the city, there are those who wield power for their own advantage and there are those who are victims of this power. The only important question—the only "real" question—is: who gets the power? By contrast, Socrates in the *Gorgias* sees ruling as a craft whereby the rulers seek to perfect the souls of the ruled. We will learn later that such perfection actually imparts moral virtue. Legislating, which is analogous to gymnastic, builds up virtue in healthy souls; judging, which is analogous to medicine, cures sick souls by restoring virtue. The contrast between the two views could hardly be greater. Socrates' view of ruling as perfecting souls is, to these characters, at best naive.

If Socrates' view is eccentric and naive to his hearers, to us it seems slightly sinister. In our culture, the office of building up virtue we give to ethical and religious teachers; the office of curing sick souls we give to counselors, confessors, psychologists, and psychiatrists. All are professionals we consult voluntarily—in most cases at least. According to Plato, however, it is those who pass the laws who are supposed to be aiming at the perfection of the souls of the citizens; it is the judges who are aiming at the healing of sick souls. Such a theory of politics runs counter to much liberal democratic theory. Modern democratic societies usually aim at regulating behavior that might harm other people. The status of the soul behind the behavior is part of the private life of the citizen and—theoretically at least—is no business of the state. For instance, in modern liberal theory, the state has no interest in psychological conditions of even a self-destructive nature as long as the person with the condition harms no one else. A person may drink himself to death; the state's only interest is to see that he does not harm other people by, for example, driving, brawling, or stealing to support his habit. Plato, on the other hand, would have the state change the drunken soul whether it harmed anyone else or not.

However, in its first appearance in the conversation with Polus, Socrates' use of the craft of ruling does not seem so sinister. In that conversation, Socrates refers to judicial punishment as a way of curing the soul of vice (477e ff.). Judicial punishment is compared to medical treatment—following the account of therapeutic craft; the former removes the ills of the soul while the latter, also painful, removes the ills of the body.[20] Indeed, even in our positivistic culture, there is some sentiment that judicial punishment has some moral purpose. At least, it should convince the criminal not to engage in crime in the future. Insofar as the springs of action are in the soul, the judge can claim to remove evil from the soul. Still, Socrates' use of the account of therapeutic craft in the conversation with Polus leaves many questions unanswered. In particular, if the therapeutic craft of judging removes evil from the soul, we do not know how it does so. We do not know what in the soul constitutes evil, what in the soul is comparable to sickness in the body. As we shall see in the sequel, Socrates eventually locates the sickness of the soul within the desires. Disorder of the desires is that which makes the soul evil; thus, the therapeutic craft of sick souls must concentrate its efforts toward such desires. However, before the dialogue arrives at that important conclusion, it goes through a rather slow and careful preparation. First, in the conversation with Callicles, Socrates introduces the desires as morally problematic, as pathological. Then, in a reprise of the account of therapeutic craft, Socrates makes pathological desires the object of the craft of ruling. So, before we can see how the therapeutic craft of the soul improves the soul, we must see that which in the soul is to be improved—that is, the desires—and their pathological state.

At this point, we can already appreciate that Socrates has set the stage for answering the question about the relation between the perfection and the welfare of those who are ruled. His argument could be something like the following: perfection is, or includes, one's desires being in a certain condition (to be reported in the next section), and this condition of one's desires is also in one's best interest, is one's welfare. Finally, the ruling craft brings that condition of one's desires into the soul. Obviously, then, the concept of desires and their possible good or bad conditions is vitally important for this account of the ruling craft. In the first place, what Plato says about these desires has implications for our understanding of the goal of the craft. As well, this preliminary assessment of desires in the moral life gives us some insight into his ideas about the good human life and happiness. Next, it gives us some insight into the relation between one's desires and virtue. In what follows we will be concentrating on the way Socrates presents, in his sketch of a moral psychology, the role of the desires. In the next three sections we will concentrate on the exchange between Socrates and Callicles and its approach to desires as the source of both moral perfection and personal welfare. We will try to come to closer grips with the way that desires form the basis of Plato's account of the perfection that the ruling craft confers. The account has roughly three stages, all devoted to different aspects of desires and their treatment. First Socrates introduces, with the image of the leaky jars, the notion that desires can be morally problematic; the image portrays desires that have grown insatiable. Next, he gives another view of morally problematic desires and a hint about their treatment in what we call the "medical analogy." Here he says for the first time that treatment of problematic desires should bring about order among the desires. Finally, he turns to the craft of ruling proper—the craft that treats desires— judging, presumably in order to tell us how it brings order to the desires. While his account of the way that judging brings about harmony of desires is disappointingly thin, it has a surprising outcome. In talking about the ruling craft, Socrates betrays his conviction that his own question-and-answer technique—called "elenchus"—is a type of the ruling craft. This fascinating claim gives us yet another view of the way that desires and their harmony contribute to the perfection of human life.

IV

While Socrates does make the desires the focus of his investigation into perfection and welfare, he accomplishes this important departure in his investigation in a somewhat indirect way. First of all, he provokes Callicles in a typically Socratic move. After Callicles has given a measured account of the kind of life that he believes worthy of pursuit—a life of political power—Socrates asks him if he would also include self-rule (491d). In explaining his meaning, Socrates asks whether a political ruler should be temperate (*sōph-*

rona onta), ruling over his own pleasures and desires (*tōn hēdonōn kai epithumiōn archonta tōn en heautōi* [491d11–e1]). The question seems calculated to provoke Callicles to a passionate outburst because Callicles virtually leaps out of his seat, to denounce all such nonsense. Rather, he says,

> the one leading the right sort of life allows his desires to grow as great as possible and does not restrain them (*mē koladzein*); and then he should be up to the task, through courage and wisdom, of supplying these desires, having grown as great as possible, and of filling each of them with whatever it wants. (491e–492a)

Finally, it is luxury, unrestraint (*akolasia*), and freedom of action, backed up by force, which are virtue and happiness (492c).

This outburst gives Socrates leave to make desires the focus of their discussion—and ultimately the focus of the craft of ruling. It is worth noting that making desires the focus in its consideration is an important development in Plato's moral theory. It may be commonplace for us to think that moral well being includes desires that are themselves well disposed. However, it is significant that the earlier dialogues that deal with the ruling craft (and—as we shall see—those that deal with the analogy between craft and virtue) do not see the desires as the ingredients of virtue. Neither the soul nor its desires are the object of these crafts. It is the genius of the *Gorgias* and the *Protagoras* to have located the discourse about moral perfection at the level of desires.

Socrates adopts Callicles' notion of unrestrained desires (*akolastos*), but he makes them out to be insatiable and tiresome instead of good. In replying to Callicles' notion of the good life, Socrates draws an analogy between desires and jars. Some people's desires are like sound jars: although the liquids needed to fill them, for example, honey and wine, are difficult to acquire, once filled up, these jars remain that way. Other people's desires are like leaky jars: they can never be filled and one must labor day and night to keep liquid in them. It is clear that Socrates means to identify the latter kinds of desires with Callicles' notion of unrestrained desire and that he means to recommend the life in which desires are like the sound jars. Callicles does not object to the image of the leaky jars probably because he believes that pleasure comes from filling up, that is, satisfying, the desires. Callicles is claiming that his hero does not seek satisfaction as the natural goal of desire. It is not satisfied desire that he seeks but the experience of satisfying desire. It is not that desires do not reach a point of satisfaction but that the point of satisfaction is not the end or goal.[21] Rather, satisfaction is but a pause in the endless process of filling the desires. Treated in this way, desires become the vehicles for attaining pleasure. The point of satisfying desires is not satiety—the state of a satisfied desire—but the pleasure inherent in the process of satisfying desires. If this reading is correct, the insatiable desires are basically the normal desires for food, drink, and sex. In normal life, one satisfies them while observing the usual limits. One stops eating when one is full, for instance. In the Calliclean life, one does not observe the usual limits. Thus, insatiable desires are normal desires that are being used in a certain way. Moreover, this distinction allows that, left on their own, these desires are basically good—that is, desires for things that contribute to or constitute one's welfare. However, when these basically good desires become vehicles for pleasure only, they become problematic. They are desires for good things that have been made to function in a way that is not for the good.

In this reading, Callicles is recommending an idealized sensual state in which the pleasure of replenishing is the goal of existence.[22] The cogency and seductiveness of Callicles' hero of the appetites reaches us over the intervening centuries. Plato has not fashioned a straw man but a still-attractive alternative to conventional wisdom. Conventional wisdom says that one cannot spend all of one's days attending to one's appetites, devoting his total efforts to finding new and more exotic experiences. The business of life is not devising more intense or grander pleasures; it is making a living, attending to one's family, being a good citizen. Of course, one satisfies one's desires, but only as a means to achieving these other goals; and the best evidence that this relation is the right one is that the level at which satisfaction of these desires naturally occurs is related to their function as means to these other goals. For example, one eats in order to have the energy to make a living; the desire is naturally satisfied when one has eaten enough food to restore one's energy. Desires are naturally calibrated to just these goals; satisfying one's hunger for food and sex, up to the natural and practical point of satisfaction, is aptly fitted to achieving these goals. Callicles' exhortation hints at another picture altogether: the life of a sensualist. From the fact that desires do have this natural, practical limit we should not derive any normative principles about how to live our lives or about how to approach the satisfaction of our desires. Why subordinate the pleasures of satisfying desire to the duty toward family and city? What is more important than the experience of pleasure? Why betray one's appetites by treating them as things to be gotten out of the way, as though the only point is to quiet and calm them?

In turn, Socrates' image of the leaky jars tries to convince us that desires treated only as vehicles for pleasure rob the one who has them of the ability to be satisfied. If satisfying a desire on a particular occasion is not the point, then satisfying such a desire is never enough. In a paradoxical but all too real sense, such desires can be satisfied but the one who has the desire will not be sated. At this stage in Socrates' exposition, we might say that the desires are insatiable at least in the sense that satisfying them is never enough for the one who has them. Socrates is urging that it is not the filling up that is the goal of life—the process of satisfying desire. Rather—as Socrates says at 493d—the temperate person is adequately provided for and is satisfied with what he has (*ton kosmiōs kai tois aei parousin hikanōs kai ezarchountos echonta bion* [493c6–7]).[23] Socrates seems to be calling to Callicles' attention the value of satiety, the state of having satisfied desires. He is promoting the value of satisfaction as a kind of end, in contrast to treating satisfaction as a pause on the way to more replenishment-generated pleasures. In this picture, then, Socrates seems to be hinting at something like Epicurus' teaching that the tranquil life of satisfied desires is preferable to a life of exotic pleasures associated with replenishing desires. If the point is to have satisfied desires, then the kind of desires to have are moderate ones rather than ones that require extravagant means for their satisfaction.[24]

Epicureans made a distinction between the kinetic pleasures of replenishment and the static pleasures of satiety. The distinction is between, for example, the pleasure of eating a gourmet meal and the pleasure of satisfaction once the meal is over. They thought the latter superior to the former. For them, one should attempt to have a life in which the pleasures of satiety outweigh the pleasures of replenishment. The best way to have such a life is to have desires that could be easily satisfied, whose replenishment was easy, and whose satiety was valued for itself. One can see an entire attitude toward life in this account. Such a life would treasure what satiety it had at any moment rather than be constantly seeking new and more exotic pleasures. The latter bring with them too much anxiety because they are difficult of attainment. It is better to have a life of simple pleasures that can be attained without the trouble and anxiety of the exotic pleasures. Moreover, one should not seek to have one pleasure after another; one should savor the satisfaction of the pleasures one has. The image is not of an ascetic life but of a simple life. If an Epicurean were arguing with Callicles, he would probably say that Callicles is mistaken in failing to recognize the static pleasure of satiety. This mistake, in turn, leads him to make kinetic pleasures the goal of life, rather than static pleasures. However, as we shall see, Socrates cannot make this kind of argument for the good of satiety. So, if the image is telling us that satiety is a good, we are still unclear what the good of satiety is. The image is much better at suggesting that something is wrong with insatiable desires than at suggesting what is wrong— just as it is better at suggesting that something is right about satiety than at suggesting what is right about it. At the most, the image suggests that insatiable desires are malfunctioning. The analogy—by comparing desires to jars—focuses on the individual desire and its function. The sound jar—the analogue of the desire not in need of restraint—is able to fulfill its function as a jar whereas the leaky jar cannot attain what jars are supposed to attain—that is, to hold what is valuable. By analogy, the insatiable desire, which substitutes the pleasure of replenishment for satiety, is incapable of fulfilling its function. By making satisfaction a way station in the endless seeking of pleasure, Callicles has robbed the desire of its function, just as making a sound jar into a leaky jar robs the jar of its function.[25] But if it is malfunctioning, we still do not know what malfunctioning amounts to.

As murky as the notion of the function of a desire might be, it is one visited again in the *Republic*. Here Socrates seems to be struggling with the possibility that a desire, considered in itself and apart from its relation to other desires, might function correctly or incorrectly, as though it were like a tool. If that correct functioning were distinct from providing the pleasure of replenishment, then Socrates has an argument against Callicles' ideal of the sensualist life. However, at this point in the dialogue we should not expect more than a preliminary suggestion about the malfunctioning of insatiable desires. What is really important at this point is that Socrates presents desires as morally problematic. Although to us it may seem obvious that desires are the source of moral problems, to his hearers it would have been unusual for Socrates to present them as such. With this development we have a departure in Plato's moral theory. According to most commentators, until he wrote the *Protagoras* and the *Gorgias*, Plato had been following the Socratic teaching, from earlier dialogues, that desires are not morally problematic. Desires seek what is good; when one does something that is not for the good, the problem is not that the desires have misled but that they have themselves been misled. However, in allowing that desires can sometimes be like leaky jars, Plato now seems to be admitting that desires are not always for the good.[26] Certainly, desires themselves are presented as in need of attention; in their lack of restraint, these desires seem to have a direction of their own, not always aimed at the good. Indeed, the very notion of the craft of ruling implies that desires can become in themselves problematic.

In order to understand the way that desires have become problematic in Plato's account, let us look at the notion of desires in the earlier dialogues. What we will see is that there has been a subtle, but not seismic, shift in Plato's conception of the relation between desires and the good. First, we will look at the so-called Socratic paradoxes—the teaching that assumes that desires are morally unproblematic because they are always desires for the good. Then we will be able to see in what way the *Gorgias* modifies this assumption; while the modification is not radical, still the relation between desires and the good becomes problematic. However, it is the consequence of this modification that holds the most interest. Having made the relation between desires and the good problematic, Socrates must now redefine that relation; redefining that relation is the purpose of the next section of the dialogue.

The teaching from earlier dialogues on the relation of desires and the good is sometimes known as the Socratic paradox. In one of its expressions the teaching is the paradoxical statement that no one voluntarily pursues evil.[27] Thus, if anyone actually pursues what is bad or evil, he or she is either forced or fooled into pursuing it. Either this evil-doing person is physically or psychologically forced to do what is evil or this person is under the illusion that what he or she is doing is good when actually it is evil.[28] It is really the latter alternative that interests Plato because Socrates seemed to believe that the only reason someone does what is bad or harmful is that he or she does not know that what is being done is bad or harmful. He or she is mistaken about the goodness of what is being done. If such a person knew that the action were bad or harmful, he or she would not do it; indeed, he or she would not even want to do it. Thus, when a person pursues evil, he or she does so unknowingly; in turn, we would say that such a person pursues evil involuntarily because he or she would not pursue evil if she or he knew that it was evil.

In this account of the Socratic paradox, the basic assumption is that desires are always desires for the good. Thus, desires are not the problem; it is not desires that mislead. The problem is in our knowledge. So someone like Socrates, who wants to help people avoid evil, should work to overcome ignorance, to help people understand where the true good lies. Then their desires will follow the lead of such knowledge about the good, just as they followed the lead of the mistaken belief about the good. Desires are not, then, a drag or obstacle; they are unhesitating in their pursuit of the good. In one version of this charming view of life, a person's desire for, for example, chocolate brownies is basically the desire for something that is good for her. Such a person eats brownies thinking of them as something good for her. If, at some moment, her reason decided that eating brownies was bad—for example, was leading to being dangerously overweight—she would not only stop eating brownies; she would also stop desiring to eat brownies. Her desire to eat chocolate brownies would simply cease; after all, the desire is basically a desire for the good and brownies are no longer seen as part of or leading to the good.

Santas holds that there are two versions of this paradox—the prudential and the moral versions.[29] The prudential version holds that no one desires what is bad for oneself; the moral version holds that no one voluntarily does what is unjust—that is, what is wrongly harmful to another. He argues that Plato makes the latter dependent on the former; Plato tries to show that what is harmful to others is harmful to the one who perpetrates the harm. However, we will concentrate on the prudential paradox because it exposes an important aspect of desires in Plato's account at this point.

In one way of looking at it the prudential paradox does not seem paradoxical at all. After all the claim is not that no one desires what is harmful to oneself. Rather, the Socratic paradox is the claim that no one desires anything that one knows or believes is harmful for oneself.[30] Thus, a famous argument in the *Meno* (77b) holds that no one wishes to be harmed and thus no one wants to do what one knows is harmful to oneself. But the argument does allow that someone might do what is harmful in the mistaken notion that what one does is not really harmful. But in this case, one does not knowingly desire what is harmful to oneself. Still, the claim that no one knowingly desires what is harmful can strike us as paradoxical when we think of people who eat unhealthy food or smoke cigarettes, when they know that such actions are harmful to themselves.[31] Surely one can object that in these cases, the person knows that some foods are unhealthy but continues to desire and to eat these foods. The paradox is that the claim that no one knowingly does what is harmful is contradicted by the example of this person who knows that eating the food is harmful and still desires to eat it. The Socratic claim flies in the face of our experience.

In fact, Callicles seems to present just such a case. According to him, desires can be made into vehicles for seeking the pleasures of replenishment; if the pleasures of replenishment are not the same as the good—even when 'the good' means one's own good—then desires are not for the good. In this way there arises the possibility that desires can be good-independent, merely pleasure seeking rather than seeking one's over-all good.[32] Desires can be made into desires for pleasures that are in fact harmful for one and one can know that fact and still desire them. Thus, instead of being allies in seeking the good life, desires become enemies. Perhaps this is the challenge that Callicles is presenting—the very notion of the life of unrestrained desire exposes the fact that desires are not for the good.

In fact, the claim that no one knowingly desires what is harmful to oneself is ambiguous.[33] In one of its meanings, it is the uninteresting claim that whatever one desires one does so with the notion that it is, in some sense, a good. Thus, even the person who desires to eat unhealthy food and who, in some part of her mind knows that it is unhealthy, sees the healthy food as something good. Perhaps, she sees the unhealthy food as pleasant tasting and just insofar as it is pleasant tasting she sees it as good, not as harmful; what she desires then is that good. She does not look upon eating, for example, the sweet chocolate brownie the way she might look upon eating a bowl of broken razor blades. Thus, in this sense of the claim that no one knowingly desires what is harmful, 'knowingly' has a rather weak sense that makes the claim true in an uninteresting way. It might well be true—and is certainly not obviously false—that whenever one desires to do something one has some sense that what one is doing is, in some way, a good. But this claim does not seem to tell us anything very important. In the second sense, the claim is stronger; but it is also less clearly true. In this sense, no one desires to do what one recognizes to be harmful after considering all the relevant factors. In this sense, 'knowingly' means that one has considered the proposed actions and soberly assessed its consequences for one's overall welfare. The claim then says that, after such an assessment, no one will desire to do what is harmful to one's overall welfare. In this sense, desire is always for *the* good, or for the best; the latter phrases imply that the object of desire is one's considered welfare.[34]

Now we can see what is at issue between Callicles and Socrates. Callicles is saying that the pleasure of satisfying desires is the point of having desires. Moreover, the pleasure of unrestrained satisfaction should be taken to be one's overall good, in spite of what Socrates, or anyone else, might call the "overall good." On the other hand, Socrates argues that one should not substitute the good of pleasure for the overall good. Thus, Callicles and Socrates are not arguing about the Socratic paradox—about whether desires seek the good and follow the lead of reason; they are arguing about what the good is. What is at issue between Socrates and Callicles is whether one's overall good is the same as the pleasure of unrestrained satisfaction of the elementary desires for food, drink, and sex. For Callicles they are the same (495a); moreover, this opinion seems to be a reflective one. Obviously he has thought about it. For Socrates, on the other hand, these pleasures and the good are not the same.

That the difference between pleasures and the good is the issue between Callicles and Socrates is shown by the sequel. At this point in the *Gorgias*, Plato is aware that the distinction between the pleasure of satisfying desires and one's overall good must be made.[35] After the initial characterization of insatiable desires as leaky jars, Socrates engages in an extended two part argument with Callicles to show that there is a difference between good and pleasure (495a ff.). We will not give the details of these arguments. The upshot of the second argument is that, given Callicles' identification between pleasure and the good, there is no difference between the coward and the brave man since both experience about the same amount of pleasure and pain. Such a conclusion seems unacceptable to Callicles because he wants to distinguish between the coward and the brave man. Presumably either he genuinely believes that there is a difference between the coward and the brave man or he is ashamed to admit that there is no difference between the coward and the brave man.[36] Given the way that Plato presents his character, it is probably the former; Callicles seems to think of himself as a brave man or at least as aspiring to the standing of one.

After arguing that pleasure and the good are different, however, Socrates makes an important concession—a concession that implies a new relation between desires and the good. Socrates tries to convince Callicles that pleasure pursued for its own sake in some way renders the desires pathological. Socrates develops this strategy in what we have already called the "medical analogy." He compares unrestrained desires to the desires of a sick person—a person whose desires are pathological and in need of medical treatment. The unrestrained desires of Callicles' account need a kind of treatment that is analogous to medical treatment; these unrestrained desires are, morally speaking, pathological.

Characterizing insatiable desires as pathological has two consequences that are significant for understanding the new, problematic relation between desires and the good. First of all, desires are not naturally good-independent; second, they can, nevertheless, be corrupted so that they become good-independent. First, the very idea of treating insatiable desires like the desires of a sick person implies that the desires are by nature sound. They are perfectly normal desires for, for example, food, drink, and sex, that have become pathological; they are not naturally pathological. As we have argued, the desires for food, drink, and sex are not in themselves desires for bad things; they are made bad by being used as vehicles for pleasure. Treatment is the way of returning them to their inherent, proper functioning. Indeed, in the *Gorgias*, Socrates explicitly says that everyone desires (*boulesthai*) the good. In the conversation with Polus (467c ff.), Socrates presents a fully developed argument that depends on the claim that people desire the good, concludes that they can be confused about what the good is, and thus they sometimes desire what turns out to be bad. Second, however, the notion of treatment for insatiable desires also implies that such desires can become, in themselves, impaired. It is not sufficient merely to show the person who does so that using desires as vehicles for pleasure is wrong—as it presumably would have been in the early dialogues. The treatment for insatiable desires is not simply intellectual; it is not directed solely at what one believes. As we shall see, treatment must discipline the desires by punishment, as though the desires themselves have become corrupted. When the person who would use desires as vehicles for pleasure must be restrained by experiencing pain, we can conclude that the lesson is not merely intellectual.

It is not altogether clear what is going on when we say that desires are somehow in themselves impaired. We are not saying just that desires can be used as vehicles for obtaining pleasure but that this use can harm the way the desires function. One way to put this harm is to say that desires that are used as vehicles for pleasure can take on bad habits. They come to function in such a way that pleasure substitutes for the usual ends of desire. If this way of putting it is plausible, then Plato would be suggesting that desire can have dispositions—an idea that is to have great importance in ancient moral philosophy. Even if the natural disposition is to function well—that is, for one's overall good—it is possible for desires to take on a bad disposition. Incorrect belief about one's overall good might be the beginning of the corruption of desires; but after awhile the desires malfunction on their own—so to speak. They become insatiable.

Thus, we can now see the new, problematic relation between desires and the good. While desires are naturally for the good, they can be corrupted so that they do not seek the good. To corrupted desires, pleasure becomes a rival goal to the good; its influence is more insidious than that of other goals that rival the good because, once instituted, its influence is not so easily dissipated as the influence of a wrong belief. The upshot of this new relation between desires and the good is very important for Plato's moral theory. Up to this point, the dialogues said that as long as they were not misled by belief, the desires sought the good. However, having allowed that desires can be corrupted to seek only pleasure, Plato must redefine their relation to the good. He must give an account of the way that insatiable desires fail to obtain the good and an account of the way that moderate desires contribute to the good. Redefining the relation between desires and the good is the burden of the medical analogy. It is in order to fulfill that role that harmony and order among desires make their debut.

V

In the medical analogy, Plato elaborates on the pathology of desires and suggests a way of understanding nonpathological desires—that is, that condition of desires that corresponds to health in the body. Here he presents the notion of harmony and order among the desires. This way of presenting the good condition of the soul is important for our understanding of the way the ruling craft treats desires and for our understanding of the relation between desires and perfection. Moreover, it prefigures the conception of psychic harmony in *Republic* IV, there portrayed as health in the soul. Socrates begins his explication of the medical analogy for the treatment of unrestrained desires by reiterating the complex analogy, which he originally elaborated for Polus (464a ff.), between therapeutic crafts that care for the healthy and those that care for the sick. Then, by developing the notion of a craft, he makes an extremely important advance in his account of the ruling craft. Contrasting the uncraftlike sophistic rhetorician, with the craftlike good man (presumably someone speaking in the assembly or in the law courts) Socrates says that the good man has as his whole endeavor to make the souls of his fellow citizens as good as possible (*to paraskeuazein hopōs hōs beltistai esontai tōn politōn hai psychai* [503a7–8]).

Invoking the notion of perfection, *to beltiston* (503d), Socrates next characterizes that perfection in a way that will have important implications for all of his subsequent accounts of the moral life. The perfection that all crafts seek is an order within the object of the craft.

> . . . each sets into place whatever he sets into place according to a particular order, and forces different parts to fit together and harmonize (*prepon te einai kai harmottein*) until he has combined the whole into an ordered and arranged thing (*tetagmenon te kai kekosmēnenon pragma* [503e–504a]).

Citing the order and arrangement of houses and ships, Socrates next extends this motif of order and arrangement to the body and the soul. It is the comparison between order in the body and order in the soul that is the import of the whole passage. In the body, order and arrangement are health; in the soul it is lawfulness, justice, and temperance.

In order to understand this crucial comparison, we need to elaborate carefully what Socrates says about the body. Disorder in the body is sickness and calls for medical treatment to restore order. Now there seems to be a leap in the progress of thought; Socrates seems to be saying that restoring order in the body entails restraining appetites—as though there is some causal relation between the appetites and bodily disease. He says that the physicians allow the healthy person to eat and drink his fill (literally to fill up his desires); the sick person, however, they do not allow to satisfy completely his appetites (literally to fill up his desires completely). About this diseased appetite, Socrates says that it is not clear that filling it with a lot of drink, for example, will profit the sick person and may even harm him (504e). Perhaps Socrates has in mind people whose appetites have grown excessive because of their disease; at the same time, satisfying these excessive appetites contributes to making the disease worse. For example, a person with a high fever can have an insatiable thirst (cf. *Philebus* 45a–c). In such a disease, the sick person drinks water beyond the capacity of the stomach to hold the water. Grown pathological, such a desire does not cease at the appropriate point; the appetite is not in relation to what the body needs. Moreover, the excessive drinking can make the person even sicker. The job of the physician, then, is to moderate the appetite. He does not keep the patient from drinking at all; rather he allows the patient to drink only a moderate amount. The healthy person, by contrast, can be allowed to drink his fill because the limit of the appetite is in relation to what the body needs.

After this rather short reference to the role of appetites in bodily disease, Socrates then turns to "sick" souls.

> And does not the same treatment apply to the soul, my good friend? Whenever it is in an evil state, being ignorant, undisciplined, unjust, and impious, it is necessary to restrain the soul from its desires and not to allow it to do anything but what will be for its improvement? (505b)

Now we know why Socrates implicated desires in the pathology of the body; he wished to draw an analogy between treatment of desires in bodily disease and treatment of desires in the soul. Let us try, then, to fill out the analogy between restrained and unrestrained desires of the sick person and the restrained and unrestrained desires of the vicious person—the ignorant, undisciplined, unjust, and impious person. Desires grown pathological through disease have lost their natural limit, that is, the point at which satisfaction and the good of the body coincide. The job of the physician is to substitute for and ultimately reestablish that limit. Without its natural limit, the appetite has a dysfunctional limit—a limit with no value for the body.[37] If we draw out Socrates' analogy between disease and moral unrestraint, we would say that appetites that have become insatiable through disease are like appetites that have grown insatiable through unrestraint—through ignorance, undiscipline, injustice, and impiety. The pathology of the former has rendered them without a limit that is functional for the body. Desires grown insatiable through unrestraint have lost their natural limit as well; if one draws out the analogy, their natural limit is defined by its relation to the good of the soul; they are dysfunctional for the soul.[38] Presumably, then, a person who has unrestrained or undisciplined desires will harm his soul in some way in attempting to satisfy their excessive demands.

However, Socrates does not give us a very clear or explicit picture of what harming the soul amounts to here. Thus, it is not clear how desires can be dysfunctional for the soul.[39] Of course, in introducing the medical analogy Socrates has, at least, suggested a way in which unrestrained desires are dysfunctional. Socrates has said that the craftsman arranges everything according to a certain order, and forces the parts to fit together and harmonize, until he has combined the whole into a well-ordered and well-arranged production. He has also said that the craftsman of the soul will restrain the desires that have grown excessive through vice. Thus, the craftsman of the soul will doubtless work on the excessive desires so that they fit together and form a well-ordered and well-arranged whole.[40] The implication is that these desires are the source of lack of order and arrangement.

Socrates does not explain exactly how these desires could be the source of disorder. Presumably they would come into conflict with other parts of the soul. But Socrates does not explicitly identify the other parts of the soul with which insatiable desires would conflict. Irwin points out that insatiable desires might well be incompatible with other more moderate desires.[41] There may be other possible conflicts but for the purposes of illustration we will concentrate on this one. This incompatibility could occur in several ways. It can be imagined that an insatiable desire can be incompatible with other desires at the same level—that is, with the same scope of activity. An insistent desire for food, for example, will conflict with a desire whose satisfaction is incompatible with the activity or consequence of overeating—for example, the desire to fit into a certain bathing suit. As well, one can imagine higher order desires—for example, the desire to be healthy—that might be incompatible with the unrestrained desire for food. The desire for health is higher order because it is more general than the desire for food, involving more facets of one's life. It is, perhaps, in this sense that we are to understand the insatiable desire to be dysfunctional for the soul; it is the source of incompatibility among the desires, either with desires of the same level or with higher order desires.

The sort of incompatibility at issue here is between insatiable desires and moderate desires. Thus, it is the incompatibility between desires that are used only to achieve the pleasures of satisfaction and desires that function in the normal way. This incompatibility or conflict is the pathological condition that the craft of ruling must overcome. Of course, there are other incompatibilities between desires with which the ruling craft is not concerned. There is the incompatibility of moderate desires—for example, the desire to hear this one-time concert and the desire to attend my daughter's fifth birthday party, scheduled at the same time. The latter is not considered to be pathological. Why the former incompatibility is to be considered pathological is not altogether clear.[42] At least one reason suggests itself. Moderate desires may be incompatible with one another because of the object of the desires; both objects cannot be attained at the same time. Such incompatibility is not systematic since it depends upon the incompatibility of the objects; a change in the objects—location or time, for example—would avoid the incompatibility. However, when an insatiable desire is incompatible with a moderate desire it is not because of their respective objects. The insatiable desire is incompatible with the moderate desire because of the way that it functions as a desire. Being insatiable, it pursues its object in season and out; being insistent and without limit—at least theoretically—it simply crowds out the moderate desire. It is for this reason that the latter kind of incompatibility seems pathological. In turn, it looks more like a remediable condition, one that a therapeutic craft could address—especially if, when the insatiable desires are returned to normal function, they cease to be systematic obstacles to other moderate desires.[43] The obverse of this picture of incompatibility is that a certain kind of compatibility of desires is good for one's soul. The sort of compatibility that does not systematically frustrate the desires is good for the soul. It is one thing to have frustration of incompatible desires because of their respective objects;

it is another to have the frustration of incompatible desires because of the way that one of the desires functions. At the very least, the soul should not stand in the way of itself, so to speak. Not standing in the way of itself is good for the soul.

Now we can see the new relation between desires and the good. Formerly desires were desires for this or that object that, when guided by knowledge or true belief, contributed to or constituted the good; all desires thus being for the good, their systematic compatibility was assumed. Systematic incompatibility now being possible, desires are not automatically for the good. Thus, systematic compatibility of desires becomes an important indicator of the good; desires that do not systematically frustrate one another are either a means to the good or actually constitute the good. Certainly, the text makes clear the importance of compatibility of desires. In Socrates' analogy, the desires, at some level, should fit together the way the parts of the ship or of the house fit together. At this level, at least, the soul should have an integration of desires. The soul should form a *kosmos,* an ordered arrangement (*Gor.* 506e). The notion of *kosmos* within the soul is repeated throughout this passage. It is obviously a powerful idea, capable of evoking strong assent. The particular *kosmos* of each thing is what makes it good, indeed is the virtue of the thing (*taxei ara tetagmenon kai kekosmēmenon estin hē aretē hekastou* [506e1–2]). Later in the same passage, *kosmos* is again invoked to characterize the entire scheme of being.

> Wise men say, Callicles, that both heaven and earth and gods and humans, communion holds together, and friendship and orderliness (*kosmiotēta*) and temperance and justice; and because of these they call the whole thing a *kosmon,* my friend, not a "disorder" nor an "undiscipline." (507e)

Here the entire moral universe is represented as a *kosmos,* a beautifully ordered whole. The proximity of this image of the moral universe to the passage in which Socrates praises the *kosmos* of the soul can be no accident.

The *kosmos* of the soul evokes no less strong an assent, then. In turn, the notion that the soul's desires should fit together to form a *kosmos* has a certain appeal. The appeal probably is best appreciated from its absence. A life of frustration or a life dragged in opposite directions by large-scale and fundamental desires seems to most people to be bad. On the other hand, a life in which one does not experience such frustration or such contradictory pulls has an integrity that might be comparable to the integrity of a well-made ship. Most people would prefer a life with such direction and integrity. Certainly many of those who are counted as saints or heroes and heroines seem to have this "well-fit-together" aspect to their lives. However, as powerful as the image may be, it is only an image. It does not amount to a theory about psychic perfection and how to attain it. At this point in the dialogue we have the very compelling notion that, in order to have the good, one must have a certain order and harmony among the desires. Exactly what this order and harmony are is unclear. But even more obscure is how the one practicing the ruling craft goes about bringing such order and harmony into the soul. We need to get beyond the medical analogy to the ruling craft proper.

VI

At best then, in the medical analogy, Socrates has given us a type of psychic disharmony. At best, he has hinted at a type of psychic harmony. The medical analogy has all the drawbacks of analogies, then; but we should not forget that it is used to introduce the notion of judging, a species of the ruling craft properly so called. The latter is the therapeutic craft whose object is sick souls. Judging is analogous to medicine; it will do for the soul what medicine does for the body. Thus it will do for morally pathological desires what medicine does for bodily pathological desires. In elaborating Plato's account of this species of the craft of ruling, we will see that, in talking about judging, Socrates does not greatly advance our understanding of order and harmony among desires and the method for attaining it. However, Socrates' method of refutation, by means of question and answer—called Socratic elenchus—is presented as a type of the ruling craft. In exploring this development we attain an important glimpse of one way in which the ruling craft can attain harmony and order among desires.

In the following passages Socrates gives us—albeit in an incomplete form—an account of the method that the craftsman of soul uses to restrain desires that have been corrupted. The method is, in a word, *punishment*. In the earlier conversation with Polus, Socrates identifies the judge as the one who treats the soul of the unjust person; just as the medical treatment for the body is painful so is the punishment inflicted by the judge (478d–e). However, while this punishment is said to cure its victim of injustice, Socrates does not explain how punishment effects the cure; he does not tie the punishment to the discipline of overweening desires. As we know, of course, it is only later, in the conversation with Callicles, that Socrates identifies the desires as the object of treatment in sick souls. So in the conversation with Polus, he is not in the position to make the connection. However, what Socrates says to Polus about the role of the judge in curing sickness in the soul and to Callicles about the function of the desires in the soul's sickness would allow us to conclude that the punishment inflicted by the judge has the effect of disciplining uncontrolled desires. There are indications in the text, after the introduction of desires as the objects of the therapeutic craft, that just such a conclusion is Socrates'.

At 507d, Socrates refers back to his conversation with Polus and to one of its more scandalous paradoxes, that is, that the good person who has done injustice should turn himself over to the judges to be disciplined. Clearly referring to the expected effects of the punishment to be meted out by the judge, Socrates says, the unjust person should seek punishment, thereby "not allowing his desires to be unrestrained and, in attempting to fill them—an endless evil—living the life of a robber." In this passage, Socrates seems to be referring back to the leaky jars, desires whose filling are an endless task. Thus judging might here be supposed to restrain the appetite so that satisfied desires would be its goal. Nothing is said about compatibility of desires however. While this passage does not refer to compatibility of desires, Socrates hints at compatibility when he recounts the myth at the end of the dialogue. There Socrates outlines a therapeutic craft exercised by the gods of the underworld. When an unjust soul arrives in the underworld, it bears the marks of its past life. In some cases the judge sees "that because of the power, the license, the wanton violence, and the lack of self-control of its actions, the soul is filled with disproportion and ugliness . . ." (525a). The judges must decide whether such a soul is curable or not. If such a soul is curable, it is subjected to punishment that will return it to health. If we assume that it is the desires that are disproportionate and ugly, the punishment will return proportion and beauty to the desires. Finally, disproportion among desires means that some desires are out of proportion to others; thus disproportion might well be a form of incompatibility of desires—an incompatibility that the judge cures.[44]

Somehow, then, punishment would restrain the insatiable and disproportionate desires. However, Socrates does not offer a theory to explain why punishment has this effect.[45] He leaves us wondering what restraining the desire by punishment amounts to and why doing so should lead to a cure. Presumably, in any theory of punishment, one is expected to make a connection between the crime and the punishment. In the most superficial of theories, the criminal comes to realize that because he commits the crime he suffers the punishment. He then has some motivation to avoid committing the crime in the future, provided that punishment reliably follows the crime and the pain of the punishment outweighs the pleasure of committing the crime. Of course, it is natural for us in this century to think of judicially inflicted punishment in a different way—as something like negative reinforcement. On the negative reinforcement model, the criminal is supposed to make a further connection between the desire to commit a crime and the pain of the punishment. The pain of the punishment restrains the desire by establishing in the mind of the criminal an association between the crime and the pain of punishment. The desire to commit the crime lessens because the prospect of the pleasure of its satisfaction is dimmed by association with the pain of the punishment. The trouble with Plato's accounts of punishment and his talk of restraining desires is that we get no such theoretical connection between the pain of punishment and the restraining of desires.

While the explicit account of judging does not advance the notion of the ruling craft very much, Socrates' own practice of elenchus in this dialogue does. As we shall see, not only does Socrates present elenchus as a kind of ruling craft—in particular, as a kind of judging—he does so in such a way as to add a new level of meaning to the notion of ruling craft. Indeed, towards the end of the dialogue Socrates makes the astonishing claim that he is the only true practitioner of the craft of ruling (*politikē technē*) (521e). In claiming that he is the only true statesman existent then in Athens, Socrates presents himself as someone who does not pander to the desires of his audience but tells them what they need to hear. The implication is that what he has to say is painful but necessary to hear. If we remember that Socrates characteristically does not make speeches but refutes his interlocutors through his method of question and answer—the method of elenchus—it appears that Socrates is basing his claim to superior statesmanship—to be a better practitioner of the craft of ruling—because he practices elenchus.

This passage seems to invite us to apply the account of therapeutic craft to Socratic elenchus. Indeed, such an invitation is only to be expected since the central contrast in the whole dialogue is between craft and routine, between Socrates and Gorgias. Since Gorgias' rhetoric is routine, Socrates' philosophy—that is, elenchus—should be craft. In turn, if Socratic elenchus were a therapeutic craft, it will be a therapeutic craft of the soul and one which cares for sick souls. It will be analogous to medicine, which metes out painful treatment to the body; as a therapeutic craft of the soul, it will, like the craft of judging, inflict punishment in order to restrain desires. Of course, unlike judging, which uses corporal punishment, elenchus uses the punishment of contradiction. We find just such a presentation of elenchus throughout the dialogue.

In this regard, then, elenchus fits the account of craft already outlined by Socrates early in his conversation with Polus (464b ff.). Elenchus does what it does not with the aim of pleasing those who are its objects. Like a craft, then, it aims at the good not just at pleasure. Indeed, as we shall see, Socrates holds consistency to be a great good. Elenchus might be supposed to have that good as its craft goal. Of course, all elenchus does is to point up inconsistency in beliefs. However, insofar as pointing up inconsistency leads to one achieving consistency of beliefs, elenchus has the good of its objects in mind. However, a craft is supposed to be able to give an account of its procedures, to explain why it provides what it provides. Here elenchus does not fit the account of craft so well. It is not clear that Socrates has a theory to explain why he does what he does.[46] He, of course, characterizes elenchus in various ways—as we shall see; but he does not offer a systematic account. He seems to rely on suggestions and hints about his purposes in practicing elenchus. At the most we can say that Socrates sees his craft as providing consistency of beliefs, which he presents as a great good, as we shall see. Indeed, throughout this dialogue, Socrates does seem very adept at his craft. He seems highly capable at ferreting out the important beliefs of his interlocutors and at showing an inconsistency in their beliefs. He is also skilled in showing not just any inconsistency in their beliefs but the kind of consistency that calls into question central beliefs.

However, what is missing is the sense that Socrates can give a theoretical account of what he is trying to accomplish besides showing an inconsistency. He seems to believe that what he is trying to accomplish by his elenchus is important for his interlocutors. He does not seem able to explain exactly why it is important. Of course, given his avowals of ignorance, it should not be surprising that Socrates has no theory to explain his elenchus; indeed, this Socratic ignorance cannot be overcome until the theory of Forms is introduced. In any event, in the sequel, we will concentrate on those ways in which Socratic elenchus seems to be a therapeutic craft of the soul, admitting that there are also ways in which it does not seem to be a craft.

First of all, in the conversation with Polus, as we have already seen, Socrates characterizes the judge in the court as using punishment to relieve the soul of evil; the judge is like the physician in that both must require painful treatment in order to return the patient to health, whether psychic or bodily health. Then, Socrates characterizes himself as someone in a court trying to get Polus to testify. Polus, he says, is the only witness he needs to establish his point (472b–c; 474b; 475d–e). Finally, in a sly self-reference, Socrates compares his own elenctic treatment of Polus in the same terms he uses for the judge and the physician. At the point where Socrates gets Polus to admit to a contradiction of his previously avowed belief, he cajoles

> Do not hesitate to answer, Polus. For you won't be harmed. Rather submit nobly to the argument, as to a physician, and answer, and either affirm or not what I ask. (475d)

Evidently, being a witness for Socrates can also be a painful kind of treatment.

If, in his conversation with Polus, Socrates is implicitly compared to a practitioner of the craft of ruling, in his conversation with Callicles, Socrates explicitly claims to be such. In the denouement of this passage in which Socrates has badgered Callicles into admitting that, in the sick soul, the desires must be restrained, Socrates next makes a passing comment that, in the first place, characterizes Callicles himself; but it also characterizes Socrates' elenctic procedure. Callicles, objecting to the direction that the Socratic elenchus has taken, says, "I do not know what you are talking about, Socrates; ask one of these others." Socrates replies, "This man will not submit to being improved and himself undergoing the treatment we have been talking about—being disciplined" (505c).

Clearly then Socrates is also characterizing his own practice of elenchus. Bringing Callicles to the point of contradicting his previous statements about the superiority of undisciplined desires is, in itself, a kind of discipline. The pain of the treatment comes from having to admit the contradiction, of course. Since the strength of Callicles' reaction shows us that Socrates' elenctic conclusion is painful treatment, Socrates looks like a judge meting out punishment.[47] If Socrates' elenchus is an example of the ruling craft, the pain that it inflicts ought to be a means for restraining desires that need restraint. Indeed, in this passage Socrates is rather explicit about connecting his elenchus with the treatment that restrains desires. The "treatment we have been talking about" is the treatment that restrains desires and makes the soul a harmonious unity.

However, on the surface, elenchus simply seems to be a method for exposing the inconsistencies in the moral beliefs of his interlocutors. In the introduction to his conversation with Callicles, he jokes that they both love two things: Callicles loves Demos, the son of Pyrilampes, and the Athenian *demos*—that is, the Athenian mob; Socrates loves Alcibiades and philosophy. Because Callicles will not contradict his beloved Athenian *demos*, he involves himself in inconsistency. Socrates' unflattering description of Callicles, however, becomes considerably more pointed when he challenges Callicles to refute the claim that wrong doing and not paying the penalty when one has done wrong are the worst evils. Otherwise,

> you, Callicles, will not be in agreement with yourself but you will be out of tune in your whole life. And I think, oh most excellent one, that it is better for my lyre, or a chorus that I sponsor, to be disharmonious and out of tune—or many men to disagree with me and contradict me—than that I, being one, should be out of tune with myself and contradict myself. (482b–c)

The address to Callicles at the beginning of their conversation is clearly meant to show the direction that Socrates will try to take. Consistency, then, is a value to be highly prized; but the consistency is not just a consistency of any opinions whatsoever. Since the consistency is of vital importance for Callicles' whole life, surely the opinions are fairly important, presumably moral, beliefs. What is even more arresting about this address is the way that Socrates implies that Callicles already harbors an inconsistency in his moral beliefs.[48] Socrates says that if he cannot refute the claim that wrong doing and not paying the penalty when one has done wrong are the worst evils, then he will be out of tune with himself. Surely Socrates is then assuming that Callicles will be out of tune with himself because this opinion is inconsistent with some other belief he holds. So, a few pages later, when Socrates catches him in an inconsistency, we can read his address as prophetic.

However, as we have already seen, at the conclusion of the elenchus Socrates also says that exposing this inconsistency is a way of disciplining Callicles in the way that the physician disciplines the desires of the sick person. We should not pass over this juncture lightly. The implication is that exposing a contradiction in one's beliefs will have an effect on what one desires. There is here an important assumption about the connection between what one believes and what one desires, about the way one affects the other. In this dialogue, at least, elenchus is not just a question of propositions; it is also a question of attitudes.

Recently, commentators have emphasized the way in which elenchus in the *Gorgias* has psychological, as well as logical, significance.[49] They note that the elenchus implicates the interlocutor's deeply held preferences or deepest desires. The following is an attempt to elaborate on that insight. Although the commentators point up the relation between beliefs and desires, what they do not tell us is just how contradicting a belief affects a desire. The answer, of course, begins with the fact that, in the *Gorgias*, the beliefs that are the object of elenchus are not merely notional or speculative. The rendering of the characters makes it clear that these beliefs are intimately related to what the characters desire; the beliefs express what the characters desire. Indeed, the desires seem to be rather large scale—desires about the shape of one's whole life. It is the nature of such beliefs that when one attacks the belief one also attacks the desire. In the case of Socrates' elenchus of Callicles, we know that Callicles believes that the life of unrestrained desires is the best life. As Socrates makes clear at 505b–c, it is this belief that is contradicted by having to admit that the soul whose desires are restrained is better off than the soul whose desires are unrestrained. Now if we suppose that this first belief is motivated by, and expresses, the desire to lead such a life then it is this desire that is the focus of the elenctic attack. Socrates' elenchus of Callicles, then, not only contradicts his belief that the life of unrestrained desires is the best life; it also attacks his desire to lead such a life. Indeed, insofar as attacking the belief requires Callicles to give up or modify his belief, attacking this belief entails giving up or modifying the desire to lead a life of unrestrained desire.[50]

If Socrates' elenchus restrains Callicles' desire to lead a life of unrestrained pleasure, then a significant shift has taken place in Plato's account of the ruling craft. The desires that are the object of elenchus are of a different order from the desires that were of concern in the image of the leaky jars and in the medical analogy. The latter were presented as insatiable desires; but the desire to lead a life of unrestrained pleasure—the desire that is the object of elenchus—is not itself an insatiable desire. In the first place, it is not a desire used only as a vehicle to attain the pleasure of satisfaction. More importantly, however, the desire to lead a life of unrestrained pleasure is something like a second order desire. It is more comprehensive and, potentially at least, more considered than any particular insatiable desire. An insatiable desire can, of course, determine the course of one's life; however, it may not be a desire to lead that kind of life. It has no goal more long range than the next cycle of pleasurable satisfaction. The desire to lead such a life, on the other hand, encompasses that pleasure and all that follow—and other consequences as well.

If elenchus is a type of ruling craft and if it works on these second order desires, then the account of the ruling craft is more complex than it was previously. Not only is the level of desires different but what makes them problematic is different. The desire to lead a life of unrestrained pleasure is not itself an insatiable desire; if it is morally problematic, it must be problematic for reasons different from those that make insatiable desires problematic. Moreover, if the desire to lead such a life is problematic but not insatiable, restraining that desire is different from the restraint appropriate for insatiable desires. As second order, these desires are the sort that get expressed in beliefs about what it is best to do. That these kinds of beliefs are the object of elenchus is not surprising, then. Indeed, it is these sorts of beliefs that Socrates refers to at 466e ff., where he talks about the distinction between what one thinks best and what one wants (*boulesthai*). What one wants is the good; and what one wants is not always the same as what one thinks best. Beliefs about what one thinks best can also be without intelligence; presumably it is their being without intelligence that explains why they can be at odds with what one wants. One can see here a possible role for elenchus. Since Socrates says that these beliefs are without intelligence, he might well see elenchus exploiting that fact in an attempt to point out their lack of correspondence with what one wants.[51]

If this account of elenchus is correct so far, then several results follow for elenchus as a craft for harmonizing desires. Elenchus works primarily at the level of second order desires. Socrates seems to aim at beliefs that express certain second order desires and attempts to show a contradiction between that belief and some other belief the interlocutor holds. Socrates seems to assume that pointing up a contradiction will force a choice between beliefs and that the interlocutor will, or ought to, give up the belief that expresses the targeted second order desire. Further, if the interlocutor gives up the belief he will also give up the desire. In this way elenchus brings a certain harmony into beliefs and, in turn, into second order desires expressed by beliefs. It is less clear how elenchus might discipline insatiable desires themselves—what we might call "first order desires." Of course, if elenchus causes Callicles, for example, to give up the second order desire to lead a life of unrestrained desires, then elenchus indirectly affects insatiable desires. It is not clear that Callicles has such desires already; but if he did, the pain of contradiction might be a kind of punishment that disciplined them—analogous to punishment inflicted by the judge.[52] Such a view makes the punishment inflicted by the craft of elenchus an internal one instead of external. If it were external, Callicles would be shamed by having to admit, before his peers, to a contradiction in his beliefs. It is not that Callicles is actually made uncomfortable by discovering a contradiction; he is made uncomfortable by having to admit in public to a contradiction. On the other hand, if the punishment of elenchus is actually internal, it works by making Callicles face something about himself that it is painful for him to face. In this reading, Callicles feels pain because he sees a contradiction between two beliefs, at least one of which expresses how he wants to live. Since the contradiction is of a deeply held belief, one central to his conception of his life, Callicles is forced to make a momentous choice. Callicles is being made to face the fact that his desire for a certain kind of life is at odds with something else he believes. It is in this way that the craft of elenchus disciplines desires by pointing up a contradiction in beliefs.

At this point we can summarize the major features from our investigation of the therapeutic craft of ruling. While it is clear that the desires are the focus of this craft, it is not quite so clear how the craft will approach the desires that are thought to need treatment. First of all, Callicles presented an ideal account of the desires as unrestrained means for enjoying pleasure. Both Socrates and Callicles took this condition to be one of unrestraint. However, Socrates characterized lack of restraint to be insatiability, an inability to attain the goal of desire, satiety. The contrary ideal, held up by Socrates, is a life of moderate desires, a life of satiety— in which, it is suggested, each desire is able to fulfill its goal as a desire. There is contained in this ideal the notion of correct functioning for each desire. Later Socrates presents insatiability as a pathological condition in need of treatment. The treatment Socrates prescribes in the medical analogy is restraint of insatiable desires by a sort of discipline, like the discipline imposed by the physician. The latter treatment attempts to render insatiable desires compatible with other parts of the soul, including presumably other less insistent desires. Even though this account is at best suggestive, it does introduce for the first time the notion that the good state for the soul is an integration of certain kinds of desires. Here the goal of the craft of ruling is said to be a fitting together and harmonizing, by restraining them, of desires grown excessive. The ideal of psychic harmony makes its first appearance.

Finally, in elaborating the therapeutic craft of judging, Socrates says that punishment is the way that this craft achieves restraint of desires. Although his account is not explicit as to how punishment achieves restraint of desires, Socrates compares his own elenchus to a type of judicial punishment. The pain of the punishment is the pain of contradicting one's deeply held beliefs about the conduct of one's life. Socrates seems to assume that the contradiction will discipline and restrain desires. This development suggests that contradicting beliefs disciplines the desires these beliefs express and that the desires are second order desires about the kind of life one would lead. Disciplining these desires affects the first order desires—for example, the actual or would-be insatiable desires.

For the present, however, we can at least see the outlines of the answer that the *Gorgias* offers to our question about the perfection at which the political craft aims and its relation to the welfare of the ruled. Even though much about this account of perfection is still schematic and thus problematic, we can, nevertheless, see— if only dimly—the relation of perfection to welfare intended by the account. The ruler, as the shepherd of the people, seeks their perfection (*to beltiston*), according to Socrates in *Republic* I. But the perfection, according to the *Gorgias*, is a psychological perfection; the ruler seeks to bring the desires into order. The gap between perfection and welfare seems to have been narrowed. If the perfection sought by the craft of ruling is the moderation of the desires and if that moderation produces a certain compatibility of desires, perfection is closer to being the welfare of the person whose desires are perfected. Thus, Socrates' notion of moderation in the desires seems to honor a genuine sense of subjective welfare.[53]

VII

We can close this section by looking at a major problem this account of perfection leaves open, however. It is one related to a recent controversy about the efficacy of elenchus. Gregory Vlastos pointed up what he called "*the* problem of Socratic elenchus." If elenchus only shows a contradiction between beliefs, it cannot show which of two beliefs is the correct one.[54] Vlastos' interpretation makes Socratic elenchus both naive and indefensible.[55] One way to put this problem is to say that elenchus itself just does not seem effective in the way in which Socrates seems to think it effective. It depends on consistency; but Socrates does not seem aware that there is more than one way to achieve consistency of beliefs. Even if his interlocutor does hold the second belief—the belief that entails the denial of the interlocutor's original belief—he may well be prepared to give up the second belief—rather than his original belief. In fact, this problem seems even more pronounced if we suppose that the belief in question is an expression of a desire to lead a certain kind of life. Why should Callicles give up his desire to lead a life of unrestrained desire just because his belief that this life is the best contradicts some other belief he holds? Why should the second belief—that the soul with restrained desires is better than the soul with unrestrained desires—have such a profound effect on the soul of Callicles? If his desire to lead the life of unrestrained desires is so strong, why does he not just give up the second belief? Indeed, he might be imagined to be grateful to Socrates for having shown him that he holds an incompatible and unnecessary belief.

Charles Kahn, one of those commentators who hold that the elenchus has psychological implications, comes to the defense of Socratic elenchus. He holds that the elenchus exposes not just an incompatibility of beliefs but also an incompatibility of desires.[56] According to this interpretation, besides the desire that Socrates is attempting to restrain, there is another desire—one incompatible with the desire to be restrained. Referring to the passage at 466e, Kahn says that Socratic elenchus assumes that everyone wants the good. Not only does elenchus assume that everyone wants the good but it also assumes that everyone identifies, at some level, the good with virtue.[57] This interpretation can be incorporated into our previous account of elenchus. We would say that the two contradicting beliefs, exposed in the elenchus, both express desires of the interlocutor. We have assumed that Callicles' belief—that the life of unrestrained desire is the best life—is an expression of his desire to lead such a life. We could also assume that the second belief, which elenchus leads Callicles to assert and which contradicts the first belief, also expresses a desire. In the case of Callicles, his reluctant, elenctically produced admission that the soul whose desires are restrained is better off than the soul whose desires are unrestrained would, in some way, express another, unconscious, desire. Kahn would say that this admission expresses the unsuspected desire to lead a life of harmonious and ordered desires. Thus, Callicles is in the grip of incompatible desires.

However, if Callicles' situation is stated in this way, this approach does not really escape something analogous to *the* problem of Socratic elenchus. Even if we suppose that the contradictory beliefs expose incompatible fundamental desires, and even if we suppose that the exposure is painful, it is not obvious why Callicles should choose one desire over the other. That he must choose one is obvious; but why he should choose the one he chooses is not obvious. Elenchus alone is no more able to show which of two incompatible desires to choose than it is able to show which of two contradictory beliefs is correct. Just as the efficacy of elenchus as a mode of demonstration depends on an additional assumption about which of the two contradictory beliefs is correct, so the efficacy of elenchus as a discipline of desires depends on an assumption about which of two incompatible desires is preferable. Elenchus cannot be efficacious by exposing an incompatibility of desires alone. In order for elenchus to be efficacious in disciplining vicious desires, one must assume that the comparison of the two desires will also show that the desire for virtue is one's strongest, or authentic, desire.

Indeed, Kahn's interpretation anticipates this objection. Socratic elenchus assumes a determining role for the overarching desire for the good. Under the guidance of elenchus, then, Socrates' interlocutor might come to see that, in comparing the life of unrestrained desires with the life of balanced and harmonious desires, the latter and not the former fits with his fundamental desire for the good. What is assumed is that the desire for the good has this determining force in his interlocutors.[58] Indeed, if we assume a universal desire for the good, it makes some sense to say that exposing the incompatibility of desires is a way of making the interlocutor realize which of the two desires he actually prefers. It is by no means necessary but it is not unlikely that, faced with two such desires, one would achieve the requisite clarity about which desire is one's true or authentic desire. Moreover, Socrates might plausibly be presented as believing that one's desire for the good plays the decisive role in this realization. It is even plausible to say that the desire for the good would incline one toward the desire for virtue. Kahn warns, however, that the process would be protreptic rather than deductive. His reason is that verbs for desire govern opaque contexts.[59] Just because Callicles desires the good, it does not follow that he desires the harmony and balance of desires—even if the latter are the good. After all, he might not know that the good is the harmony and balance of desires. If he did not know this vital fact, then he could not be led deductively from his desire for the good to a desire for harmony and balance of desires. The most that Socrates can hope is that elenctic questioning can bring Callicles to realize the identity of the good with harmony and balance of desires. Absent such a realization, Callicles cannot conclude from a desire for the good to a desire for harmony and balance of desires.

There is a problem, however, even with this scenario. If we assume for the moment that elenchus is deductive, it might have the following shape. The desire for the good would function as the standard in a compatibility test. When elenchus reveals two contradictory beliefs, these beliefs express incompatible desires. Socratic elenchus would then bring the desire for the good to the fore and the resolution is effected by comparing the two desires to the desire for the good. If the interlocutor sees that one of the two desires is implied by the desire for the good, then he could see that the other desire is incompatible with the desire for the good. Since he desires the good, he will see which desire is preferable. Thus, when Callicles sees that his desire to lead a life of unrestrained desire is incompatible with the desire expressed in his belief that a soul with restrained desires is better than one with unrestrained desires, he is forced to see the relation of the two desires to the desire for the good. He then sees that the desire for the good implies a desire for a soul with restrained desires and that the desire for a life of unrestrained desire is incompatible with the desire for the good. He now knows which desire is preferable. However, the problem with this model is that the desire for the good does not seem determinant enough to have the required deductive force. The difficulty is that, in order for the deductive model to work, the desire for the good would have to have enough content to make the determination of implication and incompatibility possible. On the surface, at least, it does not seem to have such a content. The desire for the good does not seem to have enough content to imply the desire for a restrained and balanced soul.

No wonder that Socrates is such a threatening figure in this dialogue, the subject of so much anger. He listens intently to his interlocutor, searching for the belief that betrays what he believes to be a morally corrupt desire. Then he moves in with his elenctic questioning and shows how the belief contradicts another belief the interlocutor holds. The first belief is, however, not just a randomly chosen belief; it is the articulation of a deeply seated and centrally important desire. The genius of Socrates' elenctic method is that he can expose such desires. Such behavior is threatening, of course, because deeply seated and centrally important desires—especially ones with broad implications for one's whole life—are usually guarded closely. No one wants those desires ridiculed; no one wants anyone taking—or even trying to take—these desires away. Yet this kind of diremption is precisely what Socrates seems to aim for.

Because we all have such deep-seated and important desires, we can understand Callicles' anger. Each of us probably would at least wonder why Socrates should be allowed to probe our very souls, seeking out those desires he thinks evil. We might easily become angry with him because we might find him to be meddling. Each of us might feel that Socrates is dealing with things—our heart's desires—about which he cannot possibly have proper understanding. It seems presumptuous in the extreme for him to expose and attempt to modify or extinguish a desire so important to one's whole life. But, more to the point, why should we allow him to characterize the exposed desire as fit to be extirpated? There is something arbitrary at the very heart of Socrates' procedure. The elenchus at most shows an incompatibility of desires; but the elenchus by itself cannot show the interlocutor which of the incompatible desires should be abandoned. Nevertheless Socrates decides which desire is the culprit and therefore which desire should be abandoned. We might want to ask why he thinks it obvious that, if one feels the contradiction, the desire for the good will lead to the Socratically determined outcome. Indeed, one of the salient features of this dialogue is the final disposition of the character Callicles. Socrates has made little progress in convincing Callicles that a life of unrestrained desires is not worthy of pursuit. Socrates may compare unrestrained desires to disease; but it is not clear that Callicles ever agrees to the comparison. He has yet to renounce a life of unrestrained desires—a life of the greatest possible influx—as his ideal merely because his belief that such a life is desirable seems to run afoul of other beliefs he holds. If anything, Callicles seems inclined to modify these other beliefs or to seek to evade in some other way the contradiction. Callicles seems to want to cling to the ideal of a life given over to the endless filling of those empty jars.

In one way of looking at it, this problem casts doubt on what we said previously about the relation between perfection and welfare. At the end of the last section we said that the gap between perfection and welfare is narrowed if perfection moderates desires so that they are compatible and if compatibility of desires constitutes, or is a part of, one's overall good. However, if there is more than one way to achieve compatibility of desires—by, for example, giving up the moderate desires—then it is possible that one would achieve compatibility of desires by letting immoderate desire define an alternative good. Thus, insatiable desires might come to define in the mind of Callicles the good life as the life given over to the pleasures of replenishment—as long as he is willing to give up whatever belief he has about the value of bravery. Seen from this perspective, the welfare of the soul would be different from its perfection, when the latter implies restraint and moderation. Thus, the gap between perfection and welfare opens again.

These issues in moral psychology are ones that must be addressed in the *Republic*. In the latter dialogue, Plato makes significant advances in moral psychology, introducing a more complex account of the parts of the soul. Presumably, the craft that orders these parts is accordingly made more complex; it must order more and quite different parts. These aspects of the mature moral theory are addressed in Books II–IV. It is, of course, an important part of this more complex moral psychology that we get a better view of what moderation in the desires is and how to go about achieving it. At the same time, we learn that there is more to the political craft of soul-tending than merely moderating desires. The other parts of the soul present further aspects for balance and harmony. It is in the context of this advanced moral psychology that Plato addresses anew the issue of the relation of desires to the good of the whole soul. As well, the *Republic* revisits the issue of consistency of moral beliefs and compatibility of desires as the content of the good life. Since there are different ways to achieve compatibility, mere compatibility of desires is not enough. There needs to be a standard whereby one can judge among the possible ways to make one's desires compatible. The standards are the Forms; they are presented in Books V–VI of the *Republic* as the guides that the rulers use in making their decisions for the city. As well, these are the standards that the rulers use in establishing and maintaining the correct ordering of souls of the citizens.

Having seen what headway the *Gorgias* has made in explicating the relation between perfection in the soul and human welfare, we need now to recall that in this dialogue Socrates also identifies the perfection of the soul, the disciplining of desires, as virtue, *aretē*. And while, in this passage, *aretē* is first of all used in a general sense to apply to every kind of excellence, including that of inanimate objects, when Socrates turns to human *aretē* it is clear that he means the usual panoply of virtues, that is, justice, temperance, bravery, and piety. We need to remember that Socrates is making a rather bold claim, that is, that psychic health will result in a certain kind of behavior toward others. The person with moderated desires will treat other humans justly, the gods piously. Such a person will act courageously in, among other things, the affairs of the city. The relation between human welfare as psychic health and the practice of these virtues is, of course, a vexed question both in the *Gorgias* and the *Republic*. For it is not obvious that psychic health will automatically result in that kind of conduct that we identify as virtuous. When we turn to the latter dialogue, we will need to see in what way it allows us to have a better view of the most difficult issue, the relation between psychic health and the virtues—the relation between disciplined desires and treating others justly, acting courageously in the affairs of the city, treating the gods piously.

NOTES

All translations, unless otherwise noted, are the author's.

1. We will follow the order of the dialogues outlined in T. Irwin, *Plato's Moral Theory* (Oxford: Clarendon Press, 1977), 291–292. Although Irwin does not agree with those who take *Republic* I to be an early dialogue, we will treat it as one. The difference on this point is not significant; even Irwin admits that the dialogue is Socratic in the way that it presents the craft analogy (178). What we say about *Republic* I needs only this concession.

2. This distinction between the craft analogy and the craft of ruling is not one properly understood by many commentators. Cf. *Plato: Gorgias*, T. Irwin, trans. and ed. (Oxford: Clarendon Press, 1979), 214, n. 503de and C. D. C. Reeve, *Philosopher Kings* (Princeton: Princeton University Press, 1988), 19–20.

3. Cf. Michael J. O'Brien, *The Socratic Paradoxes and the Greek Mind* (Chapel Hill: University of North Carolina Press, 1967), 58 ff.

4. No claim is being made about the relative dates of these two dialogues but only about the relation of relative complexity of accounts of the ruling craft. Such a claim is consistent with the notion that *Republic* I is a "Socratic" dialogue, even if it was written after the *Gorgias*.

5. Cf. David L. Roochnik, "Socrates' Use of the Techne-Analogy," *Essays on the Philosophy of Socrates*, Hugh H. Benson, ed. (New York: Oxford, 1992) Roochnik gives a helpful list of citations of the craft analogy. However, his thesis about the implications of the analogy contradicts the aims of the present book; I will address his thesis about these implications in the next chapter.

6. The following references are by no means exhaustive. Horse training: *Apo.* 25a–c, *Rep.* 342c; medicine: *Charm.* 171a, *Euthyd.* 291e, *Euthyphro* 13d, *Gor.* 501a, *Rep.* 341e; physical training: *Crito* 47b, *Gor.* 464b; huntsmanship: *Euthyphro* 13e; farming: *Euthyd.* 291e; shep-

herding: *Rep.* 345d; building: *Euthyphro* 13e; working in brass, wood, and wool: *Charm.* 173d; calculation: *Charm.* 165e, *Gor.* 453e.

7. Cf. J. Gould, *The Development of Plato's Ethics* (Cambridge: Cambridge University Press, 1955), 16 ff.; J. Lyons, *Structural Semantics* (Oxford: Basil Blackwell, 1963), 139 ff. While Lyons says that "the field of *epistēmē* is divided by the fields of *technē* and *gnōsis*" (178), it must be remembered that he is talking about the whole Platonic corpus; the present qualified claim is about the early dialogues only. Cf. *Charm.* 165c4–e1; *Euthyd.* 281a1–b2.

8. Cf. Aristotle's *Metaphysics* Book I, 980b25–981b15. See also Martha Nussbaum, *The Fragility of Goodness* (Cambridge: Cambridge University Press, 1986), 96 and J. E. Tiles, "*Technē* and Moral Expertise," *Philosophy* 59(1984):60–61.

9. Cf. D. S. Hutchinson, "Doctrines of the Mean and the Debate Concerning Skills in Fourth-Century Medicine, Rhetoric and Ethics," *Apeiron* 21(1988):34–35.

10. Cf. Kimon Lycos, *Plato on Justice and Power* (Albany: State University of New York Press, 1987), 109 ff. for an attempt to defend this argument.

11. For a very helpful discussion of Thrasymachus' position see P. P. Nicholson, "Unraveling Thrasymachus' Argument in the *Republic*," *Phronesis* 19(1974):210–32. See also F. Sparshott, "An Argument for Thrasymachus," *Apeiron* 21(1988):55–67.

12. Cf. Lycos, *Plato on Justice*, 46–47.

13. Such would be the implication of Nicholson's analysis of injustice in "Unraveling" 216: "What then is justice for the ruler? Since justice is the advantage of another, justice for the ruler must be the subject's advantage. It is because this is so, that Thrasymachus always prefers injustice to justice, that is, prefers the promotion of one's own advantage."

14. Cf. J. R. Bambrough, "Plato's Political Analogies," in *Plato: A Collection of Critical Essays*, vol. 2. Gregory Vlastos, ed. (Garden City: Anchor, 1971), 187–205. Bambrough argues that Plato is making only an analogy between ruling and craft. According to Bambrough the problem with the notion of ruling as a craft is that craft is necessarily instrumental; it can have no internal standard for what it is supposed to accomplish. This point, if true, would work against Socrates' argument here. Socrates wants to argue that the craft of ruling does have an internal standard for what it is supposed to accomplish, that is, the good of the ruled. Against Bambrough's position, Tiles ("*Technē* and Moral Expertise," 49–66) holds that craft entails an understanding (*epistēmē*) of the end of the craft. In what follows, I am trying to add plausibility to this position by pointing up the shift from *to sympheron* to *to beltiston*.

It seems more reasonable to think of a craft having an end if the end is thought of as *to beltiston*.

15. This reading of *to beltiston* is based on the following facts. (a) *To beltiōn* is formed from the comparative of *agathos*—'good'—and means literally 'the better.' (b) In this sense, then, to seek, literally put, the better of an object is to seek the improvement of an object. (c) *Beltistos* is the superlative of which *beltiōn* is the comparative. (d) *To beltiston* means literally 'the best.' Therefore, if to seek the better of an object is to seek its improvement, then, by extension, to seek the best of an object is to seek its perfection, its coming to full flower.

16. Cf. R. J. R. Kraut, "Reason and Justice in Plato's Republic," *Exegesis and Argument*, Lee, Mourelatos, and Rorty, eds. (Assen: van Gorcum, 1973), 220.

> Suppose, however, that the artisan does his job because he loves it. He starts learning his trade during childhood and becomes enthusiastic about it. Then, having mastered it, he pursues it with the same single-minded devotion shown by the carpenter who rejects lengthy medical treatment. Unlike an artisan who is concerned primarily with making money, the devoted craftsman would go to great lengths to make the best product he can.

17. For an interesting attempt to untangle this particular feature of Socrates' argument against Thrasymachus see Lycos, *Justice and Power*, 106–119.

18. However, if this new claim is plausible and proof against Thrasymachus' objection, it itself is open to another objection. Even if Socrates substituted perfection for welfare in his argument, surely he did not mean to abandon the claim that craft seeks the welfare of its object. Surely he meant something like the claim that craft seeks the welfare of its object by seeking its perfection. Yet, it is not so clear that just because a craft seeks the perfection of its object that it is therefore also seeking the welfare of its object. After all, it is not logically impossible—at a first glance, anyway—to try, and succeed, in making a race horse a perfect race horse and make it die before its time—or a student into an excellent philosophy major and make her unhappy, haunted by the eternal puzzles of philosophy. Cf. Irwin, *Gorgias*, 134, n.464c. Perhaps we can explain this difference between perfection and advantage by saying that perfection is defined in terms of function. There are many functions an object may fulfill and there are crafts to perfect those functions. But it is clear that fulfilling—and *a fortiori* perfecting—at least some of those functions would be to the disadvantage of the object. Quite clearly, our own contemporary debate about social policies impinges on this same issue. When we try to perfect children into good citizens, are we merely domesticating them to the demands of a dysfunctional adult world or rather are we doing some good for them as human beings? Unlike the charge of

Thrasymachus, this charge does not say that anyone else is benefiting from this domestication, only that those perfected to functions within the adult world are not benefited.

Socrates has shifted the ground of his argument from the claim that ruling seeks the welfare of the ruled to the claim that ruling seeks the perfection of the ruled. Thereby he has sidestepped the grosser implications of Thrasymachus' argument; but he has opened himself up to a more profound objection. The rulers might not be self-serving; but they may still be making victims of their subjects by, even unwittingly, accommodating them to an inhuman fate.

19. Cf. Basil O'Neil, "The Struggle for the Soul of Thrasymachus," *Ancient Philosophy* 8(1988):167–185. O'Neil also notes the vital link between ruling in *Rep.* I and in *Gor.* However, he presents the link in a different order of development than from the one presented here; but then his focus is not so much the ruling craft in the city as ruling craft in the soul. On this point he admits that Book I anticipates the rest of the *Republic.*

20. Mary Margaret Mackenzie, *Plato on Punishment* (Berkeley: University of California Press, 1981) shows how punishment, for Plato, has therapy for the criminal as its function. Although an acceptable theory of punishment, she also shows that it is in competition with theories in which the welfare of the criminal is not paramount.

21. If pleasure comes only from satisfying desires, from filling the jars, once the filling is over so is the pleasure. For example, the pleasure of a good meal comes from eating, which satisfies the emptiness of hunger; once hunger is satisfied pleasure ceases. Taken literally, the image implies that the jars can be filled up once and for all; then the pleasure of that jar (desire) is over once and for all—as though it would be possible to eat one meal that would be sufficient for the rest of one's life. Irwin, *Gorgias*, 196, n.494ab "But Socrates has assumed that happiness consists in a permanent state of being filled—if I could desire and get everything I need all at once and then always remain filled, I would be well off." But whatever else she might have meant by her solemn vow never to be hungry again, Scarlett O'Hara surely did not mean she wanted to be finished with eating once and for all.

Of course, it must be admitted that Callicles seems to take Socrates to be urging just such a life. He rejects it because such a life, having no replenishment, is devoid of pleasure; it is the life of a stone. However, we are not forced to accept Callicles' understanding of the image as authoritative. He can easily mistake Socrates' meaning; this claim is not diminished by the absence of Socrates' attempt to correct his mistake. We need not expect Socrates to take on the task of correcting Callicles' misunderstanding, if he indeed misunderstands. After all, Socrates seems intent on pushing Callicles to draw out the consequences of the Calliclean position; he need not pause to explicate fully his own.

Irwin's reading is based on the assumption that filled jars are to be equated with desires that have been satisfied once and for all. In turn, it would follow that leaky jars "that can never be filled" are desires that are never satisfied. According to this reading, in Socrates' portrayal of Callicles' ideal life, the intemperate person never experiences satisfaction of desire. Such a person would be hungry no matter how much he ate, thirsty no matter how much he drank. This literal reading of the image cannot be right. It should be clear that Callicles' hero of the appetites does satisfy his desires fairly regularly. Even Socrates seems to say as much when he says that, according to Callicles, the happy person is supposed to fill his desires, grown as great as possible, from whatever source (*heōnta de autas hōs megistas plerōsin autais hamothen ge pothen hetoimazein* [492d 6–7]). Cf. Irwin, *Gorgias*, 195, note 493bc, seems to agree with this reading. On the other hand, in his critical edition, *Plato "Gorgias,"* (Clarendon Press: Oxford, 1959), 304, n.493d5–495b9, E. R. Dodds holds the stronger, and somewhat stranger, thesis that Callicles believes that "without a constant process of replenishment (*plerōsis*) there can be no pleasure, and without pleasure one might as well be a stone." If we take "constant" literally, the pauses dictated by satiety would make pleasure impossible. Surely Dodds meant a continual process of replenishment.

22. It is clear, then, why Callicles would seek to lead the life of a tyrant; only such a person would have the material resources and the power to make the process of satisfying desires the whole of his life. He could allow his sexual appetite, for example, to become insistent and incessant. There would be no need to restrain it because of the lack of willing partners, occasions, settings, or accouterments. Nor would he need to worry about the censure of the community or legal sanction. The only obstacles to the constant pursuit of sexual pleasure would be imagination and physical strength. Moreover, in order to avoid becoming jaded, the tyrant should follow Callicles' advice and seek to make his appetites grow—to push the limits of satiety farther and farther out.

23. Dodds, *Gorgias*, 305, note e4–6. Dodds seems to agree with this reading in his translation of 493e4–6; "'The one man, having once got his jars filled, conducts no more supplies to them nor gives them a further thought; his mind is at rest so far as they are concerned.' The middle *plerōsamenos* is used with reference to the agent's interest."

24. Certainly this picture is the one we find in Xenophon's *Memorabilia*, I. 3. 5–6. Irwin's commentary also supports this Epicurean reading of Socrates' account at this point in the dialogue. Irwin, *Gorgias*, 194, n.492e.

25. What is wrong with these corrupted—and thus in need of restraint—desires, then, is not the object of the desire. Rather, the desire is bad because it seeks to have too much of a good thing. The desires for food, drink, or sex are not, in themselves, bad; they are bad because they lack restraint. These desires are not, then, fundamentally good-independent; they have been corrupted. By contrast, Irwin's discussion of these desires leaves one with the impression that there is a class of desires that are by nature good-independent. The good-independent desires are defined by the objects they seek. Moreover, some of these desires are actually desires for things that are bad for the person having the desires. These desires are good-independent and bad because what they desire is both independent of and deleterious to the good of the person having them. Thus, such good-independent desires are not good desires that have been led astray or even perverted; these good-independent desires are simply bad desires, incapable of changing or being changed, because they are defined by their objects, which are bad for the person having the desires.

26. Cf. T. Irwin, *Plato's Moral Theory*, 124.

27. This discussion reflects considerations brought forward by the following: J. C. B. Gosling, *Plato* (London: Routledge and Kegan Paul, 1973); Gerasimos Santas, *Socrates: Philosophy in Plato's Early Dialogues* (London: Routledge and Kegan Paul, 1979); *Plato "Gorgias,"* T. Irwin, ed. and trans.; T. Penner, "Thought and Desire in Plato," in *Plato*, G. Vlastos, ed., 96–118.

28. Norman Gulley, *The Philosophy of Socrates* (London: Macmillan, 1968), 87–93.

29. Santas, *Socrates*, 184 ff.

30. Santas, *Socrates*, 185–186.

31. Cf. Irwin, *Gorgias*, 143.

32. Cf. Irwin, *Gorgias*, 190–191, n.491d4e, uses the notion of good-independent desires, meaning desires "which aim at some pleasure rather than at the agent's good, as the agent conceives it. . . ."

33. Cf. Gosling, *Plato*, 29–30.

34. Commentators are not always very clear about this condition. Cf. Santas, *Socrates*, 200; Irwin, *Plato's Moral Theory*, 124; Penner, "Thought and Desire," 101; Irwin, *Gorgias*, 191. While this claim is more substantive than the previous, it is also at odds with our experience. Cf. Dodds, *Gorgias*, 235–236, n.467c5–468e5. The person who eats the brownies might well soberly consider the effects on her weight and cholesterol level, think about blood pressure and heart disease; yet she might go right ahead and eat the brownies. She seems, on the face of it, someone who knowingly decides to do what is harmful to herself. Not only does her desire remain after her assessment of her overall welfare; it determines her choice in the matter. However, a Socratic answer to such

an objection is to say that, in these cases, one still desires the good but that one's knowledge of the good is obscured—for example, the harmful consequences of satisfying such desires are masked in some way. In our previous example, we supposed a person continuing to eat brownies even after she recognized that eating them was not good overall. Still a defender of the Socratic claim that desire is for the good could say that the reason for her behavior might be that she decided for the good of pleasure. Two goods are presented to her—the good of health and the good of the pleasure of eating the brownies. The prospect of the good of the latter clouds her grasp of the good of the former; she mistakenly decides for the latter. Still, her desire is for the good; it is her poor grasp of the good that is the problem in this case. She has come to believe that the pleasure of eating the brownie is the good. Thus, she does what she believes to be good, although her belief is wrong; still, she does not knowingly do what is harmful to herself. Cf. Penner, "Thought and Desire," 99. See also Santas, *Socrates,* 188–189.

However, it is still possible to hold that even this milder claim is wrong. Some people hold that some desires are not, in any sense, aiming at the good. To use Irwin's terminology, we can say that some desires are good-independent. A good-independent desire is simply one whose satisfaction has nothing to do with the welfare of the agent; and the agent knows that fact clearly and unequivocally. In our previous example, we need not think that the person who ate the brownie had finally decided (even mistakenly) that the good of pleasure was better than the good of health; she might well have understood fully that the brownie was bad when she decided to eat it. Thus the strong counterclaim against Socrates' claim: it is possible for someone to desire to do what is harmful to himself or herself even when that person is fully aware that the action is harmful. In such a case the desire is not for the good, nor is the person simply misled about the good. Indeed, in his commentary on the *Gorgias,* Irwin claims to find evidence in the text for just such a position; he hints that in this dialogue Plato may already be abandoning the Socratic position that desires are always for the good. Cf. Irwin, *Gorgias,* pp. 191 and 195 where he claims to find ambiguity on this point.

35. Cf. J. C. B. Gosling and C. C. W. Taylor, *The Greeks on Pleasure* (Oxford: Clarendon Press, 1982), 69–82. They argue that Socrates' counterargument is not antihedonist but rather is only an argument against the shortsighted hedonism of Callicles.

36. Cf. Dodds, *Gorgias,* 314, n.497d8–499b3.

37. It is unclear from the example whether Socrates means an appetite that is merely dysfunctional but not insatiable or an appetite that is dysfunctional because insatiable. If he meant for the diseased desires to be compared to leaking jars, Socrates would be here assuming that their

being insatiable has made them dysfunctional or pathological. However, Socrates makes no such explicit characterization of them.

38. Cf. Mary Margaret Mackenzie, *Plato on Punishment*, 185:

In the discussion with Callicles, Socrates returns to the subject of punishment. At 504 he is trying to establish the prudence of having a well-ordered soul. In the process he suggests that the satisfaction of bodily appetites is often less useful than abstention, particularly when abstention promotes health. For health is desirable; sickness makes life wretched. So it is with the soul, that when it is evil, its appetites should be restrained, and it should do only those things which improve it.

39. Indeed, the analogy seems to break down at this point. In the case of the body, the desires and the health of the body are conceptually separate so that satisfying the first is conceptually separate from the second; thus we make a causal connection between the first and the second. However, in the case of the soul, desires are more nearly constitutive of the soul rather than being separate things that can affect the soul. If desires are constitutive of the soul then what counts as being dysfunctional desires is different from the case of the body. Since being a desire is, by definition, being part of a soul, then the definition of the desire as being "dysfunctional" must be in relation to the soul of which it is a part. Thus, being a dysfunctional desire must be defined in terms of what it is to be a part of a whole. Since the desire is constitutive of this whole, it cannot be defined separately from this whole. Thus, we are thrown back on our concept of the nature of desire and of what it is for a desire to be functional within a whole of which it is an essential constituent.

40. This concentration on desires and their satisfaction raises the issue of hedonism. In *Plato's Moral Theory*, Irwin argues that, in the *Protagoras*, Plato accepts hedonism as a way of defending the Socratic argument against *akrasia* (106). This position is contested by both Vlastos (for instance in his introduction to *Plato, Protagoras* (Indianapolis, 1956) and Zeyl "Socrates and Hedonism: *Protagoras* 351b–358d," *Phronesis* 25(1980):250–269. In his commentary on the *Gorgias*, Irwin inclines toward the notion that, while Plato accepted hedonism in the *Protagoras*, in the *Gorgias* he changes his mind (205, n.499ab). Still, he believes that Plato "leaves open the possibility that a more sophisticated hedonism, with a different conception of pleasure, might avoid Socrates' objections . . ." (197). One possibility for such a more sophisticated hedonism might arise from the notion of moderating excessive desires. When such desires are moderated, they can be made to fit with other desires; the result might be more pleasant than indulging just one, immoderate desire. Thus, a sophisticated hedonism might be the motivation for the craft of making desires to fit and harmonize with one another. However, the present passage does not offer support for this position since it is vague about the parts of the soul that will be made to

fit together. Not only may immoderate desires be moderated in order to fit with other, moderate desires; it is possible that immoderate desires may be moderated in order to fit with other kinds of parts in the soul— as they are in *Republic* IV. In the following discussion, we concentrate on desires; but we should not forget that other parts of the soul may be the subject of the craft of ruling.

41. Cf. Irwin, *Gorgias*, 195, n.493a: "Though Socrates does not say so, these desires seem to be liable to conflict with other desires; if some desires are insatiable and others are not, conflict is liable to result." See also 220, n.506e–507a.

42. There is a concept of psychic health at work in this passage. Here Anthony Kenny ("Mental Health in Plato's *Republic*" *Proceedings of the British Academy*, 55[1969]:229–253) sees only an allegory for psychic health; fullfledged theory comes in the *Republic* (230). The theory builds on an analogy with health in the body, which is sometimes a "balanced constitution . . . of wet, hot, dry, cold, sour, and sweet," other times "a harmonious mixture or blending of the humours (phlegm, blood, yellow and black bile") (231). John Anton ("Dialectic and Health in Plato's *Gorgias*: Presuppositions and Implications," *Ancient Philosophy*, 1[1980]:49–60) argues that the *Gorgias* in fact has a theory of health, tied up with its theory of dialectic. For more on this topic, see below. See also Anthony Preus, "Socratic Psychotherapy" *University of Dayton Review* 16.1(1982–83)15–23. Although helpful, none of these articles addresses directly the role of desires as the source of pathology in this dialogue.

43. In any event, our original account of the malfunctioning of unrestrained desires seems somewhat different from what is now being proposed in this account of the treatment for pathological desires. The image of the leaky jars seemed to suggest strongly that insatiable desires were malfunctioning because they could not fulfill the function of desires; with insatiable desires one never has satiety. According to the image, the good is a moderate life in which the pleasure that comes from the process of satisfying desires is not the goal of life but, rather, having satisfied desires is the goal, that is, satiety itself. This malfunctioning belongs to individual desires. By contrast, the implication of the medical analogy is that the pathology consists in a type of relation among desires—that is, the systematic incompatibility of insatiable desires with other moderate desires.

Of course, the two conceptions of malfunctioning are not inconsistent. As we have said, having insatiable desires—desires that have become merely vehicles for the pleasures of replenishment—may be a sufficient condition for having incompatibility among desires. Indeed, the image of the leaky jars does suggest the possibility that insatiable desires would monopolize one's time and energy, thus keeping one from pursuing any other goals. Cf. Santas, *Socrates,* 190. And while the image did not explicitly represent problems of compatibility among desires, the elenchus that immediately follows the image does exploit the notion that insatiable desires would be incompatible with such higher order goals as bravery.

44. The other political craft, law making, restrains desires in another way. Even if it does not involve judicial punishment, it seems to be similarly severe. Referring to the political craft (that is, the therapeutic craft of the soul) at 513d, he says that those crafts aim at what is best: "not indulging in pleasure but battling against it." At 517c, Socrates rounds out his criticism of Pericles, Cimon, Themistocles, and Miltiades by saying that they merely indulged the desires of the Athenian people, instead of doing the job of a real statesman, that is, "giving those desires a different direction . . ." (*metabibadzein tas epithumias*). In this passage, it is clear that Socrates believes that a good orator should direct the desires toward what will make his audience better—toward virtue— instead of toward such things as ships, walls, and arsenals. If the nature of moderation is unclear, the relation between it and giving the desires a different direction is also unclear. Socrates might mean either redirecting immoderate desires or giving proper directions to desires not yet made immoderate. If he meant the former, then—given that the desire he is talking about in this passage was actually satisfied by buildings, ships, walls, and arsenals—this desire, grown immoderate by these public defense projects, might have been disciplined and thereby redirected toward virtue. Being sick, this desire must be subjected to drastic and painful treatment. On the other hand, if Socrates meant that these statesmen should have given a different direction to desires they found uncorrupted, he might mean that, for example, the healthy desire for self-defense should have been directed to acquiring virtue rather than ships, walls, and arsenals; perhaps there is implied here the claim that virtue is a better defense than ships, walls, and arsenals. Thus, only virtue would truly satisfy the desire for self-defense. Of course, the preceding is speculative. Since Socrates talks more about restraining and disciplining desires than about directing them aright, it will be more promising to concentrate on the former topic.

45. Cf. Mackenzie, *Plato on Punishment,* 185. In her book on Plato's theory of punishment, Mackenzie confines herself to a somewhat more general description of punishment and its effects than the one we are seeking in this chapter. She holds that Plato has in mind some combination of conditioning and education, but she does not go much further in specifying either notion. See also Dodds, *Gorgias,* 254, n.477e7–479e9.

46. This issue is also related to a problem about Socrates in contemporary scholarship: the conflict between Socrates' claim of ignorance

about virtue and his reliance on certain propositions of morality in his elenctic practice. Thus in *Socrates, Ironist and Moral Philosopher* (Ithaca: Cornell University Press, 1991) Vlastos addresses this issue by distinguishing between knowledge that entails infallible certainty and knowledge that is elenctically justifiable but not infallibly certain. Socrates' claims of moral knowledge belong to the latter category (32). In their book *Socrates on Trial* (Princeton: Princeton University Press, 1989) Brickhouse and Smith believe that Socrates is certain of the moral rectitude of his Delphic mission, although it is not elenctically justifiable; this certitude they attribute to divine origin (107). In his article, "Socratic Reason and Socratic Revelation" (*Journal of the History of Philosophy* 29[1991]:345–373) McPherran also attributes Socratic beliefs to divine origin, especially his belief in the reliability of his *daimonion*, although this belief is still to a degree rationally justifiable (356).

In his book *Socrates in the Apology* (Indianapolis: Hackett, 1989) Reeve's thorough account of what he calls "expert knowledge," which he identifies with craft knowledge, is closer to the mark, however (37–53). Indeed, Reeve claims that expert knowledge must have an explanation of its procedures that is elenchus-proof (38). Reeve contrasts this elenchus-proof expert knowledge with the knowledge that Socrates uses in his elenctic practice—for instance, that it is better to suffer injustice than to do it. The latter, although it is a strong conviction, is not expert knowledge; it lacks certainty, explanatoriness, and teachability (52–53).

In the *Gorgias*, the value of consistency might be one of those moral beliefs for which Socrates cannot give an explanation. Although it does not appear to have a divine origin, this belief is not relevant to our account. This account focuses on the beliefs of Socrates' interlocutors, not on those of Socrates. Finally, it is significant for our claim about the distinction between the craft of virtue and the craft of ruling that Socratic ignorance about virtue does not keep him from claiming to be a practitioner of the ruling craft.

47. Cf. Irwin, *Gorgias*, 218, note 505c, where he reads Calllicles' desires as the object of this restraint. Mackenzie,(*Plato on Punishment*, 185) seems to dismiss this very important self-referential passage as a joke. While the passage is amusing, it is also more than a mere joke.

48. Recently commentators have lavished a good deal of attention on the way Socratic elenchus brings about the awareness of this inconsistency. Gregory Vlastos, "The Socratic Elenchus," 29–58, and Richard Kraut, "Comments on Gregory Vlastos 'The Socratic Elenchus'," 59–70, in *Oxford Studies in Ancient Philosophy*, vol. 1, Julia Annas, ed. (Oxford: Clarendon Press, 1983).

49. Cf. Charles Kahn, "Drama and Dialectic in Plato's *Gorgias*" *Oxford Studies in Ancient Philosophy*, vol. 1, 75–121; Richard McKim, "Shame and Truth in Plato's *Gorgias*" in *Platonic Writings/Platonic*

Readings, Charles L. Griswold, ed. (London: Routledge, 1988), 34–48; John Anton, "Dialectic and Health," especially 56.

50. Cf. Irwin, *Gorgias*, 233, n.513c: "Though Socrates has previously suggested that Callicles' desires may be disordered (505c), and mentions here the misguided 'love' (*erōs*; see 481d) that prevents him from being convinced, he still insists that rational persuasion can make Callicles re-direct his desires."

51. Recent discussions have centered on how real the distinction between what one wants and what seems best is. Cf. Kevin McTighe, "Socrates on Desire for the Good and the Involuntariness of Wrongdoing: *Gorgias* 466a–468e," *Phronesis* 29(1984):193–236 and Naomi Reshotko, "The Socratic Theory of Motivation," *Apeiron* 25(1992): 145–170. My discussion does not turn on whether the good is the apparent good (McTighe) or determined objectively (Reshotko). Although I am more sympathetic with Reshotko's (and Penner's) reading, all my discussion needs is a possible variation between what one thinks initially about what is best and what elenchus will show one about the compatibility of that initial belief and one's desire for the good.

52. Charles Kahn, "Drama and Dialectic," emphasizes the psychological function of elenchus.

> Once Callicles admits that some pleasures are better, some worse (at 499b), he has in effect accepted *boulesthai* or rational choice as the decisive criterion of virtue and happiness, in place of *epithymia* or sheer desire. We thus return, immediately to the notion of the good as the end and goal of action (499e–500a), and eventually to the rational desire (*boulesthai*) for happiness, which can be realized only in the practice of the virtues (507c9 ff.). Hence, 'no one truly wants (*boulomenos*) to do injustice, but all who act unjustly do so involuntarily (*akōn*)' (509e5–7). As we know, this rational desire for the good may be partially unconscious, as it clearly was in Callicles' case. But it is the function of the elenchus to bring this desire to consciousness, as Callicles is reluctantly obliged to do.

Cf. McKim, "Shame and Truth." "His [Socrates'] method is therefore psychological, not logical—not to argue them into believing it [the Axiom that virtue is always supremely beneficial to the moral agent himself as well as to those toward whom he acts virtuously] (35) but to maneuver them into acknowledging that, deep down, they have believed it all along. . . . His chief weapon in this psychological warfare is not logic but shame" (36). This psychological warfare brings Socrates' interlocutors to recognize something about their basic attitudes. "Socrates does not deny that men often in fact choose injustice over justice; thus his argument *is* designed to encourage Polus to choose justice instead. But this encouragement consists of a psychological demonstration that it is *already* the choice that Polus and everyone else would always make, even at the expense of suffering injustice, *if they followed their own better judgment* as to their bests interests" (37).

53. Cf. *Gor.* 506e ff., where orderliness of soul leads to temperance and justice, to goodness, to doing well, and thus to happiness. As well, in *Republic* I Socrates says that there is proper (*oikeios*) function for each thing. This is the function that it alone can perform or that it performs best of all. He goes on to claim that there is such a function for the soul: to manage, govern, and rule—finally to live. Now fulfilling that function well is the proper (*oikeios*) virtue of the soul. Fulfilling that function well is also said to be happiness. This theme of proper function and proper virtue is also found in the *Gorgias*. The course of the argument at 506c ff. shows us that Socrates identified the virtue of an object with a certain order of parts. In turn, the virtue is the source of, or the same as, whatever good the object has. Finally, its order is proper and peculiar to each object. "Hence a certain order (*kosmos*) coming to be in each thing, which is proper to each (*ho hekastou oikeios*), provides the good for each" (506e). We can see, then, that Socrates' position is that whatever good an object has is due to its having its proper order. Of course, if 'proper' (*oikeios*) means only 'what the object ought to have,' such a position would be minimally informative. We might have found out only that Socrates held that an object is good because it has the order it ought to have. But 'proper' does not mean only 'what it ought to have.' It also means 'belonging to one,' 'one's own,' and 'one's peculiar'; that 'proper' has also this sense can be seen from the next lines where the peculiarity of the order is even more strongly emphasized. "So the soul which has the order which belongs to itself (*kosmon echousa ton heautēs*) is better than one which is unordered" (506 e). Here, the claim is being made, first, that an ordered soul is better than an unordered one and, second, that the order in question is one peculiar to the soul, is its own. Moreover, the contrast seems to presuppose that there is no way, other than by having its peculiar order, that a soul can be ordered and, thereby, good. The choice is between either the soul and its peculiar order or the soul without order since the thrust of the argument is to present two exclusive and exhaustive alternatives, only one of which is the true good.

54. The controversy surrounding Vlastos' article on '*the* problem of the elenchus' is precisely whether elenchus achieves anything more than a demonstration of inconsistency of beliefs. Socrates seems to claim that elenchus achieves not only such a demonstration but also the further conclusion that one of the inconsistent beliefs is false. See also Thomas Brickhouse and Nicholas D. Smith, "Vlastos on the Elenchus," *Oxford Studies in Ancient Philosophy*, vol. 2, Julia Annas, ed. (Oxford: Clarendon Press, 1984), 185–195, and Hugh Benson, "The Problem of Elenchus Reconsidered," *Ancient Philosophy*, 7(1987):67–85. The controversy about whether elenchus can achieve anything more than a

demonstration of inconsistency of beliefs is aimed at Socrates' claims for elenchus. In fact, whatever the resolution of that controversy, it still leaves open the response of the interlocutors. Socrates may or may not believe that his interlocutor has hostages to fortune among his moral beliefs. It is another question altogether whether his interlocutor actually does have just such compromising beliefs and, more importantly, whether he is able to give up the very belief that Socrates believes he should retain and thus is able to retain the very belief that Socrates thinks he should discard.

55. Gregory Vlastos, *Socrates, Ironist and Moral Philosopher*, 113–114.

56. Cf. Kahn,"Drama and Dialectic," 118: "So behind the refutation of Callicles we catch sight of a fundamental distinction between two conceptions of desire, and the inadequacy of one of these conceptions as the basis for a coherent theory of the good life." See also Kim, "Shame and Truth," 39: "Whereas shame is for Callicles an unnatural feeling that inhibits our real preference for vice, Socrates believes to the contrary, on my reading, that our shame about vice is a natural sign that deep down we really prefer virtue."

57. Kahn, "Drama and Dialectic," 113: "I want to recast it [the basis for Socratic dialectic] in terms of a doctrine that is explicitly attested in the first paradox of Act Two: the claim that all human beings desire the good and pursue it in all of their actions (*Grg.* 468b–c, 499e: cf. *Meno* 77c–78b, *Rep.* VI. 505d11). In this perspective, the deposit of truth on which the elenchus relies will be some recognition in all of us of what is truly good; and the truly good, for the *Gorgias*, can be identified with Socratic *aretē*, the moral and intellectual excellence of the soul." Richard McKim, ("Shame and Truth," 42) expresses a similar notion. "Indeed, courage is the "natural" virtue that he [Callicles] admires and covets most, an ironic contrast to his own fear of frankness in dialectic. That his thesis should commit him to a moral equivalence between courage and cowardice, then, is a consequence that even Callicles finds too morally shameful to stomach."

58. Kahn, "Drama and Dialectic," 114–115: "Perhaps we should construe Plato's use of such an argument as protreptic rather than deductive. If you come to see that virtue is good (and hence good for you), you *will* desire it. The function of the elenchus, reinforced by the presentation of Socrates as the embodiment of virtue, is to bring the interlocutor and the reader to the point where they see this. And the motive force is not provided by Socrates' dialectical skill alone but by his ability to draw upon that deep desire for the good that motivates every rational agent, even when the agent himself is ignorant of the nature and object of this desire."

59. Kahn, "Drama and Dialectic," 114.

CHAPTER 2

The Craft Analogy in the Early Dialogues and The Craft of Justice in Republic IV

At the beginning of the last chapter we made a distinction between the use of the notion of craft to explicate ruling and its use to explicate virtue—the latter being the craft analogy properly speaking. Our task in the last chapter was to elaborate and develop the craft of ruling. In this chapter we turn to the craft analogy properly speaking—the way in which Plato uses craft to explicate the notion of virtue. This use of the notion of craft we will call the "craft of virtue."[1] As we said in the last chapter, Plato's fully developed craft of justice in *Republic* IV combines both the craft of ruling and the craft of virtue from the earlier dialogues. So we want to investigate the craft of virtue in order to see those features that become part of the fully developed craft of justice. As well, in looking at the craft of virtue, we will expose some of the problems the notion raises. Raising these problems is also preparatory to our explication of the way that Plato combines the craft of ruling and the craft of virtue into the craft of justice. Presumably, Plato will address these problems in his new craft of justice.

In the early dialogues and in the *Gorgias* and the *Protagoras*, virtue is compared to craft in a number of ways. In many of these comparisons the notion of craft is used to illustrate some one point about virtue. For instance, in the *Charmides*, the young man Charmides says that temperance is quietness. Socrates subjects the claim to elenchus by pointing out that playing the lyre, wrestling, boxing, and the pancration are best done quickly, not quietly. Again, he says that learning writing or music is better done quickly than quietly (159c–160b). Thus, temperance cannot be quietness. Charmides then offers the definition of temperance proposed by his friend, Critias, that is, that temperance is doing one's own. In refuting this statement Socrates cites the schoolmaster, the physician, the builder, and the weaver, all of whom do not do only their own (161d–162a). Thus, temperance cannot be doing one's own. In a more general vein, at 165c Socrates compares temperance to medicine and architecture. Since each of the latter has a specific goal, Socrates wants to know what is the goal of temperance, which Critias now says is the knowledge of one's self. These comparisons are characteristic of early dialogues in which virtue is compared to craft on some one point. The purpose of such comparisons is to establish a step in an elenchus.

In the *Euthyphro,* at one point Euthyphro says that piety is that part of justice that has to do with service or care (*therapeia*) of the gods (13a). In order to refute this claim, Socrates attempts to establish the kind of care meant by listing those crafts that render care—the craft that takes care of horses, the one that takes care of dogs, and finally the one that takes care of cattle. The comparison produces a result that Euthyphro does not accept. Again, referring to what medicine produces, to what shipbuilding produces, to what house building produces, to what generalship produces, and finally to what farming produces, Socrates asks Euthyphro to characterize the result produced by piety (13d). These cases seem to make only the one point of comparison between piety and craft; the one point is part of the larger elenchus.

Both of these dialogues are representative of the way Socrates uses the craft analogy in an elenchus. The assumption seems to be that virtue is analogous to craft in some way. However, the analogy seems superficial because it is focused on only one point of comparison and that point is used primarily to establish what virtue is not. It is not clear whether the comparison allows us to say what virtue is. Are we to draw out implications from the comparisons? From the *Charmides,* we might conclude, for instance, that temperance is quick and decisive—like wrestling and boxing. We might conclude that temperance is not just doing one's own but perhaps involves caring for others or even the body politic. From the *Euthyphro,* we might conclude that piety provides a service to the gods, even if it is not like the service rendered to animals. We might conclude that piety produces a good, even if it is not like the good of farming and generalship. However, even if we can draw out such implications, it is not clear that we ought to.

At other points in the early dialogues, Socrates seems to be saying something more substantive about virtue when he uses the analogy with craft. In the *Charmides*, for instance, Socrates finally draws out Critias on the topic of temperance as knowledge of self. The knowledge of self becomes knowledge of knowledge (164d ff.). Socrates develops this notion, in turn, so that it becomes a way of knowing whether one knows something about a topic. The usefulness of this knowledge of knowledge is that it keeps one from believing that he knows when he does not. Armed with such knowledge, we could keep ourselves from acting in those areas in which we do not have knowledge (171e). The result would seem to be beneficial. "Our health will be better than now; we will be saved from dangers at sea and in battle; all attire, garments, and shoes, and all implements, will be made skillfully for us, and we will do many other things through genuine craftsmen" (173c). However, even regulated in this fashion, we will not necessarily be happy. Presumably the reason is that happiness is not the same as health, safety in battle, and skillfully made coats, shoes, and tools. Socrates then pushes Critias to redefine this overarching knowledge. Finally, he says that the knowledge that presides over these others will have to be the knowledge with which we discern good and evil (174c). At this point the dialogue ends in *aporia* because they cannot discover this knowledge of good and evil. Even with this disappointing result, the reader has a sense that something important and positive has been said about virtue. Temperance is presented as a kind of craft knowledge of good and evil, which will guide the other crafts so that they will provide advantage. Here we do not have virtue compared to craft on some one point but there is adumbrated a more complicated comparison between craft and virtue. Like craft, virtue will have a goal—good and evil or advantage and disadvantage; and like craft, it will have an object upon which it works, the other crafts that are subordinated to it.

We find the same pattern in the *Laches*. There are superficial comparisons between craft and virtue. For instance, in trying to decide whether courage is endurance, Socrates asks Laches about a physician who perseveres in the painful treatment of his reluctant patient—even when the patient is his son. Even though the physician perseveres—as a physician ought—he is not thereby courageous. However, towards the end of the dialogue, Nicias says that the courageous man is the one "who has mastery (*epistēmoni*) of the things to be feared and not to be feared" (194d 9). This knowledge Nicias differentiates from the specialized knowledge of, for instance, the physician, who may know how to cure but does not know whether being cured is always better for someone. Socrates subjects this notion of courage to elenchus by arguing that what is to be feared and not feared has to do only with what will happen in the future. However, a craft must know about past, present, and future. The conclusion is that courage must be concerned not only with the future but with the past and present (199c). However, then courage becomes the whole of virtue and not just a part of it (199e). At this point, the dialogue ends in *aporia*. Still, the reader has the sense that something substantive has been said about virtue. As in the *Charmides*, it is a craft knowledge of good and evil. Moreover, it is superior to the other crafts because it can achieve human advantage, although Socrates does not say that it guides or governs these other crafts. In fact, the *aporia* at the end of the *Laches* does not show the craft knowledge of good and evil to be a problematic concept; the problem is that it cannot be courage and courage was the virtue they set out to understand.

Nevertheless, it is probably because of these characterizations of virtue as a craft knowledge of good and evil that many people are tempted to believe that the craft analogy has a positive side, that it is not used just to make dialectical points about virtue.[2] The matter might have to be left indeterminate if there were not a fuller positive statement of the craft analogy. If there were, on the other hand, such a positive statement of the analogy we would be warranted to think that these implications were part of an account of virtue that found the comparison with craft fruitful because it told us something substantive about virtue. In fact, there is just such a positive statement in the dialogue *Euthydemus*, a statement echoed in the *Meno* (87c ff.).

I

Indeed, the clearest and best example of what we are calling the "craft of virtue" is in the Socratic dialogue *Euthydemus*. Another contrastive dialogue, like the *Gorgias*, but a less serious one, it contrasts the method of Socrates and the method of Euthydemus and Dionysiodorus. The latter practice eristic, a form of verbal combat whose goal is not to discover truth but to win arguments. Thus, they are shown as reckless and ambitious young men who have gone from a profession of physical combat to one of verbal combat. They enmesh their opponent in contrived and superficial contradictions by trading on ambiguities in meanings of words. They seem to most readers to be thoroughly repellent characters, especially in their treatment of the young Cleinias. The dialogue itself is protreptic, designed to convince readers and at least some of the characters that one ought to pursue wisdom. If we understand philosophy in its literal sense—love of wisdom—such a dialogue urges one to become a philosopher. However, a protreptic dialogue does not also tell the interlocutors exactly what the wisdom they ought to pursue is. In his two exchanges with Cleinias, Socrates is the spokesman for pursuing wisdom. However, Socrates achieves this task in an uncharacteristic capacity. Attempting to defend Cleinias from the verbal attacks of Euthydemus and Dionysiodorus, Socrates uses his question-and-answer method, at first at least, not in an elenctic but actually in a positive way. Indeed, under the cover of question-and-answer, Socrates lays out an account of the relation between virtue and the good life, which becomes—as we shall see—an important part of Plato's account in *Republic* IV. In what follows we will concentrate on the two exchanges between Socrates and Cleinias—the two protreptic interludes—and will leave the eristic exercises aside.

At 279a Socrates begins by asking Cleinias whether all men wish to do well (*eu prattein*). The latter phrase in Greek is ambiguous: to do well in the sense of prospering or to do well in the sense of acting well or competently?[3] In the first sense, to do well means to be successful, to be happy, and this can mean, and does mean for many people, material success—money and possessions. In fact, Socrates begins by having Cleinias list all those things whose possession most people count as doing well: riches, health, beauty, good birth, talents, and honors. However, Socrates does not stop with these goods but has Cleinias include the usual virtues: temperance, justice, bravery, and wisdom (*sophia*).[4] Finally, Socrates has Cleinias add good fortune (*eutuchia*) to the list; indeed, he says that it is the greatest of the good things. So far the list seems standard enough. Socrates has included the usual worldly goods, ranging from wealth to standing in one's community. To this list he adds the usual virtues, just as a parent might hope for a child to have material success and a good character. These are goods of different categories, of course; but most reflective people want both material success and integrity of character, as long as they do not have to choose between the two. However, good fortune seems another kind of good altogether. First of all, to have material success frequently requires good fortune. Acquiring wealth or keeping or enhancing the wealth one is given (cf. Cephalus in *Rep.* I) may require some good fortune or luck. Business affairs may depend greatly on one's acumen—but not entirely. Physical beauty—and even its maintenance—depend on good fortune. The role of good fortune in acquiring and maintaining moral virtue is less clear but is nevertheless real. If one is to be born with virtue, then one is obviously at the mercy of good fortune. If virtue is taught or acquired by training, one depends upon good fortune for getting the right teachers or trainers.

At this point Socrates does something unexpected. He says that they have been foolish in adding good fortune to their list. They have already counted it once when they listed wisdom. He says that wisdom (*sophia*) is good fortune (*eutuchia*) (279d6). Given that wisdom was previously listed among the virtues, Socrates means to say that the virtue of wisdom is good fortune. But his argument for this claim depends on the craft analogy. Socrates offers an inductive argument (*epagogē*) to establish the claim that wisdom is good fortune by citing a series of craftsmen: flute players, grammar teachers, sea captains, generals, and physicians. Each is wise (*sophos*) in his subject; in turn, one has good fortune when dealing with the wise practitioner rather than with the ignorant. The argument sets the stage for the central use of the craft analogy. It assumes, first of all, that we can generalize from the cases of wise craftsmen to a quality they all possess, wisdom. So far wisdom seems to be something common to all the craft knowledges practiced by all these craftsmen. Socrates develops this common characteristic later in the argument. At this point, it is also clear that this common characteristic is meant to throw light on the moral virtue of wisdom. Socrates does not hesitate to talk as though this common characteristic of "craft" should be called by the same name as the moral virtue of "wisdom" since he backs up the claim that the virtue of wisdom is good fortune by citing cases of craftsmen, who are by definition wise (*sophos*). Exactly what light this common characteristic does throw, we see later. For the present Socrates concentrates on craft itself. Craft knowledge provides some good result and it does so in a regular and dependable way. At least that seems to be what lies behind the extraordinary claim that wisdom is good fortune.

Now there is an ambiguity in the notion of good fortune in this passage.[5] Good fortune can mean the chance occurrence that results in something good happening to one; it can also mean the good result itself. Thus, winning the lottery is good fortune, in one sense, because it provides wealth; in another sense, the winner might call the wealth itself "good fortune." To say that wisdom is good fortune (279d) means something like wisdom—understood as the common characteristic of craft knowledge—is equivalent, in one important respect to good fortune; wisdom, like good fortune, provides one with a good result. What one can obtain by good fortune can be obtained by wisdom. What the lottery puts in one's lap can be gotten by the craft of money making. On the other hand, Socrates also says that wisdom always makes men to enjoy good fortune. (280a) Here, good fortune is a result; but instead of being the result of chance, it is the result of craft.[6] The reasoning seems to be something like: when one goes to the craftsman, things turn out well; when things turn out well, one has good fortune; so when one goes to the craftsman one has good fortune. However, the intent here seems the same; with wisdom—understood as a general way of referring to all the crafts—one can obtain the same results as with luck; in these cases, at least, one does not have to depend on luck.[7]

However, at 280b, Socrates puts his conclusion in an even stronger form: the person who has wisdom does not also need good fortune. If good fortune means the chance occurrence that provides good things, then he means that wisdom provides all the good things that chance occurrence can. Socrates backs up this extraordinary claim by arguing that wisdom always succeeds, always leads to doing well and having a good result; otherwise it is not wisdom. (280a) We have seen this notion of the infallibility of craft before, in *Republic* I (342a).[8] In the present case, it is difficult to see how this claim can always be true, given his own list of goods—for example, health, beauty or good birth. On the one hand, good fortune could provide one with a healthy constitution, free of congenital defects; good fortune could keep one from getting the plague. Socrates seems to be saying that, in some ideal state, a physician would be so skilled that he could achieve by the craft of medicine any of these things that good fortune could bring about. On the other hand, good fortune could give one the beauty of an Alcibiades or of a Helen. Is there a craft that could give one such beauty? Is there a craft that could give one the good birth of a Plato?

In any event, it is obvious that Socrates is depending on an important characteristic of craft—its infallibility—in order to arrive at what is a significant step in his argument. In the next sec- tion of his argument, he continues to develop this notion of wis- dom, understood as craft knowledge. In order to do well, one must benefit from the goods one has; and merely having goods is not enough in order to benefit from them. One must use these goods. Clearly returning to his previous account of wisdom, Socrates illustrates this point with instances of crafts. If craftsmen (*dēmiourgoi*) possess what they need for their crafts but do not use those things, can they do well? The carpenter (*tektōn*), for instance, who, having gotten all his tools and sufficient wood, did not use them to build anything, would not benefit from the mere possession of these things. So it follows that one must not merely possess all of the goods just mentioned; one must use them. No benefit is gained from mere possession of riches, health, beauty, good birth. In fact, Socrates says that in order to be happy, one must use these good things. Then, in a very important step in his argument, Socrates makes the connection between the common characteristic of craft knowledges and the virtue of wisdom. The use of these good things is not enough; their use must be right use, otherwise they will result in harm. Moreover—drawing on the craft analogy—he says that right use is brought about by knowl- edge.[9] In the case of carpentry, what accomplishes right use (*orthōs chrēsthai*) is the knowledge (*epistēmē*) of carpentry (281a3–4). Thus, in the right use of the other goods—for example, health, wealth, and beauty—it was knowledge that guided and ruled over (*hēgoumenē kai katorthousa*) their use. So it is knowl- edge that provides right use (*eupragian*) and good fortune (*eutu- chian*) in all possessions and practices. Socrates then connects knowledge with the moral virtue of wisdom by concluding that one can gain no benefit from possessions without understanding (*phronēseōs*) and wisdom (*sophias*) (281b1–6).[10]

The account is rich in possibilities. A good carpenter knows about tools, the difference among tools, the task each is made for; he also has "a feel for" tools, how to handle them, what amount of pressure is appropriate. A good carpenter also knows about materials; the different kinds of woods and their different uses. Of course, he also has a detailed notion of how the tools and materials go together to produce a table or a house; in fact, all of his knowledge points toward such a goal. It is a peculiar kind of knowledge, which discounts properties and facts not relevant to the end in view and fastens on properties that are relevant. If we turn back to the list of goods that originally constituted doing well, we can see the appeal of this analogy. Most people agree that mere possession of wealth, or beauty, or good birth is not enough. If one has that kind of insight, she would not be tempted to treat health, wealth, and good looks as ends; she would be interested in them insofar as they could contribute to a more general goal of her life. This notion of mere possession being inadequate has a peculiarly contemporary ring to it. In a consumer society, there certainly are people who seem to believe that mere possession of material goods makes one happy. Spiritually poverty stricken, they do not seem to know what else to do with their possessions than to sit among them; they have missed the point that they must also have the wit to use them well in order to derive real benefit from them. Worse still, sometimes people who are deceived into believing that mere possession is happiness become something like the servants of their possessions. We have to think only of the furniture that can never be used, but only cleaned, polished, and protected; the owners have become the servants of the furniture.

Moreover, the one who could identify a goal other than mere possession might well see that these possessions must be used well to achieve that goal. In Plato's analogy, she would need a craft knowledge that would guide her use of them so that she would act with the deftness that a good carpenter shows in his use of tools and wood. With understanding and wisdom the good person will know how to use assets of body and of soul so that they are beneficial and not harmful. The fact that these assets can be harmful gives us a little better sense of what right use might be then. The good person has an understanding of her true welfare and of the way to use her assets to achieve that welfare. No matter how varied the attractions that the uses of, for example, wealth may present, the good person can discern the difference between the uses that are harmful and those that are beneficial. Not only is she skilled at discerning the difference, she is also skilled in making the means achieve the preferred end.

Indeed, we can all understand how the material goods can be misused. Wealth is the most obvious example; news stories and movies are filled with accounts of people who not only spend money unwisely, in the sense that they get nothing important in return, but who spend money for things that actually hurt them. *The National Enquirer* tells us all the time about the ways that beautiful people are made unhappy precisely because of their beauty. The same sort of thing can be said for good birth; here perhaps the journal of record is *Paris Match*, in which the vicissitudes of European nobility are chronicled. On the other hand, there are examples of wealthy people who use their wealth wisely. They buy things that they really need; they do not buy things that harm them. Their being able to do so depends apparently on their understanding their real needs. Perhaps, for instance, they prize their own characters and use their wealth in accordance with their conception of that character. Perhaps they use their wealth for philanthropic purposes, thinking that generosity is an important virtue. In general, then, they acquire possessions that serve their reflective conception of the good life instead of becoming the appendage of possessions that impose an unconsidered and harmful style of living. As well, there are movie stars who are not absorbed or destroyed by their own physical beauty; rather they use it to serve their various projects as well-rounded persons.[11]

Most people can see the need for a sense of the true value of our assets—whatever they might be—for living a happy and fulfilled life. There is something compelling, then, about having such a clear sense of the direction of one's life that one can make whatever material possessions or whatever physical or mental talents one has fit into a pattern that will reflect one's conception of the good life. We can all admire the well-made cabinet, run our hands along its surfaces, and admire the skill and intelligence that brought all these elements together. It is not without its seductiveness to think that one's own life could have the same aspect of a well-made project. Unfortunately, in this passage we find little else besides this tempting prospect. While wisdom and carpentry have been compared with respect to materials, tools, knowledge of right use, and doing well, nothing very detailed has been said about the product of wisdom, other than that it is happiness or advantage. The product of carpentry is, of course, something like a table or a house. If Socrates had been able to complete the comparison, he could easily have said that happiness or welfare was something like a table or a house, that is, an identifiable product separate from the exercise of the craft. Then he could have gone on to specify the nature of the happiness that is the product of wisdom. Pleasure, for example, might be such a product; the wise man, then, would use health, wealth, and good looks so that he would have the greatest pleasure, perhaps in the fashion of an Epicurean. However, Socrates did not draw out the analogy by specifying the goal of the craft in this or in any other way.[12]

In passing, it is worth pointing out the difference between this account of the virtue of wisdom and the account of virtue in the *Gorgias*. In the *Euthydemus* the virtue of wisdom is a craft of managing one's material and spiritual assets; in the *Gorgias* virtue, the product of the craft of ruling, is not itself a craft but a characteristic of the soul consisting of a harmony of desires, perhaps of other parts of the soul. In the *Euthydemus* we are told that happiness consists in or is the result of this management; however, we are not told how to manage those assets so that we will be happy. There is a gap in the account about the nature of the goal and about the means to attain it. In the *Gorgias*, on the other hand, the goal of the craft of ruling and how to attain it are at least sketched in. The goal is a psychic harmony, including desires as components, and the means is a disciplining of the desires.

In fact, another version of this problem of specifying the goal of the craft of wisdom is taken up in a subsequent passage of the *Euthydemus*. At 288d, Socrates begins the second protreptic interlude with Cleinias; they are to take up where they left off, that is, where Cleinias became convinced by the protreptic argument that one ought to seek wisdom. At 289b, Socrates says that they are looking for a craft knowledge (*epistēmē*) that makes but also knows how to use what it makes. It is not like harp making, which can only make but not use what it makes. The subsequent discussion becomes an extended search to find any craft that both makes and uses its product. In each case, the candidate craft only makes something; it turns over what it makes to another craft to be used—for example, hunting turns over its catch to the cook. After ascending a hierarchy of such crafts, they find that the kingly craft—also said to be the craft of ruling—is the only craft that does not defer to another craft but uses what the other crafts make.

However, the craft they are seeking must not only use what others make. It must use what it makes. So at 291e, Socrates says that they started to look for what it is that the craft of ruling makes. At this point the argument becomes rather complicated through the use of previous assumptions, suppressed premisses and truncated arguments.[13] It is agreed that what the craft of ruling makes must be beneficial; that the only candidate for such benefit is knowledge—clearly understood to be a craft knowledge—of some sort; that the only candidate for such craft knowledge is a kind of craft knowledge that is always beneficial. The conclusion is, then, that the craft of ruling must impart itself. The reasoning for this problematic conclusion seems to be that all the other craft knowledges can either benefit or harm (292d). It is because they can either benefit or harm that what they make is turned over to another craft to be used for benefit. The top of the hierarchy, the craft that does not turn over what it makes to another higher craft, is the ruling craft. At this point, the conclusion seems to be that only the ruling craft is invariably beneficial because only it uses what the other crafts provide without turning over to a higher craft. Thus, if the ruling craft confers some craft knowledge on the ruled that is always beneficial, it can only confer itself on them.[14] Let us, for the sake of illustration, take the broad hint to the effect that the ruling craft just is wisdom. The conclusion of this argument says that the ruling craft will confer wisdom on the ruled; it will make them wise. In turn, the ruling craft will use what it makes, that is, the wise citizens. But this conclusion only postpones the important question. Since we do not know the content, as it were, of the ruling craft itself—we have no account of its wisdom—we do not know what it confers on the ruled. The ruling craft will confer something that benefits the ruled, makes them better in some way. But in what way will they be made better? Using the previous conclusion, we can suppose that they are made better by receiving a craft knowledge—that of ruling—that allows those upon whom it is conferred to confer that same craft knowledge on others (292e). If we do not know in the first instance in what way the craft knowledge of ruling is a benefit, the benefit conferred seems to recede, like an infinite regress. Thus the search for what the ruling craft makes, that is, the knowledge inculcated *in* the ruled, and how *that* will make the ruled better, is the problem that finally ends the investigation on an aporetic note.

In this search, then, happiness seems like a goal ever receding before the succession of crafts—exactly like the lark being chased by children (291b). The inability to bridge the gap between craft and goal can only leave us with the conclusion that Socrates cannot specify the nature of the happiness that is the goal of wisdom; as well, and perhaps for this reason, he cannot specify the knowledge whereby wisdom will attain this goal.[15] Socrates does not provide for wisdom an understanding of human advantage and the way to attain it that is comparable to the understanding a carpenter has of houses and how to build them or a physician has of health and how to attain it. The craft analogy in the *Euthydemus* is incomplete, then, on these two counts. The effect of this account is twofold. First of all, we are attracted by the promise that there is such a knowledge that will give us this sense of the true value of our physical and spiritual assets and of the way to use them so that they will serve our true advantage. The second effect is in contrast to the first; we are disappointed by Socrates' inability to tell us exactly what this wisdom is, to fill in the details so that we may begin to live just such a life as the wise person of his account. So far we are left to suppose that Socrates does not complete the account because he cannot do so. Being unable to do so presents a problem for the craft analogy. Moreover, the problem poses an obstacle for our interpretation of the moral theory of the *Republic*. Presumably, if we are to interpret the craft of justice as a combination of the craft of virtue and the ruling craft, then somehow this problem of filling out the account of the craft analogy must be addressed. Before proceeding, let us look more closely at the problem.

We can begin our analysis of the problem with a prior question that generates the problem: whether or not craft is only instrumental.[16] Its being instrumental means that craft only knows how to produce a result without knowing whether the result is good or bad—an idea we have already seen in the *Euthydemus*. Thus, in the *Laches* (195c), Nicias says that the physician knows about health and disease but does not know whether being healthy is better than being diseased; there may be cases in which it would be better to die than to live.[17] The same idea comes up in the *Charmides* (173d), where Socrates says that even if experts in each kind of craft knowledge—for example, medicine, military strategy, and tailoring—took care of us, it would not follow that we acted well or were happy. Both of these dialogues end problematically; they both suggest that what is needed is a general sort of knowledge of good and evil (*La.* 199d; *Charm.* 174b). The instrumentality of craft seems to be connected to something else odd that Socrates says about craft. In the *Lesser Hippias*, Socrates

argues that the skilled person is the one who can voluntarily produce harm; the physician who can voluntarily produce harm for
the body knows more of the healing art than the one who cannot
(375b). In *Republic* I, the one who knows how to guard against
disease, *scil.*, the physician, is the one who can most skillfully
inflict it (333e). If craft is instrumental then one can explain this
odd fact about its practitioners. Since what the craft produces is,
in itself, neither good nor bad, it is open to the craftsman then to
use the craft to produce what is bad.

These arguments point up a flaw with the craft analogy, of
course. If virtue is a craft and if it is instrumental in this way, then
its goal could be a matter of indifference to its practitioner. It
would be possible, then, for the virtuous person to do evil voluntarily. Indeed, that strange conclusion is the one Socrates draws in
both of these passages. Of course, such a conclusion contradicts
Socrates' central thesis that a virtuous person never voluntarily
does evil. Moreover, such a conclusion would doom any attempt
to interpret the moral theory of the *Republic* as a craft of justice.
If craft in the early dialogues is necessarily instrumental, then
there is no way to salvage that notion of craft for further development in Plato's mature moral theory. We will end this section by
looking closely at this issue.

First of all, the claim that craft is necessarily instrumental
seems to conflict with another feature of craft. In the early dialogues, therapeutic crafts in particular are said to provide always
good things. In the *Euthyphro* (13a ff.), Socrates says that the care
provided by the therapeutic crafts of horseman and huntsman are
for the good and welfare of their charges. In the *Lysis* (217a ff.),
he says that medicine is a friend to the sick person because it is useful and good in providing health, something good for the sick person. Even in the passage from the *Charmides* he says that what the
physician, general, and tailor provide is good. Finally, in the *Gorgias*, craft is virtually defined as always seeking what is best for its
object (*Gor.* 464c). How can a craft, whose goal is to provide
good for its object, be instrumental toward an end that is neither
good nor bad in itself? The answer seems to involve something
like the notion of context. The good of health, which the craft of
medicine exists to provide, is not necessarily, or by itself, good
when it is considered in the context of one's whole life; the good
of health is qualified by the larger context. Even goods of the soul,
such as courage and temperance, must be judged from that larger

context. (Indeed, it is at least possible that the larger context might include more than just the life of the individual in question.) Medicine provides health, which is good from the point of view of one's body; but from the point of view of the project of one's entire life, health might not always be good. Suppose, for instance, that the physician restores one to health only so that one's torture may be completed. Again, just by itself, health might not be good. Suppose that one uses health to ruin her soul. There is a larger context in which the good of health must be judged.

Crafts like medicine are instrumental, then, in a qualified sense. Such crafts, in themselves, always seek the good of their objects. However, the good that they seek is restricted to the context of each craft, is restricted to the specific kind of good that the craft can provide. Such crafts are instrumental in the sense that the good that they provide is not necessarily good if one takes a larger perspective.[18] The problem of the evil craftsman should be read in this way, then. Craft itself does not indifferently produce good or bad. It is the craftsman who does so. If the craftsman were to work within the context of the craft, so to speak—if he accepted the goals of the craft as his own—he would always provide the good of that craft. In the case of medicine, the physician who worked within that context would always heal patients. However, it is possible for the physician to work outside the context of medicine; then he can harm patients. He is able to do so because, outside the context of medicine, he can adopt another goal besides health, thereby perverting the craft.

Thus, it is the problem of instrumentality that leads to the positing of a very general knowledge of good and evil in the *Laches* and *Charmides*. Such knowledge is an attempt to capture this larger context, as is the distinction between crafts that produce and those that use what is produced.[19] We have seen the latter notion already in the *Euthydemus*; but it is also found in the *Cratylus* (388c ff.) and in *Republic* X (601c ff.). In these two dialogues, the latter craft instructs the former so that what it produces is useful and good; the using craft has a notion of what the product is to be used for. In the *Euthydemus*, Socrates does not say that the using craft instructs the producing craft; he simply says that the using craft uses what the producing crafts produce in order to provide benefit. Obviously, the notion of the using craft is an attempt to address a problem, to overcome the instrumentality of the producing crafts.

We now can state the problem of the craft analogy. If craft is necessarily instrumental, it would follow that there will not be a using craft—the knowledge of good and evil—which overcomes the instrumentality of craft. This problem presents a crux because different commentators take different paths at this point. Some hold that, indeed, Plato came to see that all crafts are instrumental and concluded that virtue cannot be a craft.[20] Others hold that Plato saw this property belonged to some crafts but concluded that there would be at least one craft that is not just instrumental.[21] The *Euthydemus* can be seen as illustrating this crux. In the first protreptic interlude Socrates presents a full account of wisdom as a kind of craft. However, Socrates does not specify what the goal of that craft is, other than to say that the craft makes one happy. Socrates does not elaborate in what this happiness consists. According to one line of interpretation, the trouble is that a craft cannot give the kind of account needed at this point. Like carpentry, the wisdom that is modeled on craft can provide a product; it cannot tell what the product is good for. Thus, according to this line, the failure recorded in the second protreptic interlude is not an accident; it points up a fatal weakness in the craft analogy.[22] Socrates introduces the craft that both produces and uses what it produces as a conscious attempt to overcome the shortcoming of the craft analogy—that is, the fact that craft is instrumental. However, the ever-receding goal of that craft shows that it is not possible to overcome the shortcoming. On the other hand, our line of interpretation holds that the problem posed for the craft analogy in the second protreptic interlude is one that Plato plans to solve. Moreover, it holds that the solution will keep what is valuable in the craft analogy by, finally, introducing a craft that is not instrumental, a craft that both produces and uses what it produces. This notion of craft will also modify the analogy by making the craft of virtue into a type of ruling craft, that—as we shall see in chapters 3 and 4—is also the knowledge of good and evil.[23]

II

It is now time for us to present the craft of justice. As we have already said, this new analogy between craft and justice in Book IV of the *Republic* combines elements from the craft of ruling and the craft of virtue. So the best way to explicate this new craft analogy is to begin by contrasting the two uses of the notion of craft we have so far seen, the craft of ruling and the craft of virtue. The craft of ruling has as its object—that is, what it works on—the soul of the ruled.[24] In the *Gorgias*, this object was shown to have parts, for example, the desires; these became the effective object of the craft of ruling. In general, its goal is to instill virtue in the soul of the ruled; in the *Gorgias*, virtue is identified with restrained desires, or with desires already moderate. The craft of virtue in the *Euthydemus*, on the other hand, has as its object the assets of body and soul; these assets belong to the one who has the craft of virtue. The craft of virtue makes the person who has it capable of using these assets for her own advantage. The craft of ruling and the craft of virtue both have as their goal the happiness of the one on whom they work. The virtue conferred by the ruling craft is explicitly identified with happiness; the advantage conferred by the craft of virtue is also happiness.[25]

Several important points must be made. First, the person who exercises the craft of ruling exercises it on another person. So this craft is distinct from the craft of virtue, in that the latter is directed towards one's own self or assets. Second, the objects on which the two crafts work are different: the soul and its desires, which are the object of the craft of ruling, are a different set of things from the assets of the body and soul, which are the object of the craft of virtue. While desires and the assets of soul are both psychological items, they are distinctly different kinds of psychological items; the assets of soul are virtues, such as courage and temperance. Third, the craft of ruling is said to produce virtue while the craft of virtue is not said to produce virtue. Fourth, as we have noted already, the craft of ruling, as it is presented in the *Gorgias*, seems closer to defining its goal than is the craft of virtue, as it is presented in the *Euthydemus*. In the former dialogue, Socrates makes some headway in defining the virtue the craft of ruling is supposed to confer on its object; virtue is, in this preliminary account, an ordering and restraining of desires. However, in the *Euthydemus*, where the goal of the craft of virtue is "doing well" or "happiness," we do not have a clear sense of the content of doing well or happiness.

Now we can turn to Plato's reconstruction of the craft analogy. In Book IV of the *Republic* he combines the craft of ruling with the craft of virtue into one craft, thereby creating a new ver-

sion of the craft analogy. As we shall see, this new craft is therapeutic and not productive; it is like medicine and not like carpentry.[26] In fact, it is said to be a kind of ruling—another species of
the therapeutic craft. Thus, it is like the craft of ruling in the *Gorgias*. However, its object is the soul of the one who is also practicing the craft; in that it is directed towards oneself, this craft is like
the craft of virtue in the *Euthydemus*. Still, even though this craft
is self-directed, its object is not one's material and spiritual assets
but the parts of one's soul. In that it is directed toward the parts
of the soul, it is like the craft of ruling in the *Gorgias*. In sum, the
new craft of virtue—what we will now call the "craft of justice"—
is a craft of self-rule within one's own soul. It should not be surprising that Plato would make justice a craft of ruling in one's own
soul. He wants to make it continuous with the craft of ruling practiced by the ruler guardians of the city. The latter is clearly presented in Book IV as a kind of craft knowledge.[27] Indeed, as we
shall see in subsequent books of the *Republic*, the craft of ruling
in the city and ruling in one's own soul are described in terms that
make them seem even more the same craft, motivated by the same
ideals, that is, the Forms. Little else could be expected from the
care with which Plato creates a similar structure between the city
and the soul. In the city, the ruler sees that all of the parts are
brought into harmony and balance, that each gets its due. So, in
the soul, an analogous task is set for the ruler in that interior
city.[28]

   Our primary source for this account of the craft of justice is
the very compact section at the end of Book IV of the *Republic*
where Socrates comes to the end of his exposition of the value of
justice in the soul (435b–448e). Here Socrates believes he has at
last brought to the first stage of completion the extremely difficult
task set him by Glaucon and Adeimantus at the beginning of Book
II. He was to show that justice is valuable in itself and in its consequences, apart from the consequences of being known to be just.
In effect, he is asked to show what value justice has in the soul,
apart from its value in the social context. After a long detour
through his theory of the ideal city, Socrates returns to the soul.
He portrays the soul as having the same parts as the city, the same
structure, and the same virtues. A person with his soul so arranged
would have every reason, according to Socrates and his hearers, to
value justice in his soul as intrinsically good, indeed as identical
with happiness. Let us turn to this account of virtue in the soul.

In an extended argument at *Republic* 435c–441d, Plato tells us that the soul has three parts. We will not attempt to disentangle the argument itself but will simply use the results—that is, the account of the parts of the soul. Unfortunately, even that modest plan is not altogether uncomplicated since it is not clear exactly what the results are.[29] Although we are told that the parts are reason, appetite, and spirited part, much controversy exists about the nature of these parts. For our present, somewhat preliminary purposes we will say that the parts are distinguishable functions within the soul and that each function has a dual aspect. Plato seems to want to attribute both some cognitive ability and some desiring motivation to each part of the soul. In the case of reason, the cognitive ability is fairly clear; for example, it discovers the truth, generally conceived. On the other hand, reason also seems to be motivated by a desire to learn the truth. In turn, appetite of course desires its object; appetite obviously has a motivation, then. However, appetite also has a primitively cognitive grasp of its object; it has a conception of what it wants.[30]

Plato establishes the distinction between different functions by showing a conflict between them. In Plato's inventory of psychological functions, there is first of all reason, which calculates consequences and takes forethought for the whole soul. It frequently finds itself at odds with the second part of the soul—the desires. Thought by Plato to consist primarily of the desires for food, drink, and sex, they seek immediate fulfillment while reason has the job of looking out for consequences. It seems fairly obvious how these two functions would conflict. When one is thirsty, one's desire for drink simply wants to have something to drink, without any consideration of consequences other than quenching the thirst. It is reason that calculates the remote consequences—such as the effect on one's health of drinking this drink. The desire wants immediate gratification and the reason thinks about long-range consequences—that is, one's overall good. The conflict between the two is classic and is one of the fundamental issues of moral thought for Plato. The resolution of the conflict is one of the results Plato wishes to provide with this account of virtue.

Nevertheless, in setting up the opposition between reason and desires, Plato makes a significant departure from his previous understanding of the relation between desire and the good. In an extended argument (*Rep.* 437e–439b), Socrates explains that the desire for drink, of itself, is not desire for good drink.[31] Of itself, desire is neither for good nor bad drink. If good drink is drink that is good for one in the long run, then the desire for drink is not, in itself, desire for drink that is good for one in the long run. Presumably, Plato's reason for so arguing is that it is the job of reason to look out for good and bad; it is the job of desire to seek drink. However, this differentiation of functions means that desire does not of itself seek the good in each category. However, this characterization of desire does not mean that desires are good-independent. Desires are not said to be desires for what is pleasant as opposed to what is good—the definition of good-independent. Indeed, the simple desire for drink is no more for pleasant drink than it is for good drink. Plato's point is that desire, in itself, is not calculative; it is, let us say, good-indifferent. It is the job of reason to calculate. Thus, desire in itself neither abets nor hinders reason in its job. It simply wants what it wants. The job of reason is to guide that want.

The third part of the soul is less familiar a notion to the modern reader than to the ancient. It is called "*thymos*," or "*thymoeides*," and is usually translated "the spirited part." *Thymos* is a character of Greek warriors—an aggressive principle impelling one to adventure across the forbidding seas, to join in awful battle. Plato makes it an ally of reason in its conflict with the appetites. In this passage it is expressed as the self-directed anger one feels when one wrongly gives in to an appetite.

Plato's tripartite soul can be seen as an inventory of psychological functions. Each person must have these three functions for living a life: (1) reason gives us the long view about courses of action; (2) *thymos* carries out our conception of the best course of action; and (3) the desires are motives whose satisfaction makes possible the bodily existence. But the three also entail three distinct kinds of needs. Given that we have these three functions, our life is also characterized by three kinds of emotional needs and their corresponding satisfactions. Plato introduces this notion later in Book IX of the *Republic*, where he says that each of the three parts of the soul has its peculiar desire and pleasure (580d). To begin with the appetites, it is obvious that we need the satisfactions afforded by fulfilling our desires for food, drink, and sex. (Plato allows, in the best kind of life, for what to us would appear to be the sublimation of the latter.) As well, we need a life that has the satisfactions of *thymos*—one that enjoys adventure, aggressive play, and risks. Finally, our lives need the satisfaction of reason—

its desire to discover, solve, resolve, and contemplate. A life without one of these three kinds of satisfactions is much poorer than a life with all three. Plato seems wise in recommending all three; he only seems unwise when we stop to think what has been left out. Much of the plausibility of the position depends on his ability to adapt this tripartite division to include other needs, notably personal affection.

Having distinguished the three parts of the soul, Plato is now ready to give his account of the four virtues: justice, wisdom, courage, and temperance. In this passage, justice is the foundation of all the other three virtues. Analogous to justice in the city, justice in the soul is each part of the soul doing its own job or function (*ta hautou hekaston tōn en autōi prattēi* [441e1–2]). Thus, justice means reason fulfilling its job of ruling in the soul, exercising forethought, endowed with the knowledge of what is good for each of the parts and for the whole formed by the three parts; the knowledge amounts to wisdom (*Rep.* 441e; 442c). As well, justice implies that the spirited part fulfills its function by following the lead of reason in fearing what ought to be feared—that is, the spirited part has courage (*Rep.* 442c). This latter means assisting the reason in keeping the desires in line, especially keeping them from trying to become rulers in the soul. Thus, each fulfills its peculiar function in the soul. In fact, the integrity of functions is the basis for the virtue of temperance (*sōphrosunē*). Temperance is the agreement among the parts of the soul—the ruler and the ruled—that reason ought to rule; and the other parts do not raise revolt against the rule of reason (442d). In this way the temperate soul is a harmony of functions under the lead of reason. While earlier in this passage reason and the spirited part treat the appetites as though they are untrustworthy, in this part the appetites seem to be tamed, agreeing to the rule of reason.

Next Socrates says that this arrangement of the parts of the soul is the source of our treating others justly. He lists the ways in which a person may commit injustice—nicely catalogued by Vlastos under the headings of vanity, cupidity, and sensuality.[32] The person, in whose soul reason rules with wisdom (the spirited part follows reason, and the desires are subject to these two) will not steal, rob temples, break oaths, commit adultery, or betray comrades. The reason, Socrates says, is that "each of the parts within him does its own (job) with respect to ruling and being ruled" (443b).

Now we can see how the craft analogy pervades this account. To begin with, reason's ruling in the soul is an adaptation of the craft of ruling. Its craft of ruling is identified with the virtue of wisdom. In the good person, reason rules, being wise (*sophos*) and exercising forethought for the whole soul (441e4–6). In the *Gorgias* (464b7), the craft of ruling has the same function—except that there it was for the souls of others. The parallel to this craft in the soul is the wisdom exercised by rulers in the city, which, in turn, is identified with good counsel (*euboulia*) (428b). But a city is well counseled because its rulers have a certain kind of knowledge (*epistēmē*). This knowledge is different from the knowledge (*epistēmē*) of the carpenter, the farmer, and the smith because, in its relations with itself and with other cities, it looks out for what is best for the city as a whole. The context clearly makes this knowledge a craft knowledge; moreover, its analogue in the soul—wisdom—is also said to be the knowledge (*epistēmē*) of what is beneficial for each part and for the whole (442a5–8).

When reason is endowed with wisdom and followed by the spirited part, it is capable of working on the desires. The latter is the largest part of the soul and the part that becomes the most insatiable (*aplēstotaton*) because of possessions.

> Reason and its ally will watch over the desires lest they become filled (*pimplasthai*) with too much of the bodily pleasures and grow so strong as to no longer fulfill their proper function but, rather, to attempt to overthrow and to rule those parts for which it is not fit and overturn the entire life of all. (442a–b)

Of course, in this description of the work of reason and the spirited part, the one taking counsel and the other executing that counsel, it is easy to see the craft of ruling in the *Gorgias*. Reason and its ally, *thymos*, now do for the soul what the good man who spoke in the assembly or law court did for the souls of others in the latter dialogue; they restrain it and bring it back to proper functioning. The chief difference is that now the parts of the soul are more complex. In the *Gorgias*, the good speaker worked on the desires only, restraining them when they had grown insatiable. In our consideration of that dialogue, we speculated that this work of restraint was aimed at bringing the desires, grown insatiable, into compatibility with the other moderate desires of the soul. In *Republic* IV, the work of reason seems to be preventive; it seeks to keep the desires from becoming insatiable and, thereby, usurp the functions of the other parts. Yet the themes are similar. In *Republic* IV, desires are to be watched so that they remain compatible with the other parts of the soul; the desires must not attempt to do the job of the other parts. Here compatibility and proper function seem to be necessary and sufficient conditions of one another. When a part of the soul does not fulfill its proper function, it usurps that of another; when a part fulfills its proper function, it does not usurp that of another. Clearly, when one part usurps the function of another, the two functions are incompatible.

Then, in a kind of paean to justice, Socrates sums up his account. Justice is really an internal arrangement. The just person does not allow any of the parts within to do alien things, to pursue promiscuously the tasks of other parts in the soul, but disposes well (*eu themenon*) what is truly his own, ruling himself, bringing order (*kosmēsanta*), being a friend to himself, and harmonizing (*sunarmosanta*) the three parts, like three notes, the lowest, the highest, and the middle. The use of *tithemi, kosmeō*, and *harmozō* shows that justice is being compared to a craft as well. Indeed, these same words or their derivatives are used in the *Gorgias* (503e5–504a4) to describe what all craftsmen do; it can hardly be a coincidence that Plato used the same words in this extremely important passage, the denouement of his account of justice in the soul. Finally, Socrates alludes to the relation between justice and wisdom at the end of his paean when he says that just and fine action (*praxin*) is any action that preserves and helps finish (*sunapergazētai*) the order,[33] wisdom being the craft knowledge (*epistēmēn*) set over (*epistatousan*) this action. Wisdom maintains its association with the ruling craft while *sunapergazētai* is clearly a craft word.

What kind of harmony will the craft of justice achieve among the parts? These parts represent directions for the soul to pursue, different kinds of life that could be realized. Besides the by now familiar life of sensuality, there are the life of seeking honor and political standing and the life of seeking knowledge and understanding. All three directions are inherent in one's soul; reason, armed with wisdom, must combine these three into a harmony. We can appreciate what this harmony might mean if we begin by considering the different varieties of disharmony and imbalance. Socrates outlines such lives in Book VIII of the *Republic*. In the best life, reason rules in the soul. Since it knows what is best for the three parts and for the whole, such a life has balance and harmony. In the other kinds of lives, other parts of the soul dominate. The first is the life in which the spirited part dominates; the goal of this life is the chief value for spirit—honor or standing in the city (*Rep.* 548c ff.). Such a person is called "timocratic"—a name based on the Greek word for honor (*timē*). This is a person who would value standing in the eyes of others as the highest value.

In the timocratic person, sensuality would be subordinated to seeking honor, of course. Indeed, sensuality, if it is not closely guarded, can cause one to lose honor; one may do many dishonorable, in the sense of cowardly, deeds at the bidding of one's desires. But in Socrates' reckoning it is reason that is neglected in the timocratic life. A life given over to honor has no time for the pursuit of knowledge. It is notorious that the Spartans lacked the instinct for the Attic pursuit of truth. Neither speculative nor interested in speculation, they stuck to their military life. While Plato seems to have found something admirable about them, their lack of intellectual distinction was not part of it. Better than sensualists—because seeking honor is better than sensuality—they still lacked an essential component of life.

Finally, there are three kinds of life in which desires dominate. First is the oligarchic, which is based on the desire for money; this desire subordinates the other desires (*Rep.* 553b ff.). The miser whose desire for money makes him neglect other desires is a good example of the oligarchic person. Then there is the democratic life, in which all desires are given equal access to satisfaction (*Rep.* 558d ff.). Socrates presents this person as a comic figure who seems to try everything. The tyrannical life is one in which some one grand desire becomes dominant; this desire is so overweening it subordinates all others to itself (*Rep.* 571a ff.). What is common to these three kinds of lives is their neglect both of honor and of reason. Of course, one whose chief aim is money, or the satisfaction of multiple desire or just one magnificent desire, is likely to be cowardly, to sacrifice his honor to these desires. In the *Gorgias*, for instance, Socrates made Callicles face the fact that sensuality militates against honor. Again, the life of pleasure means that reason cannot pursue its own goal. It certainly cannot rule in the soul; it becomes subordinate to whatever desire is in charge, little better than a procurer.

By contrast, the wise person will combine all three directions, with appropriate respect for each. It is the life of reason that gives the knowledge needed to make the combination work.[34] With such a life there is, of course, justice in the soul in the Platonic sense that each of the parts of the soul fulfills its peculiar function. But such a life also has justice in the soul in a more ordinary sense: each part of the soul receives its due. Each part is developed to the degree and receives satisfaction in the amount appropriate to it. The desires are not suppressed; they are satisfied—but not to the point that they become rulers in the soul, insatiable and overweening. The spirited part is not suppressed; it is allowed to exercise and satisfy its aggressiveness. But it does so in such a way as to respect the functions of the reason and the appetites; they are not subordinated to seeking honor. Finally, reason does not become overbearing; its rule recognizes the legitimate claims of the other two parts of the soul. Reason, guided by wisdom, does not, through contemplation, render the soul either ascetic or cowardly.

This picture of the virtuous soul is very compelling in many ways. If we accept the notion that these three parts of the soul are the complete inventory of our psychological capacities, in Plato's arrangement we have the best means for realizing each of the capacities to the fullest extent actually needed for the good of that capacity (reason knows what is for the good of each) and to the fullest extent compatible with fulfilling the needs of the others (reason knows what is for the good of the whole formed by the three). It seems somewhat pale, but nevertheless correct, to say that such an arrangement implies a well-rounded personality. Such a person will develop her intellectual capacities, her spirited-aggressive capacities, and her appetitive capacities. First of all, she will have a life in which her mind is developed in all the ways that the pursuit of truth promises, but only to the extent that the mind really needs such pursuit. At the same time, the pursuit of truth will not derogate from the development of the other two parts. Second, she will have a life in which aggressiveness and adventure will have a proper place; but the spirited part is fulfilled neither beyond what is good for it nor in such a way as to impede the other two parts of the soul. Finally, her desires for food, drink, and sex will be fulfilled, but not beyond the point at which they themselves need fulfillment. The appetites themselves do not know when this point has been reached, but they can follow the lead of reason here. In turn, this point coincides with the point at which the development of the other two parts is respected. And if we suppose that these three exhaust the soul's capacities, such a life seems to lack nothing.

At this point we can now see the congruence between this notion of justice in the soul and the virtuous soul of the *Gorgias.* As we have already noted, the words for "disposing," "ordering," and "harmonizing" are the same as—or derivatives of—the craft words used at *Gorgias* 503e5–504a4 to describe the method of all craftsmen, but especially that of the good man who speaks in the assembly or in the law court, who perfects the souls of others. In our interpretation of the *Gorgias,* the task of the good orator was to harmonize the parts of the soul, which were identified as the desires. His job included restraining any desires that had become insatiable. Such desires were, presumably, incompatible with the other moderate desires. The job of harmonizing, then, entailed making incompatible desires compatible by restraining the immoderate or insatiable ones. This somewhat speculative reading of the *Gorgias* is perhaps now justified by what we find in the *Republic.* The ruler in the soul, reason, seems to be doing the same sort of job—harmonizing and making compatible the parts of the soul. However, in the *Republic,* this task has become somewhat more complicated. The parts are no longer simply the desires, at least as these were understood in the *Gorgias.* As we have just seen, Plato has now identified two other parts to the soul, other directions for the soul to pursue. In the *Republic,* then, we see a fulfillment of some ideas that were just being developed in the *Gorgias.* The tentative and slightly primitive moral psychology of the latter dialogue is now completed in the tripartite soul of the *Republic.* The job of the good orator is now taken over—and developed—by reason seasoned with wisdom.

If *Republic* IV develops some of the underdeveloped notions surrounding the craft of ruling in the *Gorgias,* it also fills in some of the details of the craft of virtue in the *Euthydemus.* In the latter dialogue, wisdom is supposed to be a craft knowledge that uses the assets of body and soul in order to provide advantage for its possessor. Unfortunately, Socrates could not tell his interlocutors what that craft knowledge was nor, in turn, exactly what the advantage to be provided by it was to be. We knew that this advantage would be the same as happiness; however, we were still left with puzzles about what this happiness would be. In the *Republic* we have a clearer idea of the advantage to be provided by wisdom. The goal of wisdom is specified as the health of the soul, understood as a kind of order (444a13–e2). Further, the order, or health, of the soul is also the happiness or advantage of the soul. Finally, Socrates' suggestion, in the second protreptic interlude, that the craft knowledge of wisdom would be the craft of ruling has been shown to be correct. In the *Republic,* wisdom is a craft knowledge of ruling, both in the soul and in the city. In the following sections we will develop in detail the nature of the happiness bestowed by the craft of wisdom.

III

It will help us to see the intricacies of this compact craft analogy if we look at it in the context of Terence Irwin's claim that Plato, in fact, rejected the craft analogy in the *Republic.* One of his chief arguments is that Plato rejects the craft analogy because craft is only instrumental to its goal.[35] If craft is only instrumental, then no one has any reason to desire the craft of virtue for its own sake. But Plato argues that virtue is desirable for its own sake; in fact, showing that virtue is desirable for its own sake is the point of the argument ending with the passages in Book IV with which we have just dealt. So, according to Irwin, Plato rejects the craft analogy at the beginning of Book II, where the argument begins.[36]

Such a conclusion would fly in the face of the clear evidence in the text that Plato continues to use the language of craft in talking about both wisdom and justice. However, there is more than the textual evidence to deal with. Our interpretation of the craft analogy in Book IV also shows that justice, even though it is construed as a craft, is not therefore merely instrumental to its goal. Our argument for this claim uses the two characterizations given in Book IV of justice in the soul. One of these characterizations is made without comparing justice to craft; it is the Platonic definition of justice in the soul—that is, each part doing its peculiar job. The other uses the language of craft to characterize justice. What we will see is that the craft-characterization of justice does not portray a craft that is instrumental to its goal but, rather, this characterization portrays the same thing that is characterized by the Platonic definition of justice. As we shall see, the craft characterization is no more instrumental than the Platonic definition of justice.

The characterizations of justice relevant for this argument are:

(A) justice is each part doing its own function with regard to ruling and being ruled (443b);

(B) justice concerns doing one's own internally, the just man not allowing any of the parts within to do alien things or to pursue promiscuously the tasks of other parts, but disposes well what is truly his own, ruling himself, bringing order, being a friend to himself, and harmonizing the three parts (443d–e).[37]

Characterization (B) is the basis for the claim that justice is a craft. In what follows, we shall refer to justice characterized in this way as the craft of justice. "Platonic justice" shall refer to what (A) describes. We can see that what (B) describes is the same thing as what (A) describes. In doing so, we will see that (B) —the craft of justice—is no more instrumental than is (A)— the Platonic definition of justice.

First, we can see that (A) and (B) describe the same thing. When one is practicing the craft of justice, one is not allowing the parts of one's soul to engage in alien things nor to undertake promiscuously the tasks belonging to other parts of the soul, but is disposing well what is truly proper to each, ruling oneself, bringing order, and harmonizing the parts. Then one has Platonic justice—each part is doing its own function with regard to ruling and being ruled—that is, one falls under (A). The inhibiting activities of the craft of justice—"not allowing"—mean that the lower parts are not usurping the rule of reason. While all these inhibiting activities are attributed to the just man, surely they are only the outward signs of reason's ruling in the soul, with its understanding of what is beneficial for each part and for the whole.

Thus, the craft of justice is not just instrumental to justice, it is justice. Indeed, the strongest textual evidence for this claim is the fact that both (A) and (B) are called "justice" (*dikaiosunē*). In (B), justice (*dikaiosunē*) is said to be concerned with doing one's own internally. There follows in apposition to this "doing of one's own internally" that list of activities we have called the "craft of justice."[38] The fact that *dikaiosunē* refers both to each part's doing its own and to those activities listed under the craft of justice shows that each part's doing its own simply is, in part at least, doing that list of activities called the "craft of justice." Plato is explicating justice by listing these activities, which he describes using craft words he has used before in a significant passage of the *Gorgias*.

Another way to put this point is to say that the craft of justice instantiates Platonic justice. The craft of justice simply is Platonic justice. And a little reflection will show that this result is not that surprising. The craft of justice amounts to reason ruling in the soul, with wisdom as its guide, but the rule of reason in the soul is also a just rule. Since reason knows what is for the good of each and for the good of the whole formed by the three, it is reason that sees that each performs its own function and does not overstep its bounds. Reason's rule is just in two ways, then. First of all, knowing what is good for each, reason sees that each part receives what it needs to fulfill its function; this sort of justice is positive. Second, since the assumption seems to be that if each receives precisely what it needs to fulfill its own function, it will not impinge on the functions of the other parts; this sort of justice is negative. In this way, each part also receives its due. In turn, dispensing justice so that each performs its own function entails not allowing any of the parts within to do alien things, to pursue promiscuously the tasks of other parts, disposing well these parts (*eu themenon*), bringing order (*kosmēsanta*), and harmonizing the three parts (*sunarmosanta*). In addition, reason's ruling justly means that, in pursuing business or political activities, one still preserves and perfects that order that is itself justice in the soul.

In such an arrangement, reason practices the craft of justice in the soul by governing and moderating the others parts. One way to explicate this notion is to see reason as building up dispositions within the other parts. Reason would oversee and train the appetites, for example. Overseeing the appetites would entail watching them closely so that they do not overstep their bounds. Reason might keep a watch on the desire for food, for example, so that it does not take on a disposition to overindulgence and thus become the ruling desire of one's life. Oversight is negative, of course; it watches out for warning signs and reacts accordingly. Nevertheless, in doing so it can introduce dispositions into appetites. Perhaps more effective is positively training the appetites so that each functions in a moderate way. Reason might work on the appetite for food so that it is satisfied with moderate amounts by controlling eating so that one enjoys and savors what one eats—instead of rushing through a meal in order to eat as much as possible. Additionally, reason might build up moderation by concentration on the pleasures of satiety or the integration of eating with other pleasures. Whether through oversight or training, certain dispositions would build up in the appetites.

This overseeing and training the appetites so that they function in a certain way is an obvious way for reason to practice the craft of ruling justly in the soul. In building up these dispositions, reason is providing for the good of each appetite, assuming that having the disposition to function moderately is good for an appetite. Insofar as having such dispositions makes it possible to integrate the appetites into the overall functioning of the soul, building up these dispositions provides for the good of the whole as well. At *Rep.* 442d, Socrates says that temperance is each part of the soul, ruler or ruled, agreeing that reason should rule and the ruled not raising faction against it. The agreement on the part of spirit and appetites might well be a disposition to follow reason. Indeed, Plato hints at such a regimen for the spirit when he says that music and gymnastic train the spirited part and reason. The training seems to instill dispositions to behave in certain ways. Music, for instance, moderates the spirited part, reducing its tendency to more excessive forms of behavior (*Rep.* 410c ff.). Presumably reason could use other kinds of training to introduce a disposition that would avoid the excesses of the spirited part and make it a reliable ally of reason, ready to follow reason's lead. Reason too will need another education besides music and gymnastic—somewhat more theoretical but not less motivating—as we shall see.

In this interpretation, the craft of justice is not instrumental because it turns out to be a self-tending craft, a craft that builds itself up. Each exercise of justice is an instantiation of justice; moreover, each exercise of it produces justice. Exercising justice in the soul is an instance of justice in the soul because exercising it means performing some action that is itself an instance of just action—for example, a decision that evinces the justice already built up as a disposition in the soul. Exercising justice also continues the building up of this disposition of justice.[39] The just decision, for example, builds up the disposition to justice within the soul by reinforcing the habits of obedience within the other parts. Because the craft of justice in the soul is an exercise of justice, it also causes justice in the soul. Thus, even though it is a craft, it is not instrumental. Finally, then, justice is the craft which uses what it makes.

IV

So far we have argued for the place of the craft analogy in the moral philosophy of Book IV. The argument is now complete and, if it is successful, the place of the craft analogy is secure. What follows is an attempt—speculative in part—to draw out the consequences of this interpretation that bear on the notion of happiness. The distinctions at the beginning of Book II provide a beginning for this part of our investigation. There it is said that justice is good—or desirable—in itself and for its consequences. Justice's being good in itself is intimately connected to its being happiness; to show that justice is good in itself is to show in what way it is happiness. In what follows we will show what is meant in Book II when it is said that justice is good in itself and then show—in a speculative way that exploits the craft analogy—how justice in Book IV is good in itself—and thus is at least a part of happiness.[40]

At the beginning of Book II (357b4–d2), Plato distinguishes among (1) things good or desirable in themselves (*auto hautou heneka aspasomenoi*), (2) things good or desirable in themselves and in their consequences (*ho auto te hautou charin agapōmen kai tōn ap autou gignomenōn*), and (3) things in themselves laborious and good or desirable only in their rewards and other such consequences (*auta men heautōn heneka ouk an dexaimetha echein, tōn de misthōn te charin kai tōn allōn hosa gignetai ap' autōn*). We shall concentrate on the distinction between second and third categories, with special attention to the examples. The examples from the second category are seeing (*horan*), understanding (*phronein*), and being healthy (*hygiainein*). These examples are later augmented by the case of hearing (*akouein*) and an epithet is added to the whole group. They are goods that are productive by their own nature and not by opinion (367c7–d2). We may say that they have good inherent consequences.[41] However, these four capacities are also said to be good in themselves. If they are good in themselves, they ought to be good apart from inherent consequences; that is, they ought to be, let us say, intrinsically good. What exactly the intrinsic good of these activities in the examples can be, apart from their inherent consequences, is not altogether unproblematic.[42] However, what is important for the notion of happiness is that the distinction between intrinsic good and inherent consequence can be shown to hold for justice.

Now, we can contrast goods of the second category with goods of the third category. The latter are in themselves difficult and are done for the sake of their rewards (*misthoi*) and other such things as follow from them. The examples are physical exercise (*gymnazesthai*), undergoing medical treatment (*iatreuesthai*) and practicing medicine (*iatreusis*) (357c5–d2). There are two parts to this contrast. The first is based on the fact that the activities in the third category—unlike those in the second—are in themselves laborious and undesirable. It is easy to see how the examples are in themselves laborious but valuable in their consequences. However, there is another part to the contrast and it is based on a difference between the way that the consequences of the two categories are brought about. As we have seen, the consequences of the second category follow naturally and not by opinion. But the consequences of the third category are further characterized in this same passage as being done for the sake of rewards and the fame of opinion (358a4–6). By adding the notion of fame conferred by opinion, Socrates has added a new dimension to the notion of reward. As one commentator has pointed out, rewards are different from the inherent consequences of activities in the second category.[43] Rewards are like fame in that they are conferred by convention and not by nature. The reward for practicing medicine is conferred not by nature but by convention, for example. This difference is very important for what follows in Book II; however, even though it is added as almost a matter of course in the elaboration of the third category, it does not fit very well with the examples cited.

If we take rewards to be like fame, a good conferred by convention, the only example that easily fits this description is practicing medicine, where the rewards are presumably the fees earned. However, while physical exercise and undergoing medical treatment are laborious in themselves, it is hard to see how their consequences come about through opinion. If the consequences of physical exercise are health or athletic prowess, the consequences seem inherent. On the other hand, if the consequences are thought to be the praise that attends upon physical beauty or upon winning a competition, then such consequences do fit the description of rewards conferred by opinion. However, it is altogether impossible to see how the consequences of medical treatment could be thought to be a reward conferred by opinion.

In any event, even if there are two parts to the contrast between second and third category goods, it is the distinction based on the difference between inherent consequences, on the one hand, and rewards or conventional consequences, on the other, that is important for the distinction between second and third category goods.

It is this distinction that is clearly emphasized by Glaucon and Adeimantus throughout the rest of these passages. However, since the distinction between first and second category goods is based on the difference between intrinsic good and inherent good consequences, we actually have three different kinds of good: intrinsic good, inherent good consequences, and conventional good consequences.[44] This shifting in distinctions is perhaps symptomatic of some confusion, but the confusion is not fatal to Plato's argument. Thus, in the subsequent passages of Adeimantus' and Glaucon's speeches, Socrates is urged to show that justice does not belong to the third category. They invite him to concentrate on what justice is in itself—as this is understood in the third category, that is, apart from its rewards and good reputation (358b4–7; 366d7–e9; 367c5–d5; 367e1–5). However, what justice is in itself when the contrast is between second and third categories is different from what justice is in itself in the contrast between the first and second. In the contrast between the second and third categories, justice in itself is distinguished from its conventional consequences; in the contrast between first and second, justice in itself is distinguished from its inherent consequences. Throughout virtually all of the beginning of Book II, the only operative distinction is between the second and third categories. Thus, when Glaucon and Adeimantus ask Socrates to praise justice in itself, apart from the rewards of being known to be just, they are referring indifferently to the intrinsic good and to the inherent consequences of justice in the soul; when the contrast is between second and third category goods, then, justice in itself includes both its intrinsic good and its inherent good consequences. Still, there is a distinction between the intrinsic good of justice in the soul and its inherent good consequences. Moreover, that distinction is important for understanding the notion of happiness in this account because happiness is tied to the intrinsic good of justice in the soul. If we can understand in what way justice is good in itself—intrinsically good apart even from its inherent good consequences—we can understand how it is also happiness.

Having established that Plato distinguishes justice as desirable—or good—in itself apart even from its inherent consequences, we can now see—by exploiting the craft analogy— how justice is intrinsically good and, thus, how it is, at least in part, happiness. There are two aspects of the craft of justice relevant for such an undertaking. The just person is, in exercising his virtue, (a) one the parts of whose soul are functioning correctly—that is, dominating and subordinate according to nature—and (b) one who at the same time knows that his soul is functioning correctly. What is described by (a) and (b) are not two separate facts about the craft of justice but two facets of the same fact. When the just soul is exercising its justice, reason is ruling the soul by monitoring the functioning of the parts. The monitoring is a necessary condition for the soul's correct functioning and not a separate occurrence from the correct functioning—not a thrill or a reflective sense of well being, although it may be accompanied by such an experience.[45] The monitoring is an integrated part of the correct functioning. The matter can be summarized: (a) implies that (1) reason dominates, (2) the other parts are submissive, (3) all parts are receiving what is good for them and are *eo ipso* flourishing; (1) means that (2) and (3) are known to the just person, that is, (1) implies (b). Finally, the intrinsic good of justice is the occurrent state described in (a) and (b). According to this interpretation, then, the virtuous person, for example, makes decisions about long-term policies and short-term choices. In doing so, her reason functions well in its job of discerning where lies the good for the parts and for the whole. In concert, the other parts work well in making their appropriate contributions to the carrying out of these policies and choices under the guidance of reason. The virtuous person's self-control is also her knowledge of her soul's capacities and abilities working well. The occurrence of correct functioning, including the knowledge of correct functioning, is part, at least, of happiness for the virtuous person.[46]

In this account, we make a distinction between the process and product of decisions. We can illustrate the distinction by means of the following contrast. To better understand the process, think of someone making a decision that is impeccable from the point of procedure; all the relevant evidence is gathered, proper weight is given to this evidence, the conclusion is drawn in a timely and nuanced manner. Finally, such a person can carry out the decision, insofar as doing so depends on her will and talents. Nevertheless, this process is still distinct from the product—what actually happens when one follows out the decision. Thus, for reasons not under the control of the person making the decision, the intended outcome can fail to be realized. By contrast, sometimes the outcome of a decision is correct, in the sense that the conclusion is drawn that will be borne out by the facts; nevertheless, one might have arrived at that decision by a flawed process, paying little attention to evidence or not weighing the evidence properly. While it is true that good decisions, in the first sense of process, usually lead to good decisions, in the second sense of product, the distinction we have drawn between the two is illuminating for our purposes. The person with justice in her soul makes good decisions in the first sense, and is *eo ipso* aware of making such decisions. It is this process that is the intrinsic good of justice in the soul. In turn, happiness is being aware that one's soul is functioning at its best level of performance in that task for which the soul is peculiarly suited—making policies and decisions about the soul itself and executing those decisions and policies with efficiency and dispatch.

An appropriate analogy, perhaps, is that of the trained gymnast. While Socrates says that exercising can be laborious, presumably he means that it is so for the person who is in poor condition. However, for the person who is in good condition already, exercising is desirable in itself. One has a sense of her body's well functioning, of the coordination and strength that previous exercise has worked into her muscles. She relies on her well-working capacities in the correct placement of hands, arms, and legs as well as in the control over the whole body as it describes arcs, poises, and drops to the intended spot. This sense of control is not an accompanying feeling; it is the awareness that guides her action. The role of this sense of well functioning is more important in gymnastics than in, for example, cross-country running perhaps. But surely the well-trained gymnast, is happy with herself as a gymnast.[47] This analysis does not exhaust the Platonic concept of happiness. It does, however, present an important component of that concept, and one that is not noted in other places—the way in which the intrinsic good of justice is also happiness.[48] If a person has as her unique function a function that also serves to achieve her natural perfection, there is some reason to think of her as fortunate. She is fortunate by contrast to the entity whose perfection depends on another entity or whose function serves the perfection of another entity. It is even better for her if her unique function is a function whose exercise both serves this perfection and is the exercise of the perfection. Finally, since human beings function so that the presence of that well functioning is known in the functioning itself, she might well be called "happy and blessed."

V

At this point it would be helpful to see what advance the craft analogy in the *Republic* has made over the craft of ruling as we elaborated it in the *Gorgias*. Already we have noticed that the structure of Plato's moral psychology has become more complicated in the *Republic* with the parts of the soul now including the spirited part and reason, while in the *Gorgias* the only parts mentioned were the desires alone. The addition of the other two parts naturally gives a different sense to the way that the craftsman of the soul, the ruler in the soul, orders and harmonizes the parts. However, now it is time to pay closer attention to the advances that Plato has made over the moral psychology and moral theory of the *Gorgias*. Our approach will be to review the therapeutic craft of soul tending, especially the way it sought an order and arrangement of the soul.

We begin with the contrast between Socrates' life of restrained desires and Callicles' life of unrestrained desires. We said that Callicles was recommending a life in which the desires are not recognized as having natural limits but are used only as instruments for pleasure. Since the latter is thought by Callicles to be the filling up of empty desires, then the point of such a life is to have desires that are as large as possible and to be able to fill them up as much and as often as possible. According to Socrates, such desires become insatiable; in opposition to such desires Socrates poses treating desires not as vehicles for seeking pleasure but as having, as their natural limits, satiety. Such desires are adequately provided for and are satisfied with what they have. In the sequel, Socrates does not exploit this account, however. Rather, in the medical analogy, he introduces the notion that insatiable desires lead to an incompatibility of desires; the insatiable desire becomes incompatible with other desires. It is the job of the physician of the soul to reduce the incompatibility. Finally, Socrates says that the physician of the soul is the judge, whose treatment for such desires is punishment. However, the best example of the soul-tending craft is Socratic elenchus, whose punishment consists of showing the patient an inconsistency in his moral beliefs. Socrates presents elenchus as a way of disciplining desires that give rise to faulty moral beliefs. It is an instance of the craft of soul tending, which brings harmony and order into the soul.

We saw that the problem with this account is that elenchus is not as powerful a notion as Socrates seems to think. It is unclear whether exposing incompatible desires—by way of exposing inconsistent beliefs—is enough to show which desire should be preferred. Even if desire for the good is supposed to be the arbiter between the incompatible desires, so far it is not clear that desire for the good has enough content to fulfill that function. If desire for the good lacks such content, then it is not clear that the desire for the good implies the desire for a balanced and virtuous life. Thus, it is possible to attain compatibility of desires by giving up the desire to lead a balanced and virtuous life. Suppose, for instance, that having unrestrained desires is incompatible with being brave. If one wants to be a sensualist, he might identify desire for the good with the desire to be a sensualist; then he could achieve compatibility of desires by giving up bravery. One simply becomes a coward for sensuality's sake. Nothing in Socrates' elenchus seems capable of preventing such a choice.

Now we can see that part of what is causing the problems in the *Gorgias* is the lack of a fully developed moral psychology. Without such an account, Socrates cannot adequately defend his claim about compatibility of desires in the soul. However, in the *Republic*, we find a theoretical account of the parts of the soul and of the role that appetites play in the soul. This account allows Plato to argue that insatiable desires are dysfunctional because they are incompatible with the other parts of the soul. In essence, Plato has replaced the inchoate notion of compatibility of desires with the more complex account of the functions of the parts of the soul and of the way in which these functions fit and harmonize with one another. In the account from Book IV, each of the parts has a function to perform and those functions are defined in terms of the larger whole of which they are a part. Plato tells us explicitly what the functions of reason and the spirited part are. They are like the functions of ruler and auxiliary in the city; reason rules and spirited part carries out the rule, in relation to the appetites for food, drink, and sex. We are not told explicitly what the function of the appetites—conceived as parts of a larger whole—might be. Of course, in one way the function seems obvious. The desires for food and drink, for example, keep the body alive and thus keep the soul engaged in its earthly enterprise. The function of sex is less clear, on this model. While its job is to continue the species, that job does not seem to be one that contributes to the commonwealth of an individual soul. Its function in the individual soul, therefore, is less clear than that of the other two desires. In fact, we are not given a positive definition of the functions of the appetites in the same way in which we are given a positive definition of the functions of the other two parts. Rather, the definition of the function of the appetites is a negative one. The appetites are dysfunctional when they impede the function of the other two parts, when they try to rule in the soul; thus, we are left to conclude that the function of the appetites is to be ruled by reason and the spirited part.

This account of correct function and of dysfunction is, then, added to the notion of insatiable desires. In a passage in *Republic* IV (442a–b), which is clearly meant to recall the discussion of insatiable desires in the *Gorgias*, Socrates says that reason and the spirited part watch over the appetites so that they do not grow insatiable and strong. So far we can recognize the description of desires from the earlier dialogue. Next, Socrates adds what growing insatiable and strong means for the function of the appetites— they do not keep to their own function but attempt to enslave the others, to exercise rule themselves, and thus overturn the life of the commonwealth of the soul. In this account, then, if the appetites become so strong that they attempt to rule, they have become dysfunctional for the soul. In this notion we see that the successor to the notion of compatibility of desires is the harmony of functions. The basic idea is that each part has a function to play in the commonwealth of the soul. Conflict within the soul arises when one of the parts attempts to assume the function of another part. The appetites are the most prone to usurp another's function because desires can grow insatiable and, thus, overweening. Such appetites will not be functional because the appetites simply do not have what it takes to rule in the soul. They cannot, for instance, exercise foresight for the whole soul. Appetites are notoriously shortsighted; they seek the immediate satisfaction in front of them, without any thought for the longer-range consequences. They cannot see beyond their immediate gratification to what is really good for the whole commonwealth of the soul. Only reason has that capacity; reason can calculate what the longer range consequences of satisfying a particular appetite will be.[49] For instance, my desire for a drink urges me to have that next glass of wine offered to me by an overly solicitous host. The desire is monomaniacal; it wants only one thing. Thus, it does not look into the future very well, that is, beyond its own satisfaction. It cannot appreciate the way in which my conversation will become less focused, or the way in which I will become more easily irritated by the comments of others. Further, it does not have a memory of the headache the morning after the last time I had just one more glass of wine. The explanation for the appetite's failure here is that it does not have the function of exercising foresight; it cannot calculate consequences.

Reason, on the other hand, can calculate consequences. Moreover, it is endowed with wisdom so that it knows what is good for the whole soul and for its parts. Just look at the way a wise soul works. If the appetites have been well trained to defer to the rule of reason, reason can make its voice heard above that of the overly solicitous host. We should here remember that a temperate soul is one in which the appetites agree to reason's ruling. If reason invokes its status as ruler in the soul, presumably appetite is well trained enough to obey reason's ruling. Thus, reason might be imagined to prompt, "You do not remember last time, oh desire for wine, what happened. Not only was I unable to follow that illuminating conversation about fairness, but we all also had a terrible, day-long headache the next day; none of us could do much of anything. We do not really want that to happen again. It is a better plan to be satisfied with what we already have—enough sociable inebriation to be a charming, but effective, participant in this important conversational investigation. That way we all get something we want." Now if desire were always for the good, as Socrates is supposed to have held, then at this point appetite would not only agree with reason, it would start desiring what reason holds up as desirable. Being basically a desire for the overall good, the desire for wine would stop wanting this glass of wine and would want no further. However, appetite in *Republic* IV has not been presented as so rational; at most it can become trained so that it agrees that reason knows best, as we have said. Thus, the well-trained appetite can be imagined to reply at this point, "You are doubtless right, oh reason, about this issue. I cannot grasp these complicated matters; however, I do grasp that you know what is best for us all and I will happily follow your lead." Of course, in the interchange reason has talked only about what is good for the whole soul but not about what is good for the appetite in particular. Suppose the appetite were to reply instead that, while restraint might be good for the whole soul, it still did not give the appetite what it wanted and thus was not good for it. To be able to answer the appetite, wise reason should have insight into the needs of the appetite so that it can claim that restraint is good for appetite as well. For instance, in knowing the good of appetite, reason should know what is the proper level of satisfaction for each of the appetites. Back at the dinner party, the desire for wine does not know that even in itself, it does not really want another glass of wine. It cannot remember how overindulgence can easily turn into revulsion for wine; nor can it draw the proper conclusion from that fact. Reason must remind it. "You do not remember, oh desire for wine—and here please pay close attention—that last time you yourself did not even find that last glass of wine all that satisfying. In fact, oh desire for wine, halfway through that last glass of wine you yourself turned into revulsion for wine. It seemed even to you that the taste was too harsh, that the exhilaration of the alcohol was giving way to a slight depression. It just was not good, even for you." Thus admonished, the well-trained desire for wine would then reply, "Of course, you're right. I just have a hard time remembering sometimes. I'll savor what I have, instead of ruining it by trying for the next level (right, right—it is illusory) of exhilaration."

With this account of correct functioning and dysfunctioning of the appetites, we have perhaps an answer to the problems raised by the notion of compatibility of desires in the *Gorgias.* If he were confronted with the account of the *Republic,* Callicles could not now answer by suggesting that one simply give up moderate desires in favor of an immoderate one. In the *Republic* the issue has become one of harmony of functions. Insatiable appetite entails a disharmony of functions. In particular, insatiable appetite attempts to disrupt the function of reason—the function of ruling in the soul. Now, Callicles cannot overcome this incompatibility between insatiable appetite and the rule of reason by proposing that one give up reason; it is impossible to give up the function of reason. It would seem, then, that the moral psychology of the *Republic* ought to silence Callicles. He will not be able to maintain now that individual appetites have their own welfare, apart from that of the whole soul. However, a determined Callicles still has something to say. In answer to the account in *Republic* IV, Callicles might say that all of this talk of correct functioning and dysfunction, while more complex and sophisticated, has done nothing to address the basic issue of contention between him and

Socrates. Callicles might argue that, in the present dialogue, Plato has given a theoretical account of what really amounts to the claim that one should try to bring one's soul into harmony—but now the harmony must include reason and the spirited part. Still, the fact remains that harmony requires appetite, in deference to the claim of reason to rule, to give up some of what it could get if it were insistent. It is the usual tactic of prudent reason to try and make this great compromise seem the best possible solution to the fact that satisfying our appetites comes into conflict with other goals, especially those of reason itself. It is typical of a compromise devised by reason that it would entail moderating appetites so that they become docile to the rule of reason—even to the point of agreeing to reason's version of what is good for them. However, a determined Callicles might offer another way to achieve compromise. Incompatibility comes from the fact that reason's need to rule is inconsistent with immoderate appetite's need to be the leading direction in the soul. Now Callicles would, presumably, not suggest that one get rid of reason as one of the parts of the soul; such a suggestion is impossible. Rather he could suggest that one subordinate reason to the immoderate appetite. Even if Callicles concedes the need for harmony of functions, he could still achieve the harmony within the soul by the simple expedient of claiming that reason's function is to calculate consequences, not to rule. Thus, one can achieve compatibility by making the immoderate appetite the ruler in the soul and reason its auxiliary. Indeed, in that way, one can avoid the worst delapidations of immoderate appetite; one can then become canny about how to lead a life of enormous pleasure, aided by the farsighted reason. So, without giving in to Socrates' plans for restraining immoderate appetite, Callicles could present an alternative way to harmonize immoderate appetite and reason. After all, why should one have to follow only one pattern in establishing harmony between the appetites and the other parts of the soul?

At this point, Plato has given us a very compelling account of what the well-functioning soul will be like. The account is compelling because it is so reasonable. Each part of the soul is given a function and each of the functions is fulfilled; it seems an economical and even elegant distribution of tasks. Our imaginary Callicles, however, has introduced doubt about whether these alleged functions are really the proper functions of the parts. The Calliclean arrangement of the soul would contradict the claim that reason should rule. Now we can see that the plausibility of this claim depends on the prior claim that, by wisdom, reason knows what is best for each part of the soul and for the whole. If this latter claim were true, it would make sense to claim that reason should rule in the soul and for appetite to defer to reason. In particular, appetite should defer to reason's rule because, by doing so, appetite would receive what is good for it. The problem is that Plato has not done enough to show that this arrangement is also what is good for each of the parts and for the whole. We do not yet have a justification for the claim that reason knows what is good for each part and for the whole. Even if this arrangement *seems* to be good for the parts and for the whole soul, it is not clear that it is *really* good for the parts and for the whole soul.

Craft entails a kind of knowledge about the goals of the craft. Medicine, for example, entails knowledge about health and how to provide it. However, craft also entails certain attitudes about the desirability of achieving the goals of the craft. The education of a physician makes him prize the health of his patients; it is part of the dynamic of his craft to love health. Knowledge tells one the goal of the craft; knowledge also affects the motivation to achieve the goal of the craft because it reveals the goal to be good. In chapter 1, we have referred to the motivational element. There we talked about the pride of craftsmanship—the desire to see the object of the craft perfected. Commentators frequently overlook this feature of craft, making craft little different from theoretical knowledge. The latter is presumably an objective, non-value-laden view, with no power to move the knower to action; craft knowledge, however, is always value laden. The goal of the craft is seen as something that is desirable to achieve because it is presented as something good. In the next two chapters we will complete the account of the craft of justice by looking at both of these features of the craft. We will see that the theory of Forms addresses both of these features. Forms are introduced as paradigms for the philosophical rulers of the ideal city. Without the Forms for justice, temperance, and goodness, the rulers will not have the knowledge necessary to be rulers—or even to be virtuous individuals. As we will see in Books V, VI, and VII, Socrates presents the Forms as models for imitation. However, these books also hint at the role of Forms as motivation for establishing justice in the city and in oneself because they also show what is good for the city and the soul. In the last chapter, we consider the *Symposium* and reconsider the *Republic* in order to see more clearly the way in which goodness inspires imitation of the Forms.

NOTES

1. For discussions of the craft analogy cf. Irwin, *Plato's Moral Theory*, O'Brien *The Socratic Paradoxes and the Greek Mind*; René Schaerer, *EPISTHMH et TEXNH* (Macon: Protat Frères, 1930); Rosamond Kent Sprague, *Plato's Philosopher-King* (Columbia: University of South Carolina Press, 1976). Cf. J. Gould, *The Development of Plato's Ethics* (Cambridge: University Press, 1955), 16 ff.; J. Lyons, *Structural Semantics*, 139 ff.; David L. Roochnik, "Socrates' Use of the Techne-Analogy."

2. In "Socrates' Use of the Techne-Analogy," Roochnik claims that the use of the analogy implies no theory of morality—no theory to the effect that virtue is, in some sense, a type of craft knowledge: ". . . the purpose of the analogy is not to establish a theoretical model of moral knowledge" (190). Rather, he says, the analogy is used dialectically, to exhort or to refute. The argument of the article is somewhat sketchy, of course, as to what is meant by a dialectical use; it would appear that Roochnik means that the craft analogy is used in the context of larger dialogical argument in order to make a point in that larger argument. The point does not require there to be a theoretical account to the effect that virtue is a type of craft knowledge. According to this view, the craft analogy is something like an undeveloped notion, useful only for comparison. It is difficult, however, to maintain such a position in the face of the great detail and care with which Socrates elaborates this comparison between wisdom and craft in the *Euthydemus*. Indeed, Roochnik admits the presence of the craft analogy in "The Serious Play of Plato's *Euthydemus*," *Interpretation* 18(1990–91):211–232: "In this passage Socrates relies exclusively on techne for his model of wisdom, soon to be defined as that knowledge of the correct use of neutral items which brings its possessor happiness." However, Roochnik does not take this passage literally but warns that it "should be read with an eye towards the possibility of irony" (219). Even if the passage is ironic, the passage certainly looks like a theoretical model for virtue—albeit one that should not be accepted. On the issue of irony, see note 8. See also Paul Woodruff, "Plato's Early Theory of Knowledge" in *Essays on the Philosophy of Socrates*, Hugh H. Benson, ed. (New York: Oxford University Press, 1992). In his thorough account of craft, Woodruff gives the theoretical basis for the craft analogy. Yet, following Roochnik, he demurs: "Socrates' theory of expert knowledge is certainly not the expressed view of any of his interlocutors; none of them proposes it, and scarcely any

shows that he understands it. Moreover, Socrates does not adjust his view of expert knowledge to meet the need of each argument; his view is much the same, no matter whose case it is used against. Nevertheless, we would be naive to conclude that this simply is Socrates' analysis of what it is to be an expert. He uses it dialectically, especially when he applies it to moral expertise. It is safer to say Socrates supplies this view of expert knowledge as necessary in his view to support the claims made by his partners" (92). Here, without much explanation, Woodruff disclaims Socrates' ownership of the notion of expert knowledge. However, after reading the article, one might wonder why Socrates would have developed an account of expert knowledge, which he himself does not hold, only in order to correct the thinking of his interlocutors, who do not really understand it. In any event, none of this keeps Socrates from using the craft analogy as a theoretical model.

3. Thus Gifford and Hawtrey. Cf. *Plato's Euthydemus*, E. H. Gifford, ed. (New York: Arno Press, 1973), 20, n.278e3 and R. S. W. Hawtrey, *Commentary on Plato's Euthydemus* (Philadelphia: American Philosophical Society, 1981), 77–78, n.278e1. Sprague believes the ambiguity is between prospering and acting rightly—the latter in a moral sense. Cf. Rosamond Kent Sprague, *Plato's Use of Fallacy* (New York: Barnes and Noble, 1962), 10.

4. It is puzzling to include virtues, especially wisdom, among the previously mentioned instrumental goods. But in the sequel, Socrates includes only the physical assets as the instrumental goods to be used by wisdom. Cf. *Meno* 88a6–c4 where the other virtues are not really virtues unless they are guided by wisdom.

5. Chance has a thorough discussion of this passage, in which he makes the distinction I am here exploiting. Cf. Thomas H. Chance, *Plato's Euthydemus* (Berkeley: University of California Press, 1992), 57–65.

6. Cf. Gifford, *Euthydemus*, 21–22, n.279d6 and Hawtrey, *Commentary*, 80, n.279e1. M. A. Stewart, "Plato's Sophistry" *Aristotelian Society* [Supplementary Volume] 51(1977):23, says that the argument is disastrous.

7. Cf. Martha Nussbaum, *The Fragility of Goodness* (95–99) where she argues that *technē*, in one sense at least, is seen as a strategy to overcome luck, *tuchē*.

8. Cf. Hawtrey, *Commentary*, 81–82, n.280a7ff. In "The Serious Play of Plato's *Euthydemus*" Roochnik sees this argument as ironic; Socrates is suggesting that wisdom is not best modeled by *technē* (219). In the first place, what makes the argument suspicious has nothing to do with the virtue of wisdom; what makes the argument suspicious is a feature of Socrates' notion of craft—that is, its infallibility. Even if he had the comparison between the virtue of wisdom and craft in mind, surely

he is not being ironic about comparing craft and the virtue of craft on the issue of infallibility; surely he believes that both are infallible. Second, Socrates, during the rest of the passage, develops the craft analogy in great detail. It is hard to see how he means to be ironic about the craft analogy at this point if he continues to pursue the analogy. After all, irony can become deceit, and Socrates can become a sophist.

9. Roochnik finds this step problematic because it implies that there is an objective knowledge of correct use (220–221). It is not that there might not be such objective knowledge but that not everyone would agree to there being such objective knowledge. Thus, according to Roochnik, the argument fails as a protreptic argument. It would appeal only to people, presumably like Cleinias but not like Euthydemus and Dionysiodorus, who believe that there is an objective knowledge of correct use. In the first place, the argument is directed to Cleinias and not to Euthydemus and Dionysiodorus (we are always being urged to pay attention to whom arguments are directed). In the second place, Roochnik's objection would be more convincing if this protreptic argument could be shown to be significantly weaker than any other protreptic argument. Does a protreptic argument have to force someone deductively to pursue philosophy or does it rather have only to introduce reasonable enough sounding premises to convince someone that it is worth it to pursue philosophy? I submit that the claim that there is knowledge of correct use of one's material and spiritual assets sounds reasonable enough to convince an interlocutor to pursue philosophy.

10. The significance of this argument is the way in which wisdom is systematically compared to craft. There is a parallel to this part of the argument in the *Meno* (87e5 ff.). Cf. Hawtrey, *Commentary*, 77. Beginning at 87c, Socrates makes an argument to the effect that virtue (*aretē*) is the same thing as knowledge (*epistēmē*). He lists a set of goods similar to the list educed from Cleinias—health, wealth, strength, and beauty of the body. However, he argues that each of these can be harmful as well as good; the difference is right use (*orthē chrēsis*). In turn, the secret of right use is understanding (*phronēsis*). With understanding, each of these attributes of the body as well as those of the soul (temperance, justice, courage, intelligence, memory, and largeness of soul) will be used to the advantage (*ōphelima*) of the one who possesses it; without understanding, the attribute can be harmful. In this passage, understanding (*phronēsis*) serves in the place held by wisdom (*sophia*) in the *Euthydemus*. Although Socrates does not use any examples of craft to illustrate this knowledge of right use, still it seems to be like a kind of craft knowledge, like wisdom. What he says about it in this passage is the same as what he says about wisdom in the *Euthydemus*. Understanding, like wisdom, results in the right use of the same set of assets as in the *Euthydemus* in order to provide happiness. Paul Woodruff sees knowledge as

technē in this passage, "Theory of Knowledge," 103–104: "The thesis that there can be knowledge without teaching, virtually explicit in 85c, is resisted in the balance of the dialogue. Socrates infers that what is not teachable is not knowledge (99ab) on the basis of a hypothesis repeated at 87c and 89d. These passages represent the pre-*Meno* theory of knowledge as *technē*."

11. It is a little less clear how one might misuse virtue, especially given the fact that Socrates usually identifies virtue with the good. Supposing one to be courageous, the misuse of that courage would seem not to be courage. To illustrate this paradoxical saying, imagine a soldier in battle: if it were possible to misuse courage, presumably its misuse would lead to either dishonor or death. If the soldier suffers dishonor, surely it is because he is not courageous; therefore he has not misused courage. If he suffers death, either death occurs through courage or foolhardiness. Neither is a misuse of courage. Fool-hardiness is not the misuse of courage but its absence. In his argument, Socrates touches on but glosses over this problem by saying that courage without understanding (*phronēsis*) is a kind of boldness (*Meno* 88B).

12. Only in the *Protagoras* in the dialogues under consideration, is happiness explicitly identified with pleasure. But this is not Socrates' position (cf. *Plato's Protagoras*, G. Vlastos, ed., [New York: Bobbs-Merrill, 1956], x1, n.50.) If this were, moreover, Socrates' real position, its discovery would be a breakthrough in the elaboration of the craft analogy. Yet pleasure is not the goal of virtue in the craft analogy in any other dialogue under consideration.

13. Cf. Sprague, *Philosopher-King*, 52–53.

14. I have not found this reading of this passage in any other commentators. Sprague in *Plato's Use of Fallacy* says that the conclusion of this argument is "that the kingly or political art possesses the special character of having only itself as subject-matter is, I think, meant to imply that it is identical with knowledge in itself and that it really is the art for which he and Cleinias have been seeking" (22). Hawtrey also sees reflexivity here because he sees a reference to the knowledge of knowledge in the *Charmides* (137–138, n.292d1 ff.). However, this conclusion is based on the premise that the ruling craft confers only the knowledge of itself. The text does not say that the ruling craft confers knowledge of itself; it says that the ruling craft confers itself (292d3–4). Cf. Chance, *Plato's Euthydemus*, 126.

In addition, one might object that, since Socrates' project is to find a successful candidate for wisdom considered as a craft, his argument here contradicts my claim that the craft of virtue and the craft of ruling are distinct. The answer is, first, that the groping for a craft knowledge which uses what it makes has led to a suggestion—that wisdom might be the craft of ruling—which is problematic. The argument, in fact, shows the problem of identifying two crafts which are distinct. Second, the sequel argues that it is the goal of *Republic* IV to answer this problem.

15. Roochnik, in his article on the *Euthydemus*, at first says that the conclusion of this argument is that "knowledge of arete cannot be completely analogous to an ordinary techne" (227). By "ordinary techne," he means, for example, carpentry and medicine. This, by itself, is an unremarkable conclusion; it leaves open the possibility that to make good on the craft analogy some modifications must be made. However, Roochnik goes on to reject the craft analogy altogether. "If techne is the only form of knowledge, then there can be no knowledge of arete and Socratic protreptic cannot be distinguished from sophistry" (227). His argument for this latter, stronger conclusion is that the result (*ergon*) of ordinary *technē* is determinate whereas the result of *aretē* is indeterminate because what it uses—health, wealth, beauty, for example—are indeterminate. It is unclear what he means by "indeterminate" in this argument. However, his argument precludes the possibility that the craft analogy can be completed by substituting for these objects others that do not suffer from the putative defect. In general, Roochnik precludes the possibility that the present argument is still a protreptic one that sets the stage for further investigation into just such questions. Compare Sprague *(Philosopher-King,* 53) on this point. In the sequel, we argue that Plato makes good on the craft analogy by substituting for such assets as health, wealth, and beauty other objects upon which the revised craft of justice works.

16. Irwin expresses a version of this objection in *Plato's Moral Theory*; we will analyze his version of it in section 3 below.

17. This passage is an example of a partial use of the craft analogy. Laches is using the case of the physician to refute Nicias' claim that courage is knowledge of what-is-to-be-feared and of what-is-to-be-encouraged-by. Knowledge here, as elsewhere, means craft knowledge. So Laches uses a counterexample from craft knowledge. Nicias finally replies that the only craftsman (*dēmiourgos*) who knows about what is to be feared and what is not to be feared is the courageous person. Clearly, Nicias, at least, believes that courage is a kind of craft knowledge. Moreover, he gives an account of its particular *ergon*; it is knowledge of what is to be feared and what is not to be feared. However, he cannot take the analogy much beyond that point. Whereas in the *Euthydemus* Socrates introduces the objects on which the craft of wisdom works—material and spiritual assets—in this dialogue no such intriguing detail is given.

18. Cf. Woodruff, "Theory of Knowledge, 94: "If *technai* are specialised, then each one has its specific goal, the good of its object, which it pursues to the exclusion of all others. . . . This leads to paradox if each *technē* operates without fault. . . . To operate faultlessly, a *technē* would need to know what really promotes the advantage of its object. It would

have to ask, for example, whether a mutilated patient is really better off alive or dead; but that would be beyond the scope of specialised doctoring." Cf. Sprague, *Philosopher-King*, 68–69.

19. Cf. Woodruff, "Theory of Knowledge," 95: "The defect of the subordinate *technai* is that they were too specialised to know how to put their skills to good use, and so would have to be subordinate to a *technē* that did specialise in the relevant good. But any true *technē*, it now appears, must aim at the good, and must therefore know what this is."

20. Cf. Renford Bambrough, "Plato's Political Analogies," 201–202. "Wherever Plato turns among the *technai* . . . he cannot find what he is seeking, a skill at determining which ends ought and ought not to be pursued. He is conscious of this difficulty, and he attempts to overcome it by distinguishing between the standard, instrumental arts, and a higher, prescriptive art, the kingly art of politics. . . . There is no prescriptive *technē* . . . for the inescapable logical reason that anything that can properly be called a *"technē"* will be by its very nature instrumental, and the decision about the purpose for which it is to be used will lie outside its own scope." See also Reeve, *Philosopher Kings,* 8 and 19. Although he does not use the term *instrumental*, he holds that the argument at *Republic* I (333e) points up a fatal flaw in the craft analogy.

21. Cf. O'Brien, *Socratic Paradoxes*, 17–18, 103–106; a similar points is made by Terry Penner, "Socrates on Virtue and Motivation," in *Argument and Exegesis*, Lee, Mourelatos, and Rorty, eds. (Assen: Van Van Gorcum, 1973), 143–146. See also J. E. Tiles (*"Technē* and Moral Expertise," 49–66) for a qualified answer to Bambrough.

22. Cf. Roochnik, "Serious Play," 222–228. Also 231, n.7.

23. This position owes much to Sprague's distinction between first order and second order *technai* (7–8) and the specification that the kingly *technē* is eventually shown to be a second order knowledge of good and evil.

24. One might object that temperance, the virtue of self-control, is an exception to this claim. If temperance were presented in the early dialogues as a craft of ruling over one's appetites in order to instill virtue, then the distinction between the craft of ruling and the craft of virtue would not be so clear; in turn, the claim that in the *Republic* Plato combined two crafts would be undermined. It would appear that before the *Republic* he already had the notion of virtue as self-rule in order to instill virtue. First, let us look at the evidence. In the early dialogues, temperance is not presented as the kind of self-rule found in the *Gorgias*. The only dialogue that comes close is the *Charmides*. At one point Critias says that temperance is self-knowledge (164d ff.); this claim eventually becomes the claim that temperance is knowledge of knowledge. In one of its manifestations this claim becomes the claim that the temperate person would know whether he has knowledge of a subject. Then at 171e,

Socrates says that such knowledge would be useful because "we would go through life, both we who have temperance and those under our command, not making mistakes. For we would not attempt the things we do not know but searching out those who do know we would turn these things over to them." Since the knowledge is compared to craft knowledge, this passage is definitely comparing temperance to a craft; and the passage does suggest self-rule. However, this self-rule would be like the craft of ruling as that occurs in the *Gorgias* only if the self-rule were a craft of ruling over one's appetites that itself instilled virtue in the soul. But nothing in this passage says anything about ruling over one's appetites nor anything about instilling virtue as control of appetites. Whatever self-rule there is in this passage, it is much closer to the craft of virtue because temperance is like the management of one's resources of body and soul. In this case, one is managing his knowledge.

In *Socrates in the Apology* (134–136), C. D. C. Reeve identifies temperance with the craft of ruling. In order to make this identification, he uses the disputed dialogue *Alcibiades* I. Still, the passage that Reeve cites, 133b7–134a14, seems to make a point similar to the one in *Charmides* Socrates says that lack of self-knowledge is lack of knowledge of our own belongings; the latter is lack of temperance. So far nothing is said about ruling. Then Socrates says that lack of knowledge about one's own belongings entails lack of knowledge of the belongings of others. The latter lack entails that one is not fit to be a politician or ruler. Again, Socrates says nothing about ruling over one's appetites in order to instill virtue; one's own belongings could easily be those material and spiritual possessions mentioned in the *Euthydemus*. While there is nothing in the early dialogues that jeopardizes the distinction between the craft of ruling and the craft of virtue, the *Gorgias* comes closer to presenting such a challenge. At 491d, Socrates, in a successful attempt to goad Callicles into speaking his mind, asks him about self-rule. In answer to Callicles' suspicious question as to his meaning, Socrates says, "Nothing complicated but as the many say, the temperate person controls himself and rules over his own pleasures and appetites." Here there are two of the elements of the craft of ruling: temperance is compared to ruling and it rules over one's own appetites. Nothing is said about ruling over one's own appetites in order to instill virtue. However, this passage allows me to make a second point: the distinction between the two kinds of craft does not rest upon the claim that temperance is never considered a type of self-rule. It rests upon the claim that Socrates elaborates a craft of caring for the souls of others and that that craft becomes fully developed into the craft of ruling in the *Gorgias*. The focus of this craft is not one's own soul but the souls of others, until Plato works out the way in which self-rule becomes the craft of instilling virtue in one's own soul—something that requires considerable ingenuity and something he does not do until the *Republic*, where the craft in question is not temperance at all but justice. If, in a transitional dialogue like the *Gorgias*, there is a hint of anticipation that self-rule over appetites and virtue are associated, my thesis is not jeopardized. In particular, the short passage at 491d does not change the fact that Socrates does not develop the notion of self-rule in this dialogue but rather the craft of ruling as a craft of moderating the appetites of others in order to instill virtue.

25. This comparison of the craft of virtue in the *Euthydemus* to the craft of ruling in the *Gorgias* makes no assumptions about the relative dates of the two dialogues, although the former was probably written before the latter.

26. The therapeutic crafts benefit their objects by providing for their welfare and their good (*Rep.* 342a1–c9); they include medicine, gymnastic, and ruling. Socrates understands this welfare in a narrow sense; the welfare of an object is its perfection according to its excellence (*Apo.* 20a6–b2; *Rep.* 335b5–c3). Socrates' reply to Thrasymachus (*Rep.* 345b10–e4) takes on a plausibility it does not otherwise have if *to beltiston* means excellence—as it does surely in the *Gorgias* (464b2 ff; 503d6 ff.).

27. *Rep.* 488a1ff. shows that Plato still thinks of ruling as a craft in Book VI. In this last passage ruling is compared to the crafts of carpentry, brassworking, and farming. Ruling is said not to be any of these crafts, not because it is not a craft, but because its object is the good of the whole state—the other crafts are too particular. I am indebted to Professor Vlastos for reminding me of this last example. Also cf. *Rep.* VI, 500c9.

28. C. D. C. Reeve (*Philosopher Kings*, 82–85) clearly presents ruling in Book VI–VII as a craft, even though earlier he rejects the craft analogy in a passage in which he conflates the craft of ruling and the craft of virtue (17–19).

29. Different commentators take different views of the nature of these parts of the soul. Cf. Richard Robinson, "Plato's Separation of Reason and Desire," *Phronesis* 16(1971):38–48; R. F. Stalley, "Plato's Arguments for the Division of the Reasoning and Appetitive Elements Within the Soul," *Phronesis* 20(1975):110–128; J. E. Tiles, "The Combat of Passion and Reason," *Philosophy* 52(1977):321–330; Terry Penner, "Thought and Desire in Plato," and "Plato and Davidson: Parts of the Soul and Weakness of the Will," *Canadian Journal of Philosophy*, [Supplementary Volume] 16(1990):35–74; Glenn Lesses, "Weakness, Reasons, and the Divided Soul in Plato's *Republic*," *History of Philosophy Quarterly* 4(1987):147–161; Julia Annas, *An Introduction to Plato's Republic* (Oxford: Clarendon Press, 1981), 137–151; Nicholas P. White, *A Companion to Plato's Republic* (Indianapolis: Hackett, 1979), 122–130. The views range from Robinson's (that Plato has only shown

the trivial claim that the soul has different aspects) to Lesses' (that Plato has shown each part is something like a mini-agent, with its own conception of goodness as its motivation and goal). Annas gives a mediating account that says that the parts should be seen as primitive agents: "And so there is nothing wrong with talking of the explanatory parts of a whole person as though they were themselves people of a very simple kind. Talking of them as homunculi is very natural and unavoidable. . . . [Quoting D. Dennett] 'Homunculi are bogeymen only if they duplicate entire the talents they are rung in to explain.' That is, we are in trouble if the homunculus reproduces the features that were found puzzling about the whole person. But 'if one can get a team or committee of relatively ignorant, narrow-minded, blind homunculi to produce the intelligent behavior of the whole, this is progress'" (144).

30. Cf. Penner, "Thought and Desire," 101. "But on certain assumptions we can show that Plato would have found it plausible to make such a move himself—in particular the assumption that desire must have (at least some minimum) conception of its object. This corresponds to the belief that would nowadays be expressed by saying that the object of desire is intentional, where this does not mean simply '*The person who has* the desire has some conception of the object of his desire.'"

31. Most commentators take this argument to be an all-but-explicit refutation of the Socratic position that desire is always for the good. Lesses, however, argues that even in this argument Plato allows that the parts of the soul other than reason may have a conception of the good. They differ from reason in that their conception of the good is limited (151).

32. Gregory Vlastos, "Justice and Happiness in the *Republic*," *Plato: A Collection of Critical Essays*, vol. 2, Gregory Vlastos, ed. (Garden City: Doubleday, 1971), 89. Of course, it is not clear that all evil doing proceeds from one of these disorders. It is a point of controversy whether Platonic justice in the soul always results in being just to others. See David Sachs, "A Fallacy in Plato's *Republic*," in *Plato: A Collection of Critical Essays*, vol. 2, Gregory Vlastos, ed. (Garden City: Doubleday, 1971), 35–51. Our own account of this issue will take place in chapter 3 with the introduction of the theory Forms as paradigms.

33. This order is proper and specific to the soul. This is a theme that begins with the *Gorgias* (506e1–5) where the order brought by the good orator—the craftsman of the souls of others—is proper and specific to the soul; it is also what virtue in the soul is. Socrates is quite emphatic about the unique relation between a soul an its order; what I have called "proper" is Greek *oikeios*. According to Book IV, the order accords with what Plato clearly thinks is the nature of the soul; any other arrangement brings ruin and decay (cf. *Rep.* 445c4 ff.).

34. If the other two directions in the soul can become overweening, it stands to reason that reason itself could also overstep its bounds. However, how it would do so is not so clear from the dialogues. Socrates will soon present one picture of the life of reason gone bad. In Book VI, he explains why philosophy has such a poor reputation. It is because those who have the talent to practice it have been seduced to lesser activities. In their place, there come minor intellects who are like mechanics who have married above their station (495c ff.). However, this is hardly a picture of reason having overstepped its bounds; one would suspect that reason grown insatiable is reflected in the life of the intensely intellectual but ineffectual scholar.

Closer to this stereotype is the uncomplimentary picture of the intellectual life in the *Gorgias* (484c ff.). Callicles opens his conversation with Socrates by painting a picture, meant to be minatory and directed at Socrates himself. He spends too much of his time whispering in a corner with young boys about questions that make no difference in the real world of politics. These are childish pursuits that will render him impotent if anyone ever tries to drag him into court. Perhaps in these pictures there also can be seen our own stereotype of the ineffectual "egghead"—someone who is so brilliant that she cannot be bothered with the mere details of daily living. Finally, there is just a hint of this theme in Book VII where the guardian who has attained to contemplation of the Forms must be forced to turn away from her real delight to the practical tasks of ruling in the ideal city. At least, in Socrates' first picture there is the sense that the life of reason goes astray if it is not really the life of reason. Presumably, the claim is that a person who really pursued the life of reason would see that the other parts of the soul had valid claims as well. Richard Patterson develops this idea in a somewhat different direction in "Plato on Philosophic Character," *Journal of the History of Philosophy* 25(1987):325–350.

35. Irwin, *Plato's Moral Theory*, 8. A significant part of Irwin's instrumentalist account of the craft analogy depends on his reliance on productive instead of therapeutic craft as an analogue for virtue. When he says that "the virtuous man does not reject the nonvirtuous man's choice of the ultimate end, but only his choice of instrumental means to it" he seems to be taking the craft of virtue to be like carpentry (82). Both carpenter and noncarpenter agree about the end to be produced, for example, a table; whatever disagreement there might be arises about means. However, therapeutic craft does not so easily fit Irwin's model of instrumentality. Even Irwin admits this when he compares virtue and medicine. Patient and doctor will not have the same understanding of health; but the variance in understanding is not substantive, according to Irwin (83). However, the latter relation between patient and doctor is not the one Socrates attributes to medicine. For Socrates, physician and

patient are not speaking the same language. The physician is talking about an underlying physical condition, whose usual manifestation to the patient might be a certain sense of well-being. The patient is talking about these manifestations themselves. But the patient's being healthy is not his having this sense since he may have this sense and be very sick (cf. *Gor.* 464a1–b1). Moreover, in the example from *Gorgias* 521a3–522a6 in which physician and pastry cook contend before a jury of children, it is not as though the physician can win over the children by redescribing health for them. According to Socrates the physician has nothing to say to the accusation after the children scoff at his plea that he did all for their health. Craft, according to Irwin's instrumentalist interpretation of the craft analogy, is supposed to be a model of rationality (86). However, in the *Gorgias*, we see that therapeutic craft is itself caught in the breakdown of rationality. For another kind of criticism of Irwin's account of the craft analogy see George Klosko, "The Technical Conception of Virtue," *Journal of the History of Philosophy* 19(1981):95–102.

36. Irwin, *Plato's Moral Theory,* 185

37. There is also a second craft characterization: (C) any action that preserves and helps finish the order of the soul is just, wisdom being the craft knowledge that guides this action (443e- 444a). However, we will not be using this one in the argument. Nevertheless, we can see that whatever is (C) is also (A); however, there is a difference in the way in which whatever is (B) is (A) and whatever is (C) is (A). This difference is due to the difference between (B) and (C). (B) is something like a person's establishing justice in his own soul (presumably, preliminary work has already been done by one's mentors); (B) describes moral self-tending, undertaken before one begins his business or political activities. On the other hand, (C) characterizes what one does after the establishing of moral virtue, when one does engage in business and political activities; (C) describes what he does in these latter activities in order to preserve and help finish the order whose establishment is described in (B). After this order is established, then preserving and helping to finish the order, with wisdom guiding this activity—that is, what is described by (C)—is also what is described by (A). If the order is preserved and perfected under the guidance of wisdom then each part is doing its own function with regard to ruling and being ruled, that is, (A). The rule of reason is not being usurped by the lower parts since the preservation and perfection is done under the guidance of wisdom, reason's peculiar virtue.

38. Of course, that 'justice' in (B) does not refer to each part's doing its own does not mean that (B) does not instantiate (A), where 'justice' does refer to each part's doing its own.

39. Cf. Sarah Waterlow Broadie, "The Good of Others in Plato's *Republic*," *Proceedings of the Aristotelian Society,* 73(1972–73):28: "Now it is clear why justice on Plato's account is necessarily self-propa-

gating within the same soul. The rational element's function is to see that each element, including itself, functions and is allowed by the others to function as it should; so that the state in which they all function properly is, like Plato's favorite simile, health, self-maintaining in one and the same individual." See also Donald Zeyl, "Socratic Virtue and Happiness," *Archiv für Geschichte der Philosophie* 64(1982):237: ". . . the product of the virtue-craft may *also* be described as virtuous acting or living. If this is right, then it will be true that virtuous action (as the practice of craft knowledge) aims at its own replication. Thus any piece of virtuous behavior may, then, be viewed *either* as the practice of the virtue craft *or* as the product of that craft. To understand this, we may . . . compare the virtuous agent to an athlete in action. The athlete's performance serves both to express his skill (and as such is the result of previous practice), and also to develop and maintain it. Insofar as it does the latter, its value is that of an instrumental good: its aim is the perfection of the skill, and the performance that such perfection makes possible. Insofar as it does the former, its value is that of an intrinsic good: possessing the skill and displaying it is just what it is to live or do well for the athlete." See also Jerome Schiller, "Just Men and Just Acts in Plato's *Republic*," *Journal of the History of Philosophy* 6(1968):6–10; Nicholas P. White, *A Companion to Plato's Republic*, 135, n.F and 236–37, n.B. For an analysis of psychic harmony as health, see R. F. Stalley, "Mental Health and Individual Responsibility in Plato's *Republic*," *Journal of Value Inquiry* 15(1981):109–124.

40. Cf. M. B. Foster, "A Mistake of Plato's in the *Republic*," *Mind* 46(1937):386–393; J. D. Mabbott, "Is Plato's *Republic* Utilitarian?" *Mind* 46(1937):468–474; M. B. Foster, "A Mistake of Plato's in the *Republic*: A Rejoinder to Mr. Mabbott," *Mind* 47(1938):226–232; I. M. Crombie, *An Examination of Plato's Doctrines*, vol. 1 (London: Routledge and Kegan Paul, 1962), 85–88; R. C. Cross and A. D. Woozley, *Plato's Republic* (London: Macmillan, 1964), 65–68.

41. Cf. Foster, "A Mistake," 392–393.

42. The successful exercise of an achievement disposition like seeing can be viewed in two independent ways. It can be seen from the point of view of what is achieved—the inherent consequences—or from the point of view of the process of achievement. The latter is the correct functioning—according to its nature—of the entity underlying the disposition. For example, the eyes underlie the disposition of seeing. The correct functioning of the eyes is due to the disposition of seeing well (cf. *Rep.* 352d8 ff.). When one's eyes function correctly one has visual information and vice versa. But "the eyes function correctly" does not mean the same as "having visual information." It is logically possible to have correct visual images even if one's eyes are not functioning correctly. The correct function of the underlying entity is *intrinsic good* and the inher-

ent consequences of the achievement of disposition is *consequential good*.

43. Cf. Foster, "A Mistake," 387–388; White, *Companion*, 78–79.

44. Cf. Julia Annas, *An Introduction to Plato's Republic*, 66–68. Mabbott, "Utilitarian?" (469–470), confessing to find the relevant passages ambiguous on the distinction, still believes that Socrates argues that justice is good in itself.

45. Cf. J. D. Mabbott, "Is Plato's *Republic* Utilitarian?" *Plato: A Collection of Critical Essays*, vol. 2. G. Vlastos, ed. (Garden City: Anchor, 1971), 63. Moreover, the monitoring need not even be a separate occurrence within the correct functioning of the parts, not an observing, for example, of oneself in action. The agent's nonobservational knowledge of his action is discussed in Ryle's *Concept of Mind* (New York: Barnes and Noble, 1949), 141–148; cf. my amendments to the account in "The Agent's Knowledge of His Action," *The Personalist* 55(1974):44–52.

46. This account of the intrinsic good of justice in the soul helps to explain the connection between virtue and happiness in one famous problematic passage. In the *Gorgias* (507c1–5) Socrates says that the virtuous life is doing well, and that, if the virtuous man does well, he will be happy (cf. *Rep.* 353e1–354a2). What is usually taken to be the problem in this argument is pointed out by E. R. Dodds (*Plato: Gorgias*, 335–336). He notes the active and passive senses of "doing well" and charges that Socrates is buying plausibility by trading on an ambiguity. Just because one does well, in the sense of being virtuous, it does not follow that one will do well, in the sense of being happy. However, if doing well is intrinsically good in the way the above account maintains, the ambiguity disappears. "Doing well" means one's soul is functioning correctly, according to the nature of the soul—and, of course, knowing that the soul is functioning correctly. To function at one's best and to know that one is doing so is an important part of what happiness is.

47. Cf. Aristotle's account of the pleasure of activity, Book X of the *Nicomachean Ethics*. As well, J. O. Urmson, "Aristotle on Pleasure," *Aristotle: A Collection of Critical Essays,* J. M. E. Moravcsik, ed. (Garden City: Anchor, 1967), 323–333.

48. This understanding of the craft of virtue, however, does not make the *Republic* utilitarian or egotistically hedonistic. The end of the craft is the perfection of the object; this perfection is good in itself and the primary goal of the craft. That the exercise of this perfection is also a good for the virtuous man does not imply that this aspect is the goal of the craft. See Jack Kelly, "Virtue and Pleasure," *Mind* 82(1973):408. The author makes a similar point to this one, but it is about virtue in Aristotle's ethics.

49. Cf. Annas, *Introduction*, 133 ff.

CHAPTER 3

The Craft of Justice and Imitation in the Republic

Plato, in fact, has already prepared us for the fact that his impressive account of justice in the soul is, nevertheless, inadequate in some way. In Book IV, just before he launches into the long-awaited comparison between the city and the soul, Socrates issues a warning to his interlocutors.

> . . . it is my opinion that we will never grasp accurately this thing from the methods we have been using in these investigations up to now. There is another, greater and longer way that leads to this thing. (435d)

In spite of this warning, Socrates plunges ahead with his account. At first, the context would make it look as though Socrates is talking only about the structure of the soul when he talks about "this thing"; however, a subsequent passage shows that he means the whole matter of justice in the soul and in the city. In Book VI Socrates refers back to this earlier warning.

> You remember then, said I, that, having distinguished the three parts of the soul, we set up what each [of these] is: justice, temperance, courage, and wisdom. (504a)

Glaucon says that he could not forget this account. Then, Socrates also reminds him that the clearest vision of this matter was available only to the one who takes the greater route. He hints that it is now time, in the dialogue, to take this longer way round. Of course, we know that the longer way round is also the greatest learning (*megiston mathēma*), knowledge of the Form of the good and, through it, all the other Forms. And while Socrates is not able actually to take his interlocutors on the longer way round, he does offer them a sketch of it. This passage in Book VI is the prelude to the metaphysical heights of the *Republic*, the analogy of the Sun, the Divided Line, and the simile of the Cave. In short, the longer way round,

the most accurate knowledge of this matter, entails that the learner
come to know the Forms, by way of the highest Form, the good.

In this way, then, Plato, in the books immediately following
Book IV, adds two more levels to his argument in the *Republic*.
The warnings just quoted indicate that these levels are offered as
means of completing the account in Book IV. First is the introduction of the Forms as paradigms, to be used by the rulers in establishing virtue in the city and in their own souls. Second is the completion of the account of Forms by the highest learning, the
knowledge of the Form of good. In this chapter, we will concentrate on the first of these two levels—the introduction of Forms as
paradigms. As we shall see, Plato sees the theory of Forms as a
completion of his account of the ruling craft. However, it is clear
that the focus has shifted from establishing virtue in the soul to
establishing it in the city, although Socrates talks as though the
two enterprises are not really separate. In this chapter we will
elaborate his account of the relation between the Forms and the
craft of the philosophical rulers—the philosopher kings. In the
next we will turn to the greatest learning—the role of the Form of
the good in the ruling craft.

I

In Book V, the interlocutors in the dialogue begin to exhibit an
anxiety about whether the ideal city they have been talking about
is possible. In particular, having been forced to address the issue
of the community of women and children, Socrates worries that
his ideas on this subject will lead some people to question whether
the ideal city is possible, indeed whether it is even desirable. In
order to address these problems, Socrates sketches his famous theory about the role of women as guardians and about the kind of
family the guardians will have. In fact, Socrates argues that
women should be guardians along with the men; then he outlines
a system of marriages and child care that explodes the private
family and in its place puts a communal family. Conceding that
these suggestions are paradoxical to his contemporaries, Socrates
compares the predictable reaction to these two doctrines to
waves—waves that he believes their discussion has successfully
withstood. However, it is the third wave of paradox that will
prove the most difficult. This third wave is the notorious Platonic

claim that, in order to make the ideal city possible, philosophers must become kings or those who now rule must become philosophers.[1] This third wave is the means for introducing the theory of Forms, in particular Forms as paradigms. In the next section of Book V, philosophers are defined as those who have knowledge of the Forms. In the rest of Book V, Socrates sets forth a complex argument to show the relation between knowledge and Forms, as well as the relation between opinion and the perceptual world. His argument is a classic statement of Platonic epistemology. However, it is also more than epistemology, in the contemporary sense, that is at stake in this passage. We must remember that the larger issue is the knowledge that the rulers must have in order to be capable of ruling in the city. By extension, it is also the kind of knowledge needed if reason is to rule in the soul. The kind of knowledge that is sought is primarily a craft knowledge, a kind of practical knowledge.

In the early dialogues craft is identified with knowledge. In part this identification marks the infallibility of craft, its reliable production of results. In the *Gorgias*, craft is defined by its seeking the perfection of what it works on and by its ability to give an account of its procedure. Medicine, for example, knows what health is and how to go about producing it; it has an account of its goal and, thus, of its procedure. The ruling craft ought to have a similar sort of account of its procedure and of its goal. In the case of the soul, the goal of the craft is psychic health and psychic health is a balance and harmony of parts of the soul. However, the warnings that Socrates gives show that what he has so far said about these topics is not sufficient to qualify as the sort of account that amounts to craft knowledge. Since psychic health is justice in the soul, we can say that we do not yet have an account of justice in the soul that counts as knowledge of justice in the soul. And since it is craft knowledge that is sought, we can add that we do not have an account of justice in the soul that would allow reason to exercise the craft of ruling in the soul.

However, the problem in the text does not present itself as knowledge of justice in the soul but as knowledge of justice in the city. In Book V Socrates is concerned to present an account of the kind of knowledge that the rulers in the city must have. As it turns out, the knowledge that the rulers of the city need is the same as the knowledge that ruler of the soul needs. All rulers need knowledge of the Forms, in particular knowledge of the Form of justice.

It is knowledge of the Form of justice that allows rulers to establish either psychic harmony or civic harmony. Something is at stake other than theoretical knowledge of justice, then. We know that something else is at stake because Plato introduces Forms into this conversation by way of a play on the notion that philosophers are, literally, lovers of wisdom. Socrates teases Glaucon about being an ardent lover of boys, one who loves all types of boys, whatever their physical characteristics. Clearly uncomfortable but willing to go along with the joke, Glaucon asks how this characteristic of lovers is found among lovers of wisdom. Socrates says that the lover of wisdom must love all of it, not just some part of it; such a lover of wisdom will seek all kinds of learning. To Glaucon, one who thus seeks all kinds of learning is something like a dilettante, who really is a lover of spectacles (*philotheamones*). Socrates counters that the lover of wisdom about which he is talking is a lover of the spectacle of truth (*tēs alētheias . . . philotheamonas* [475 e4]).

It is in explicating what he means by "truth" that Socrates introduces the Forms. As in other passages in the dialogues that refer to Forms, here Socrates talks as though Glaucon will recognize what he is talking about, as though the notion had already been discussed among his hearers.

> Concerning just and unjust, good and bad, and all the Forms (*eidōn*) the account is the same: while each of these is one, each makes many appearances by way of varied participation in actions, bodies, and such things. (476a)

Thus, besides being lovers of truth, philosophers have another feature; they can distinguish appearance from reality. Philosophers are divided from the mere lovers of spectacles because philosophers can distinguish the one from the many, the reality from the appearance. Mere lovers of spectacles can see only the many beautiful appearances, for instance; they cannot know and cling to the nature of the beautiful itself. They are compared to people who are dreaming because they cannot distinguish reality from appearance.

> To dream is this: whether asleep or awake, one believes that which is like is not like something [else] but rather is the very thing to which it is like. (476c)

The two themes of loving wisdom and of dreaming and waking are interrelated, then. The rulers in the city are to be so in love with the truth that they seek to find it in another dimension, so to speak. Because they love all of the truth they are not satisfied with the surface but must look beneath the surface to find the whole truth. Their love of the truth has an analytical and investigative bent. So far we have a familiar theme; one must go behind the obvious or patent to something more fundamental. However, at this point, the contrast between surface and what is below the surface is characterized in a peculiar way. The whole truth leads them from, for example, many beautiful things to one beauty beyond the many beautiful things. Moreover, this one beauty beyond the many beautiful things is the reality of which the many beautiful things are the appearance.

There follows a long argument to show that this characterization of the difference between the philosopher and the lover of spectacles is correct. The argument attempts to establish that if there is knowledge, it is of Forms. Whatever grasp we have of the perceptual world, it cannot, by itself at least, ever amount to knowledge. When it comes to the perceptual world, we have opinion only. It is not within the scope of this book to develop this argument at any length. There is, however, one point that is vital for our purposes.

Within the argument Socrates presents the classic theory of Forms from the middle dialogues. In what is usually taken to be a reference to Forms, he says that what wholly is (*pantelōs on*) is wholly knowable (*pantelōs gnōston*) (477a3). While the context indicates that the Forms are what wholly is, the notion of what wholly is, however, certainly seems mysterious. We will follow those commentators who say that this phrase should be taken to be elliptical; another term is meant to follow the 'is'. 'What wholly is' is elliptical for 'what wholly is F.' What 'F' stands for is problematic, however. On the one hand, it could stand for such predicates as 'beautiful,' 'just,' or 'good' that apply univocally to Forms and particulars. On the other hand, F could stand for a term that primarily designates a Form (somewhat like a name) and derivatively applies to other Fs.[2] While the latter view is more appropriate to our interpretation, we will not argue for it. At this point, we will assume that "being wholly 'F'" is a way of designating the Form of F as the exemplar of F. Thus, what is wholly knowable is what is wholly just, or wholly beautiful. To be wholly beautiful is to be beautiful at all times, from all aspects, in all relations, and so on. We capture this notion by saying that to be wholly beautiful is to be beautiful without qualification—unqualifiedly beautiful. Socrates gives such a description of the Form of beauty in the *Symposium* (211a). The notion of unqualified beauty leads naturally to the notion of perfect beauty; to be unqualifiedly beautiful is to be beautiful without exception, that is, to be perfectly beautiful. In this account, then, Forms are perfect and unqualified; the Form of F is perfectly and unqualifiedly F. Another way to put this matter is to say that the Form is real F, authentic F. Things that are ambiguously F are phony or inauthentic F. We will assume that this way of talking does not imply only a univocal reading of 'F' but is compatible with 'F' having a primary and a derivative designation.

This notion of reality is embedded in an account of knowledge. Knowledge cannot be had of what is qualifiedly beautiful but only of what is unqualifiedly beautiful. What is qualified is ambiguous and what is unqualified is clear. Knowledge is always right; opinion can be either right or wrong. Thus, knowledge goes with clarity; opinion goes with ambiguity. Finally, knowledge goes with Forms, which are unqualifiedly whatever they are. The ambiguous object of opinion turns out to be objects in the perceptual world that are both F and not F, beautiful and not beautiful. Exactly why knowledge goes with clarity is not altogether clear itself. Of course, in one way it seems plausible to say that knowledge is of what is unambiguous. If an object is just F and not also not-F, then it is a more convenient object for knowledge; once one has grasped it there is no need to separate out extraneous matter. However, it is not clear that knowledge requires such rigid clarity. After all, it might be possible for someone to know, for example, that a particular decision is both just and unjust. However, it would help to remember that what Socrates has in mind is the sort of knowledge that makes rulers able to establish and preserve justice in the city. The point of the passage is not to give a general account of knowledge but an account of what the ruler needs to know in order to establish and preserve justice, temperance, courage, and wisdom in the ideal city, as well as in his own soul. What the ruler needs is an unambiguous grasp of, for example, justice, one that will serve as the goal of his craft. The ruler wants to know primarily what justice is.

If we keep the craft of ruling in mind, we will be able to sift through the various epistemological interpretations of this passage.[3] What the philosophical ruler needs is a grasp of justice that will be useful and appropriate in all contexts. Socrates is saying that in order to find such guidance he should not rely on the many cases of justice available to even the casual observer; he must go beyond these to find something different in kind, something more reliable. Thus, the ruler is not well served by simply grasping the justice of, for example, Solon. If the ruler tried to fix her gaze on justice in this one context she might well mistake justice for what is not justice. For instance, if she fixed her gaze on Solon, she might take his just actions in reforming the city as what justice is. She then might try to replicate Solon's actions in another historical situation only to find out that his actions are not appropriate to this different situation. The goal of her craft is not Solon's justice but justice as such. This she must grasp without the ambiguity of circumstance. If she were a physician instead of a ruler, she would want such a grasp of health. Even if we take Alcibiades to be a perfect specimen of health, it would not do for the physician to replicate his condition in others. There is much about his condition that is idiosyncratic. After all, she is not interested in Alcibiades' health, she is interested in health. To grasp that item it would be better to have it isolated from Alcibiades' beauty, or other peculiarities. Isolated, abstracted, purified, health can be applied to others.

In short, what the philosophical ruler needs to guide her craft is a paradigm of justice, which affords a grasp of justice without any of the shortcomings of the particular instances. This role for Forms is found in the *Cratylus*, where Socrates wishes to illustrate his notion of the craft (*technē*) of name-giver, that is, the one who gives things their names. He is like another craftsman, the carpenter, in that, in his craft of giving names, he looks toward something. When the carpenter makes a shuttle, he looks toward (*blepōn*) something whose nature is to weave. Moreover,

> if the shuttle were broken while he is making it will he look toward (*blepōn*) the broken shuttle when he makes another or toward that Form (*to eidos*) in accordance with which he made the broken one? (389b)

The answer is that he looks toward the Form, which in turn is called "that which is shuttle" (*auto ho estin kerkis*), one of the formulas Plato uses to designate a Form. The conclusion is that the name giver also looks toward a Form, that which is name.

That is precisely how Socrates presents the philosophical rulers at the beginning of Book VI. It is the philosophers—those who know the Forms—who are fit to be rulers in the ideal city. The way that Socrates justifies this claim—so obvious in some ways—is significant. The philosophers use this knowledge in the way artists use models; the philosophers—who are able to distinguish the many appearances from the one reality—are contrasted to those who have no distinct paradigm in the soul (*mēden enarges en tēi psuchēi echontes paradeigma* [484c7–8]) and are unable, in contrast to the way the painter works with his paradigm,

> to look toward (*apoblepontes*) the truest thing, always referring back to that, and contemplating in the most exact way possible, thus to establish here the laws concerning beautiful things, just things, and good things, if there is need to establish, and carefully to preserve what has been established. (484c–d)

If we put this description in a positive form, then, we would say that the philosopher king is like a painter who looks toward a paradigm, a model, in painting a picture. Just as the painter reproduces the features of the model, the philosopher king reproduces the features of the Forms, which are his paradigms. These paradigms, however, are the truest, affording the most accurate vision for bringing forward those features; thus, the philosopher king is able to make laws for the city, which will govern beauty, justice, and goodness.

At this point in Book VI there is a long interlude in which Socrates shows why the true philosophical natures in the actual city are counted as useless. After the interlude, he picks up again the motif of philosophical rule as an imitative craft. Not only is this analogy with the painter appropriate for portraying the way that the philosopher king rules in the city, it also is used to talk about the way the philosopher king himself becomes virtuous, as we can see from a passage later in Book VI. The philosopher himself becomes virtuous because he spends his time looking upon and observing the Forms.

> (he will) imitate (*mimeisthai*) those things and make himself as like them as possible. Or do you think that there is any way for someone who associates with what he admires (*agamenos*) not to imitate that thing? (500c)

Thus, the philosopher, who associates with Forms, will become orderly (*kosmios*) and divine (*theios*) insofar as a human may do so. In turn, if such a one is put in charge of establishing human practices, both in the private and in the public realms, and not just of molding (*plattein*) himself, he would be a good craftsman (*dēmiourgon*) of temperance and justice and the other civic virtues (500d4–8). Such rulers are like painters who make a sketch according to a divine paradigm (*tōi theiōi paradeigmati* [500e3]). Socrates then elaborates on this analogy with the painter, driving home the notion that the Forms serve as paradigms for imitation.

> Then, I suppose, they [the philosophical rulers] would set about their work, frequently looking (*apoblepoien*) in both directions, toward the just that exists in reality, the beautiful, the temperate, and all such things, and then toward that thing they would create among humans. (501b)

The ruler uses, then, the Forms for the virtues—for justice, for temperance—as paradigms for his work. However, there is a curious addition to the Forms that serve as paradigms—that is, the Form of beauty. Thus, besides instilling justice in the city, and temperance, the ruler will also instill beauty. Although it is not said, it might be supposed that the ruler instills beauty by instilling justice and temperance. Nevertheless, it should be noticed that Plato has inserted a somewhat higher term of value into the account—one which has for us strong aesthetic connotations.

Given the strong way in which imitation is presented in these passages we can appreciate Socrates' account in Book V of the nature of Forms. If the Form of justice is unambiguously just, it is a perfect object of the ruler's painterly glances. When the ruler looks to the Form, she wants a clear view, one unobscured by extraneous matter. She needs to grasp a type of justice that does not come to be nor pass away, that does not wax and wane, that is not just from one point of view but unjust from another. What is significant for the ruler, then, is that Forms do not have perspectives. Once one has grasped them, there are no unseen points of view. This feature of Forms turns out to be an important contrast with ordinary perceptual objects, which are always seen from some point of view or other. That the Form of F lacks perspectives is related to its being wholly F. Unlike perceptual objects, the Form of F is not grasped from a particular point of view; there is not another point of view from which to view it. Thus, there is not the possibility that from this other point of view it will appear not F. However, there is always the possibility that some particular F will appear not F from another point of view. The Form of justice, for instance, is just from every point of view while the justice of Solon can always appear unjust from some perspective. It is because they have perspectives that particulars are liable to ambiguity.

While we know in Book VI that Forms are paradigms for imitation, we are not given much more detail about the nature of the images made by the philosophical rulers. However, producing images arises in Book X of the *Republic*. Here Socrates returns to the role of the poets in his ideal city. Now that he has established the theory of Forms in his account of the city, he believes he is able to offer further justification for his severe treatment of the poets. Using a random—and somewhat bizarre—example of the bed, Socrates says that there are three kinds of bed. First, there is the Form of bed or that which is bed. Next is the bed made by the carpenter; the carpenter makes his bed by looking toward to Form of bed (596b–c). The latter description of the carpenter resembles closely that of the philosophical ruler we have just seen in Book VI, where the ruler looks toward the Forms of justice, temperance, and beauty in fashioning the city (500c–d; 501b–c). There the philosophical ruler is said to imitate these Forms. However, in Book X, Socrates wants to restrict the word *imitation* to those who produce the third kind of bed—the mere appearance of bed. The third kind of bed is the painting of a bed. It is a copy of a copy because it copies the bed made by the carpenter, which in turn is a copy of the Form of bed. This third kind of bed is said to be thrice removed from reality (counting the Form as the first step [597e]). Socrates then develops an elaborate indictment of such imitators. Since they do not know the reality but only the appearance, they can reproduce only images that are partial and distorted. For instance, in painting a bed—which is only an appearance of the Form of bed—the painter paints only that perspective of the bed he sees, leaving out what he cannot see. The painter thereby represents only the appearance and not the reality (598b). Socrates goes on to draw out this analogy in the case of the dramatic poets, who can produce only partial and distorted images of reality (605a).

Whatever its implications for the treatment of poets, the passage does give us some insight into the difference between the philosophical ruler and other kinds of rulers. The philosophical ruler, in fashioning a constitution or a particular judgment, is looking toward the Form of justice. His constitution or judgment is not a perfect embodiment of the Form; by the nature of the case it cannot be. However, it is a distinct improvement over the constitution or judgment that comes from the nonphilosophical ruler who has only the appearances of justice to copy. If we follow the analogy with the painter, the appearances of justice, which the nonphilosophical rulers will imitate, will be the actually existing cities; the nonphilosophical ruler would use them as standards of justice, unable to see justice itself. Since he does not know the Form of justice and cannot understand what the appearance is trying to be like, he mistakes the appearance for the reality. Mistaking the appearance for the reality, the nonphilosophical ruler would produce distorted images of justice, just as the painter produces distorted images of the bed.

Thus, there would be two kinds of image. The image produced by the philosophical ruler and the image produced by the nonphilosophical ruler would differ in their approximation to the reality. The philosophical ruler produces an image of justice twice removed from the reality (counting, in the usual Greek way, the Form itself as the first step). Presumably it is less distorted than the image produced by the nonphilosophical ruler. The latter produces an image thrice removed from reality; it must be more of a distortion than the first. The reason for this difference between the work of the philosophical and the nonphilosophical rulers is that the latter cannot tell the difference between appearance and reality and mistake the former for the latter. In our interpretation, the nonphilosophical ruler is unable to distinguish justice itself from the context in which it appears. Thus, the nonphilosophical ruler confuses what is essential to justice with what is contextual in this instance. He is like the ruler who confuses Solon's justice with justice. The philosophical ruler has the advantage in that she can fit justice itself, not merely Solon's justice, to each circumstance. She goes back to the source—the essence of justice—and begins anew to replicate the justice that is appropriate to all contexts because it is not bound up with any context, aware that justice will wear a different appearance in each new case.[4]

Finally, these passages in *Republic* VI extend the analogy between craft and justice of Book IV by introducing the notion of a paradigm the craftsman copies in accomplishing his task. Indeed, this extension of the craft of justice is the way that Plato connects this craft with the theory of Forms. It is by looking upon the Forms, understood as paradigms, that the craftsman of justice, whether in the soul or in the city, is both instructed and inspired. His task then is one of imitation. Imitation of Forms as paradigms completes the account of the craft of justice from Book IV. The analogy with imitative craft is not just a device to introduce the Forms into this account, however. Plato is making an important point in his moral theory. Besides the account of justice from Book IV, with its cogent economy of psychic functions, there is another level at which we can see the value of justice in the soul. Justice in the soul, like justice in the city, is guided by the Form of justice, the way a painter is guided by his model. This analogy is not trivial; it brings into the project of acquiring and maintaining virtue a whole new dimension, as we shall see.

Imitation is, of course, a very important component of the moral life and of moral education. Most of us become aware that, in fashioning our lives, we are depending on certain individuals as models. Some of these individuals are actual people, friends or relatives; others are fictional characters. Some of these individuals are taken to be positive models—one wishes to be like Uncle Hank. Others of these models are negative—one does not wish to be like John Updike's Harry Angstrom. In these models, then, we see instances of what we admire or what we abhor. In *Republic* II and III, Socrates makes imitation the central motif in the education of the guardians (377b). He sees literature as presenting to young people models for imitation. In traditional literature, the models are morally lacking. The stories of the gods must be expurgated because we do not want young people in the ideal city imitating the deeds of Kronos or Ouranos and excusing their evil behavior by citing these latter examples. Likewise, the stories of the heroes must be changed so that morally better models will be held up for emulation. Young people should not read stories that present death to be something terrible, for such stories undermine courage by attacking the proper attitude toward death, that is, that slavery should be more feared than death (387b). Indeed, Socrates would even forbid guardians from portraying characters in plays who are not morally worthy of imitation in real life. From childhood they should imitate (*mimeisthai*) only people who are courageous, pious, moderate, and free (395c).

In this view, Plato is trying to establish the positive kind of imitation as the heart of the moral life. In this attempt, however, the models become—as it were—larger than life because they are abstracted from life. Instead of imitating Socrates' justice, the philosopher imitates justice itself—the Form of justice. Instead of trying to discern justice, for example, obscured by Socrates' bad character traits, the philosopher can discern justice unobscured by injustice. Finally, this unobscured justice, because of its abstract nature, is applicable both in the private life of the philosopher and in the public life of the city.

However, we might want to know how literally to take this talk about paradigms. Taken literally, the notion of paradigm implies that the philosophical ruler is actually in possession of an inner vision of the Form of justice. The Form of justice seen in this vision would exhibit a characteristic that all just laws and institutions would have. In virtue of this characteristic, the ruler would be able to say that just laws, for example, all share a common character—a character that is seen in a particularly pure way in the paradigm. In this naive reading, then, the ideal in some way has and thus exhibits the characteristic justice so that it can be taken in by a visionlike grasp. On the other hand, there are the sophisticated interpreters who resist such a literal reading of talk about paradigms. To these interpreters, the philosophical ruler is not looking at—even (or especially) intellectually—an object that exhibits the character of justice.[5] The talk about vision is just metaphorical. The philosophical ruler is, for example, consulting a set of propositions—or even one particularly rich proposition—that articulates the truth about justice. Then she compares the language of the proposed laws or the descriptions of the proposed institutions with the propositions of the account of justice. She tries to find out whether the former are consistent with the latter, whether the latter imply the former. The talk of vision is merely a metaphorical way of presenting this essentially intellectual process of deductive reasoning.

The naive view is naive because it takes literally Socrates' talk about imitation. The sophisticated view, on the other hand, tries to translate that talk into categories more familiar to contemporary thought. In fact, at this point in Plato's moral theory, either way of interpreting Socrates' teaching about imitation seems possible. At this level, Forms are sources of information, so to speak; they communicate to the philosophical ruler what, for example, justice is. Whether Forms are self-exemplifying paradigms or propositional formulas, they are capable of fulfilling this function.

The difference between the naive and the sophisticated view of Forms becomes important, however, later when the Form of goodness as the source of motivation becomes relevant. We will see there that when the good, along with the other Forms, is the source of motivation, Forms also need to be self-exemplifying. Accordingly, with this level of Plato's moral theory in mind, we need to adopt the naive view.

II

In the following section we will attempt to give an account of the naive view. We will assume that a paradigm actually has the characteristic for which it is a paradigm. Thus, the paradigm for justice is like, in some way, the paradigm for the capital of a Corinthian column found in the ancient Greek sculptor's shop. The paradigm for the capital displays the characteristic to be copied by the sculptor. There are difficulties, however, with trying to grasp the notion of such a paradigm when it comes to Forms. The comparison with the paradigm for Corinthian columns is helpful, but only partially. The paradigm Corinthian column embodies the relevant characteristics for being copied. But the paradigm Corinthian column is a perceptual object; it is fairly easy to see how it can embody the characteristic for which it is a paradigm. The Form of justice is, obviously, not a perceptual object. It is, thus, difficult to see how it can embody the characteristic of justice.

To help, we can start with something similar to a paradigm for justice—the personification of justice. On, or in, many courthouses one finds a statue of Justice as the blindfolded woman holding scales in one hand and a sword in the other. If it were a series of statements, it would say that courts should be blind to such aspects of a case as social rank, that claims should be carefully and accurately weighed, that punishment should be severe. Moreover, the personification is a kind of idealization. The judge can only approximate the blindness of Justice; her decisions can only be approximately evenly balanced between competing claims. However, the statue symbolically embodies these characteristics. It presents, under the perceptual guise of the statue, the characteristics of justice. These characteristics are not themselves perceptual; but they can be grasped in a summary, nonpropositional, fashion by the symbolic representation. Of course, we cannot make too much out of this example. No one would use, instead of cases and laws, such a personification as the subject matter of a law school course. No judge would walk out to the courthouse steps to contemplate the statue of Justice while trying to decide a case, looking to see if her decision compared favorably with what the statue embodied. As such, the personification reminds us of what we have otherwise agreed upon, taught, or promoted. The personification has a merely symbolic function for us.

Now, however, suppose a nonmaterial paradigm that embodied the characteristic that justice in the city (or in the soul) was striving to have, but in something more than a symbolic way. It is something that exhibits justice, then. Moreover, in this supposition, the paradigm is abstract. It is perfectly just; it exhibits justice without the taint of injustice—unlike the average court decision, which can only be approximately just. Moreover, the paradigm is unqualifiedly just; there are no other qualities mixed with justice that distract from the paradigm. This paradigm would, then, exhibit the characteristics that heretofore were only approximately embodied. The difficulty with talking in this way is that, while it makes sense to talk about justice in the laws of the city, it does not make much sense to talk about justice in a paradigm. In the city, a just law guarantees that each citizen can fulfill his function. A law, for example, about weights and measures takes into consideration the needs of market vendors for fair competition. Whatever this characteristic of justice might be in the law, it is very difficult to imagine what it will become if it is abstracted from the actual market, vendors, and buyers in our experience. If justice is found in the relations among these actual people, how can it possibly be found in a world of abstract paradigms?

At this point, of course, it is hard to make out what Plato might have meant. The dimensions of the problem are that, on the one hand, there should be a characteristic that is justice, whether it is found in the city or in the soul; on the other hand, this same characteristic—not the universal for the characteristic—can be found, uninstantiated in a city or a soul, all by itself. Finally, we should be able to recognize that the characteristic is the same, whether in the city or in the soul or existing by itself. We could leave the problem at this point and simply stipulate that the Form exhibits in some appropriate sense the characteristic for which it is a Form without any further explanation.

For the purposes of illustration, however, we will offer a version of one of the speculative answers to this problem. Although it has some textual grounding, we are not maintaining that Plato actually held this speculative account, only that it is one of the possibilities he might have considered for making the notion of Forms as self-exemplifying paradigms specific. The speculative account is simply offered as one of the ways Plato might have answered the problem as to what the self-exemplifying Form might be. Moreover, while the subsequent account of Plato's moral theory depends on the notion that Forms are self-exemplifying, it will not depend on this particular version of the way that the Form of justice, for example, is self-exemplifying. In devising this speculative answer we shall pay close attention to the way that Plato has introduced into his account concepts that we would call "aesthetic." He talks as though what justice aims at both in the laws of the city and in its legal decisions is a balance and a harmony—a kind of beauty. If we exploit this notion, we can see what Plato may mean by such language. Justice does answer a need for balance and harmony among the functions and needs of the citizens. Justice brings the different kinds of citizens together, with due respect for their differences—an attempt to make a kind of *kosmos* or order out of the chaos of competing functions. If we see justice as a kind of ordered harmony of functions, then it is possible to talk about abstracting that order and harmony. We abstract the order and harmony from the surrounding conditions in which the order and harmony are found. We abstract the order and harmony from the citizens and their counterclaims; the result is order and harmony without obscuring elements. The consequence would be that, when justice is abstracted from actual persons and their functions—and when it is, nevertheless, not a universal for justice, but still justice even in this state of abstraction—it is an abstract, but real, order and harmony.[6]

As an abstraction, the mode of existence of the Form of justice can be compared to the mode of existence of mathematical entities. A mathematical entity is both apart from perceptual existence and still exhibits the characteristic found, in a more obscure way, in perceptual existence. For example, the mathematical entity the equilateral triangle exists, in this account, abstracted from all perceptual equilateral triangles; nevertheless, the mathematical entity still exhibits, but now in a clear and pure way, those characteristics that the perceptual equilateral triangles exhibited in a more obscure way. Just so, the Form of justice exists apart from cases of justice in the perceptual world. In its abstracted state it is an order and harmony; this order and harmony exhibit the characteristic that perceptual cases of justice exhibit in a more obscure way.[7] This paradigm would be like the personification, in that it exhibits the characteristic found in just laws, decisions, policies. However, it would differ in that the characteristic would not be exhibited in a symbolic way. This Form will stand at one end of a continuum with the order and harmony of the city's just laws and decisions at the other end. While, in the city, this order and harmony can only be achieved in an approximate way, in the paradigm order and harmony are perfectly and unqualifiedly achieved. In this way, we arrive at this paradigmatic order and harmony by abstracting from the qualifying and the imperfect.

Just such a vision of the Forms seems to be the one Plato attributes to the ruler in a passage part of which we have already seen in Book VI (500c). Here the philosopher is said not to look upon the affairs of humans,

> thus he does not engage in the strife which fills one with fear and ill-will; rather looking to those things [the Forms] which are well-ordered and remain the same always and seeing that neither do they transgress upon, nor suffer transgression by, one another (*out' adikounta out' adikoumena hup' allēlōn*)—they are orderly and proportionate (*kosmōi de panta kai kata logon echonta*)—he imitates them and makes himself as like them as possible.[8]

If we read this passage in a naive way, the paradigms corresponding to justice in the soul are clearly described as orderly and proportionate. This description seems to explain the claim that the paradigms do not commit or suffer transgression. It is hard to imagine how a paradigm might commit a transgression; still it is clear that they are being characterized as themselves just. In fact, being orderly and proportionate seems to explain why they are among themselves just—as though when justice is abstracted from the context of city and soul it is a proportionate order.

Further confirmation for the naive view is found when we look to the way that imitation of the Forms is described in this passage. If the paradigm for justice is an abstract order and proportion, then these characteristics ought also to be found in the just soul. In fact, in describing the effects of imitating the Forms of justice, temperance, and beauty, Socrates attributes to the soul a divine order, which is clearly meant to be a copy of the order found in the paradigms.

> Thus the philosopher who associates with divine order (*theiōi de kai kosmiōi*) will become orderly and divine (*kosmios te kai theios*) as far as it is possible for a human to do so (500d).

We think immediately of the description at the end of Book IV, where the just soul is also described in terms of order and harmony. There Plato uses the craft words *kozmēsanta* and *sunarmosanta*—bringing order and harmonizing. When imitating the Form of justice, the philosophical ruler makes the soul orderly and harmonious. Justice in the soul—that is, each part of the soul fulfilling its function—is a kind of order and proportion.[9] Thus, in a naive reading of the passage, the Form of justice models the justice of such an arrangement, by modeling the qualities of order and proportion in this arrangement in the soul. In the naive view, it does so because justice abstracted from the soul and the city is order, proportion, and harmony. In the soul or in the city, this order and harmony are what justice amounts to. Abstracted they simply are order, proportion, and harmony; that order has some intrinsic reality apart from its instances.

Of course, to the nonphilosopher, such a paradigm might not be the subject of a law school course, nor the object of a judge's contemplation. The reason is that its existence is, at best, a hypothesis and his grasp of it intuitive and unsure. However, Plato could say that it is present as a kind of memory trace, motivating in an unrecognized way the legislator and the judge to seek more just laws and decisions. It would serve as a dimly divined ideal, then. Plato might say that if a law student never intuitively grasped this paradigm, she would have missed the point, in some real sense, to her legal education. The laws and the decisions are all trying to embody this one paradigm of justice; without intuitively grasping the paradigm, she would not understand the laws and the decisions.

Following this naive reading, we can see one of the reasons Plato might have used the notion of paradigm. Abstracted from actual situations, the paradigm gives the philosophical ruler needed clarity in her job as ruler. Imagine the ideal city ruled by true philosophers. In this city, the ruler knows directly—grasps in a clear intuition—this paradigm and does not just dimly recollect it from what she observes in the perceptual world. In looking at the Form of justice, the ruler sees exhibited that characteristic that ought to be exemplified in the city, as well as in her own soul.[10] In the Form the ruler sees clearly and fully the characteristic, perfect and unqualified, which is only dimly seen in Socrates' Athens.[11] What she sees is the Form of justice; in our speculative reading she sees an order and harmony not tied to this law or that court case, not mixed with any other elements that would obscure its essence. Thus she sees a purified and clarified order and harmony. For instance, we can imagine a court case in which the competing claims of right are particularly strong. The nonphilosophical ruler is trying to come up with a just decision—one that adequately addresses the claims—but the strength of the claims keeps obscuring what is just in this case. The ruler's mind is pulled this way by one set of claims, then it is pulled the other way by the other set of claims. It becomes increasingly unclear what justice is in this case or what it is in general. The philosophical ruler, however, has the Form on her side, the unobscured justice itself. While she too will be pulled in contrary directions by the competing claims, she has an advantage in that she can look at the Form of justice from time to time. This consulting of the pure paradigm of order and harmony will bring stability to the deliberations of the ruler as she tries various solutions to the problematic case. Her grasp of the nature of justice will not be undermined by the confusing case before her. She can continue trying various solutions to the case because she has not lost her bearings, so to speak. In turn, in this account, keeping the unobscured paradigm in her mind will give her a sensitivity to features of the case that touch on justice, an ability to notice significant but hitherto obscured details. Finally, one or two solutions will have most clearly the order and harmony she sees exhibited in the Form.

In *Republic* VII, the rulers who have seen the Form of goodness—and thus all the other Forms—behave in just this way. Socrates warns that, descending again into the "cave" of the perceptual city, after seeing the Forms, the philosophical ruler will at first experience difficulty seeing in the shadows—that is, seeing justice obscured in the perceptual world. Addressing his hearers as potential rulers, Socrates then says:

> However, having gotten used to it, you will see those things a
> thousand times better, and you will know about each of these

> images what it is and of what [it is an image], through having
> discovered the reality concerning the beautiful, the just, and the
> good things. (520c–d)

In this account, then, it is not a question of applying philosophical
definitions of justice nor of applying legal definitions of property
rights. The method is not one of deduction from a general principle to a particular case. The judgment of the ruler will be closer to
what we call "intuition." Given the doctrine of recollection, we
can presume that everyone has some intuition, however weak, of
the Forms. The philosophical ruler simply has the weak intuition
raised to the level of knowledge.[12]

III

If craft imitates a paradigm then it produces images. The craft of
justice, then, produces images of justice—images of justice in the
soul and in the city. In this section we will investigate images in
the *Republic* in order to understand the way that the craft of justice produces images of justice. Of course, it is straightforward
enough to say that imitative craft produces images. After all, the
craft intends to make copies of the paradigm; the copies are, in an
easily comprehensible sense, images of the original. The copy of
the paradigm of the Corinthian capital is an image of the paradigm. However, the notion of image in the *Republic* is more complicated than this notion of the image of the Corinthian capital.
The image of the Corinthian capital is itself another real Corinthian capital; the image of the Form of justice is not itself another
Form of justice. The image of justice is less real than the Form. In
the *Republic*, an image is an appearance of a more fundamental
reality.

That images should be appearances of a more fundamental
reality is not a necessary consequence of the notion of image, then.
However, we have already seen one reason why Plato would have
chosen this way of explicating the relation between image and
original in the *Republic*. In Book V, each of the many beautiful,
just, and pious things both is and is not what it is said to be.

> Of all of the many beautiful things . . . is there any which does
> not appear ugly, and of the just [is there any] which does not
> appear unjust, and of the pious [is there any] which does not
> appear impious? (479a)

One way to interpret this passage is to say that an F is both F and not F (where F stands for the range of terms in the above quotation) because it has the quality that properly belongs to the Form but also has other qualities that do not belong to the Form, that is, non-F qualities. The non-F qualities include qualities both contradictory and contrary to F. An F, then, differs from the Form because the Form is unmixed F.[13]

The reason that an instance of justice, for example, is both just and not just is that instances of justice are always tied to a particular context, a particular time and place. The justice of Solon is tied to the particularities of that era of Athenian history. Although what Solon did may have been just for that era, it is not necessarily just for another era. If Solon's solution to the situation of Athens in the early sixth century were imported in a literal way into fifth-century Athens, it would not work. In order to be just in the sixth century, the solution had to be mixed with much that was non-just. The non-just is not the same as what is unjust; the non-just is simply what is not an essential part of the Form of justice. One way of presenting this blend of justice with context is to say that Solon produced an image of justice, one that is an appearance of the reality of justice. Indeed, it is this ambiguous aspect of instances of justice that led Plato to think of them as appearances; they have the ability to deceive the way appearances do (*Rep.* 476c). A preliminary way to appreciate this point is to remember that an appearance both reveals and conceals reality. There are ways in which an appearance is diaphanous and there are ways in which an appearance is opaque. An appearance of justice is the same: there are ways in which it reveals the Form of justice and ways in which it conceals the Form. Understanding the relation of the appearance to the reality of justice reveals justice through the appearance; failing to understand the relation conceals the reality. As we have seen, excessive attention to the details of Solon's reforms can conceal justice because it concentrates attention on what is the non-just; one confuses justice with the particularity of the reforms. On the other hand, seeing Solon's reforms as an appearance of the Form of justice reveals the Form in those particular lives and fortunes; one sees the justice that is, as it were, beyond the particularity of the reforms. In this way, an instance of justice is like an appearance because it both reveals and conceals justice.

A good way of talking about the way an instance reveals the Form is to say that it reflects the Form, the way a mirror image, for instance, reflects the original. It reveals the Form because it is a reflection. However, it is only a reflection and not the real thing because it is mixed with other qualities that are not justice. Thus it conceals the paradigm because its justice is mixed with other qualities that tempt one to misunderstand the true nature of justice. Only knowledge of the Form of justice would allow one to disambiguate justice in the instance from its context. If we suppose justice to be a type of balance and proportion then unembodied it would be pure justice. On the other hand, when it is embodied in a material particular it would be mixed with what is not balance and proportion, with what is balanced and proportioned. One would need to know the Form as such to abstract the balance and proportion from its embodiment. Error would be to identify justice with this particular embodiment of balance and proportion, to fail to see how it is a reflection.

Thus, in order to understand images and the role of the philosopher as one who produces images we must investigate the relation between appearance and reality.[14] In this section we will explore two aspects of the relation between appearance and reality in order to understand better the relation between image and original. The first is the way that, in Book VI, an appearance is dependent on the reality. The second aspect follows from the first: the way that properly understanding an appearance—and thus an image—is to understand its relation to reality. The point of philosophical education in the *Republic* is to avoid misunderstanding the relation between appearance and reality. Misunderstanding the relation leads one to take an appearance for the reality; in this way there arises the notion of a deceptive image. In Book X we will see the way in which a particular kind of deceptive image arises. These two aspects of the relation between appearance and reality are themselves related, of course. If the justice in souls and in the city is an image of the Form of justice and if the image is an appearance of the Form, then justice in souls and in the city is dependent on the reality of the Form. Justice in souls and in the city simply could not exist without the Form, any more than the reflection of Simmias in a mirror could exist without Simmias. In turn, understanding justice in souls and in the city entails understanding their relation to the Form, just as understanding the reflection of Simmias entails understanding its relation to Simmias. Moreover, being able to reproduce images of justice also entails understanding the relation between appearances of justice and the Form of justice.

The *Republic* makes clear that appearances can either conceal the reality or they can reveal the reality. When Plato introduces the Forms at the end of Book V, he says that the lovers of truth can tell the difference between appearance and reality. The lovers of sights cannot tell the difference. The latter take the appearances for the reality. If the lovers of truth can tell the difference, they can see the ways in which the appearance is a faithful reflection and the ways in which it is not a faithful reflection of the reality. The deficiency of the lovers of sights may be due to their being obtuse; on the other hand, the appearances may themselves be misleading. In any event, the error of the lovers of sights is that they do not see—or perhaps cannot see—the relation between appearance and reality.

However, it is in Book VI that Plato elaborates the relation between appearance and reality. There he uses several different kinds of examples of the relation. They all emphasize the dependence between appearance and reality. There are the two famous examples from the Divided Line (510a)—shadows and reflections in smooth surfaces. If we construe shadows in terms of the Cave metaphor, the shadows are related to what casts the shadow in somewhat the way in which reflections are related to what they reflect. Here object; there shadow or reflection. Before these examples, however, there is the example from the analogy of the Sun (508c). In this passage, the images in the perceptual world are not shadows and reflections but are objects illuminated by different kinds of light. First, the objects are illuminated by the sun; then these objects are illuminated by the light of the stars and the moon. In the latter case, the images are actually a mixture of light and dark. There is in each a real object; but the true contours of these real objects are shrouded in shadow. Like the examples of shadows and reflections, shadow enshrouded objects emphasize the continuity between appearance and reality. When the shadow enshrouded object is seen by someone who has seen it in the light of the sun, it is possible to disentangle reality from appearance. Even though the images of the Sun passage are different from those in the Divided Line and the Cave, there is an important similarity. The similarity between the shadow enshrouded object and the shadows and reflections of the Divided Line is that in all of these cases there is a fundamental reality that is the source of the appearance. Wisdom is to see the image not as though it were a reality in its own right but to see the image as related to the fundamental reality. To see the shadow-enshrouded object correctly is to see the relation between shadows and the fundamental reality. To see projected shadows and reflections correctly is to see them in relation to their projecting or reflected objects.

To this extent, then, the notion of Forms as paradigms finds support in the reality and appearance motif of the central books of the *Republic*. The notion of Forms as paradigms has the consequence that Forms are real and copies are appearance, and that is just what we find in the text. However, if the notion of Forms as paradigms has the consequence that Forms are real and copies are appearance, this consequence itself is problematic. The distinction between reality and appearance introduces grades or degrees into reality.[15] Some things are more real; other things are less real. Such a radical distinction between Forms and copies seems to fly in the face of robust common sense. For one thing, we are expected to believe that the world in which we live is less than fully real. How can the world of our experience—usually considered to be the very touchstone of reality—be thought to consist of mere images of reality? According to this criticism of the appearance and reality metaphysics, Plato requires us to believe that the horses, humans, and beds of our experience are not real horses, humans, or beds. They are only appearances of the real horses, humans, or beds. We are then, presumably, riding around on mere appearances of horses, falling in love with mere appearances of humans, and falling to sleep in mere appearances of beds. Indeed, it may or may not be possible to defend this interpretation of appearance and reality when it is stated in this sweeping way. Certainly, we will not try. However, a narrower version of appearance and reality might have a better chance at plausibility.

We can begin by noting that, for the most part, Plato is interested in Forms for comparative terms, including evaluative terms.[16] That is to say, in the *Republic* Plato does not typically talk about Forms for substances like horses and humans; his interest is largely in terms for justice, good, beauty, equals, and halves. These terms allow for opposites; whatever is just is also unjust, for example. If his appearance-reality metaphysics is designed primarily for such terms, then it is a metaphysics that deals with the appearances of justice, of goodness, and of equals. It does not claim, in the first instance, at least, that there are no real horses or real humans—only that there are no real good things and no real just things in the world of our ordinary experience. We might say that there are no objects of real value in our ordinary experience. Horses and humans there might be, but they cannot be valuable in the fullest sense. However, even this statement can be misunderstood unless we are careful. Just because there are no real good things or no real just things in the world of our ordinary experience does not mean that there are no good things or no just things in that experience. There are good things and just things; however, they are not "good-no-matter-what," just "no-matter-what," not "good without qualification," just "without qualification."[17] So Plato's metaphysics of appearance and reality might have more plausibility if it is restricted to value terms, like *justice* and *goodness*. Certainly, in the central books of the *Republic*, where the motif of appearance and reality is used, Socrates concentrates on such notions as goodness and justice. In these books, the implication is that in our ordinary experience we just do not find items that are unconditionally good and unconditionally just.

A fuller treatment of this restricted version of the appearance and reality distinction must await chapter 4 and our consideration of the Form of the good. What we will see there is that the dependence between Form and what participates in the Form has great significance for the whole project of imitation. When Plato casts the moral life or political life as one of imitation, he has already presented these two activities in an unusual light. However, when the imitation, which constitutes moral and political life, produces images—appearances of the reality of the Form—these two activities are even more transformed. The dependence of these activities, and of their products, on the Forms of justice, moderation, and goodness has such important implications for the notion of imitation that we will explore them in detail in chapter 4. Nevertheless, at this point, we can give a general idea of the significance of the dependence between Form and what participates in the Form for Plato's moral theory. In a general and rough way we can express its importance in a two-part claim. First, the successful moral life is, to the one leading it, an image of a deeper moral reality; it depends on that deeper reality the way an appearance depends on its original. So the moral life is being guided by something more profound than the conventions of society, something that stands behind those conventions but that is not completely captured by them. Second, the unsuccessful moral life is also an image, but an illusory one. The one who leads such a life is the subject of illusion; that person's is a deceptive image, in some sense.

We will develop the first in chapter 4 when we treat the Form of the good. For now, we can anticipate the discussion of chapter 4 by quickly noting how the moral life involves imitation. Whether in the city or in her own soul, the philosophical ruler imitates an ideal that in the nature of the case cannot be fully embodied. The reason is that she looks beyond the particular instances of justice in her experience to justice itself; it is the Form of justice that directs her craft of ruling. Moreover, what she achieves is so dependent on the Form for whatever justice it has that it can be fairly called an "image of the Form of justice." As we shall see, instead of this dependency being a weakness for the philosopher, it is what gives her achievements their validity. Being an image of justice itself is no mean achievement, but it does affect how one goes about one's task—as we shall see. For the present we can dwell on the second part of the claim. If the successful moral life is a true image of a deeper reality, then the unsuccessful moral life must be a kind of false image or illusion. It is significant to note the way in which Plato frequently presents the task of the philosopher as one of being able to distinguish true from false images. If the philosopher can distinguish true images of justice from false ones, then the nonphilosopher cannot so distinguish—or cannot do so reliably. It is tragic for the city when it has the latter kind of rulers. It is equally tragic for the individual who cannot distinguish in her own life between true and false images. Such inability suggests that the nonphilosopher is liable to choose the false image and that, thus, the unjust or immoderate life is in some way illusory. It is the latter theme we will explore for the present.

In those things that are good and just, their being good or just is dependent on real goodness and real justice. This dependence allows one to choose between the good things and those that are not good. One can make an important distinction between good appearances and bad appearances—those that are faithful representations of the original and those that are not. The distinction between appearance and reality, then, is the foundation for the claim that there is a dependence between appearance and reality. The ability to see the dependence, in turn, helps one to tell the difference between good and bad appearances. Certainly, it is the case that, for example, knowing the real Simmias would allow one to recognize that a bad image of Simmias just does not look like Simmias—a knowledgeable person would not see an image of the original in the bad portrait. By contrast, the person who did not know Simmias might take the portrait to be a faithful portrait of Simmias.

However, there is another dimension to the bad or poor appearance in Plato's account; it is also deceptive in a special way. The appearance that is bad is not just a poor image of the original; rather it obscures its relation to the original in such a way that it substitutes for the original. It loses its status as an appearance and is taken to be reality. In *Republic* V, for instance, the lover of sights, taking the appearance of beauty to be the reality of beauty, is compared to someone in a dream who mistakes appearance for reality (476c). This kind of deception is not just taking the poor portrait to be a faithful representation of Simmias, for example. It is another order of deception altogether; it is to see the deceptive image not as a "good image" but as the reality itself. Perhaps we can call this "substitute deception." Plato's favorite example of this kind of deception is *trompe-l'oeil* painting, in which the eye—at least—is deceived into thinking the painting is the real thing. The remedy, of course, is to have the person liable to substitute deception come to know the original. The peasant, for example, who took the statue of Athena to be the real Athena would overcome this deception if he ever saw the original. Of course, such is the role of the Forms in Plato's account; in *Republic* V knowledge of the Forms keeps one from taking appearances of, for example, beauty to be real beauty. In the political case, the Form of justice serves a similar purpose. The person who might be deceived about the nature of justice—who might take the appearance of justice in the case of Solon, for example, to be the reality of justice—will be relieved of that tendency if he knows the Form of justice. Forms, then, arm one against this kind of deception.

However, in the central books of the *Republic* we are not really told the ways in which substitute deception arises. The context of those books leaves us with the impression that deeply intellectual people are capable of the intense study needed to discover the nature of Forms and that such people are not subject to the deception by appearances. Thus, by implication, those who are not capable of such study are liable to being deceived, of taking the appearance of justice for the real thing. It is, of course, for this reason that these intellectually inferior types need the strong hand of the rulers in their otherwise jeopardized lives. Still, while the account is rather abstract, enforced by metaphor and allegory in which deceptive appearances are shadows and reflections, the burden of the account is that the defective faculty in the inferior sort is their reason.

We get a different account in Book X, where Socrates presents an expanded account of appearances—authentic and deceptive— in his final indictment of the dramatic poets. They are indicted for being imitators. As we noted before, in this context *imitation* now seems to be used only in a pejorative sense, to mean thrice removed from reality. Elaborating on the claim that the imitator is thrice removed from reality, Socrates talks about that part of the soul to which imitation is directed. It is that gullible part that is susceptible to illusion. Socrates compares this kind of illusion to the illusion of visual perception. To the eye, the same magnitude, when viewed close up and from afar, appears not to be equal (602c–d). The untutored eye, then, is subject to an illusion. On the other hand, the rational part of the soul, which calculates, weighs and measures, is not fooled by such appearances; it knows that the different appearances are appearances of the same magnitude. However, even though the rational part does its measuring, and thus knows that the magnitude remains the same in spite of its disparate appearances, the appearances remain. The eye still sees different sizes when looking at the same magnitude from different distances.

Next, Socrates concludes that painting, as imitation, deals in appearances that appeal to the nonrational part of the soul (603b). The missing step here seems to be one Socrates has previously introduced. At 598a–b, where the example of imitation is painting, he argues that the imitator can present only aspects of an object, never the object itself. He characterizes these different aspects as different appearances of the object being painted. Thus the object appears different without being so. Since painting deals in appearances, presumably it appeals to the same irrational part of the soul as the part appealed to by the different appearances of the same magnitude in the previous example. After characterizing imitation by using painting as his example, Socrates then turns to dramatic poetry. This is the kind of poetry that imitates various types of characters. He wants to argue that it too imitates appearances, misses the reality, and appeals to the irrational part of the soul. However, here the argument is necessarily more complicated.

He starts by saying that the dramatic poets imitate people carrying out actions, either by force or willingly, who think themselves doing either well or badly, and in all of these affairs feeling pleasure or pain. That is the whole of drama (603c). Then he compares such presentations to what the good person will actually do in similar real-life situations. In such a person there is an opposition between what reason and law (*logos kai nomos*) urge and what feelings (*pathos*) urges (604a10–b1). The latter urge him to give in to his grieving and to act rather the way that characters on the stage would act, engaging in dramatic acts of weeping and wailing. Reason urges another path. Calculating that he does not know what is good and evil in such things, and that grieving can change nothing and might even prevent healing, the wise man does not give in to the irrational part that likes to dwell on grieving (604b–e). The poet, on the other hand, plays to this irrational part by representing characters acting in ways opposite to the ways that the good man acts. First of all, the poetic image is only an appearance. Like the painter, who can represent only one aspect of an object and not the object itself, the dramatic poet is confined to representing an exterior and partial view of his subject (605a). In the case of the dramatists, the exterior and partial view presents the easily observable emotional behavior of a character in a play. This behavior too frequently is the excessive expression of pains and pleasures—the weeping, the crying, the sighs of passion. While this behavior is easy to portray, the inner life of reason and law—usually expressed by a rather undramatic exterior calm—is not easily represented.

Moreover, the poetic image is directed at the irrational part of the soul (605c). This is the part that, left on its own, would give into the vicissitudes of life; it is the source of excessive crying and grieving. It is the part that takes the vicissitudes of life to be real good and real evil (603c). Presumably, the irrational part of the soul does so because it is incapable of calculating the true weight of these fortuitous events. Like the untutored eye, the irrational part of the soul is subject to illusion. Indeed, this illusion could be a case of substitute deception because the poetic image, if successful, would make one substitute *appearance* for *reality*. Certainly, it poses itself against the calculating part of the soul as presenting a contrary image, just as to the untutored eye the appearances of different magnitudes pose themselves against calculating reason. The poetic image presents apparent good against real good. The real good is virtue—not the pleasures caused by the vicissitudes of life (600e). Presumably, real evil is vice—not the equally fortuitous pain. The dramatic poets then tempt us to mistake apparent good for the real good and apparent evil for the real evil. Moreover, the apparent good and evil have such seductive force because they appeal to the irrational part of the soul.

In this account, the deceptive image is not deceptive just because the reason of the subject is too weak to comprehend the reality. The substitution of image for reality now takes place because of the pull of the desires. Now the deceptive image is deceptive because of its relation to those desires in the soul that are not identified with reason—that is, the desires associated with the spirited part and the appetites.[18] Presumably, the deceptive poetic image presents as real what these desires, left to themselves, take to be real. They present as real what the excessive grief is about, or the exhilarating erotic passion, and other such desires that, in Plato's scheme, should be moderated by reason. Here illusion is not just optical illusion.[19] Rather it is associated with the distorting effects of pleasure and pain. The illusion works its magic by presenting as real what these desires, in their shortsightedness, so to speak, take to be real, just as the noncalculating eye takes the appearance to be real.

Indeed, it is because it works on this part of the soul that the poetic image is so objectionable. Not only does the poetic image appeal, within the context of the drama, to the irrational part, it also strengthens it as a force in one's real life. Socrates says that even in the better sort of person, when this better part of his nature is not adequately educated by reason or habit (*to de physei beltiston hēmon hate oux hikanōs pepaideumenon logōi oude ethei* [606a7–8]) it will drop its guard in the face of poetic drama (606a–b). Presumably, it then entertains the poetic image and gives in to it. It allows full rein to those feelings that ought not to be indulged. In doing so it waters and fosters the irrational part of the soul. The danger here is that, when it comes to leading one's life, the irrational part of the soul, thus strengthened, becomes the ruler instead of the ruled (606e).

If the rational part of the soul were to be educated, presumably it would be able to carry out the requisite calculations and measurements. It would not, then, entertain the poetic image because it would see the image as an illusion. In that regard it would be similar to the calculating reason that can identify the same magnitude in spite of contrary appearances. In the untutored reason, however, the poetic image is allowed to become an illusion, to substitute for the reality. Thus, in this illusory image, what the irrational part of the soul takes to be good is seen to be really good and what it takes to be evil is seen to be really evil. What the irrational part weeps over is seen to be truly worth weeping over and what it rejoices in is seen to be truly worthy of rejoicing. What is interesting here is the implication that the calculating part of the soul, if it were educated in reason or habit, would be able to dissipate the illusory image. Presumably, the poetic image would be like the appearances of the magnitude to the untutored eye. To the person with educated reason, the appearances of the magnitude would not present a serious rival to what calculation holds out. Just so, to the person with a reason that could make true calculations about the vicissitudes of life, the poetic image would not present a serious picture. One would see it as only an appearance, a superficial view of what life really is.

To fill out Socrates' account let us imagine the unenlightened spectator in the Theatre of Dionysos. He would watch a tragedy and be taken in by the deceptive images of good and evil. He would think that Phaedra, torn by her passion for Hippolytus, is suffering real evil. On the contrary, if Phaedra could only realize that passion for Hippolytus, she would have real good. Of course, she cannot realize that passion; her being unable to do so is part of her tragedy. Her life is defined by her emotions and the vicissitudes of human existence are tearing her life apart. It is a strong image that is immensely enthralling because the spectator is naturally sympathetic with Phaedra. He lives his life at the same emotional level; the image appeals to those emotions and thus appears real.

However, the better sort of spectator, although capable of being caught up, and even seduced, by the tragedy (605c), might well experience something else. What about her virtue? he would likely ask. Why is she not coping better with her emotions? Where is her self-control? The answer, of course, is that Phaedra does, at least, try to control her behavior; however, Aphrodite has afflicted her with the passion for Hippolytus. Phaedra is helpless to control her passion, even if she had known that passion, when it made its first spring-like appearance, for what it was and would become.

She cannot resolutely set her face against any such emotion; she could not make up her mind, with all of the resources of her formidable strength of character, to extirpate the roots of her budding passion. If the better sort of spectator, through lack of education, accepts this premise—lets down his guard—then he will take the image, at least during the performance, to be real. He will then indulge the emotions and feelings as though they were appropriate reactions to the tragic situation. Reality would be defined in terms agreeable to the irrational part of the soul. On the other hand, if he were educated he would not accept the premise; nor could he take the image to be real. Perhaps it would just not ring true to him. He would see Phaedra making the wrong calculation, for example. He might even deconstruct the drama, asking who put the notion in Phaedra's mind that Aphrodite is irresistible. Is not that notion an illusion put forth by the *erōs* in one's soul—or perhaps by the partisans of *erōs* in the larger culture—in order to undermine reason's ability to curb passion?

In Book X Socrates does not further elaborate on the way that poetic images mislead. In particular, he does not say how such images generate illusion within one's actual moral life. However, in Book IX Socrates does touch on illusion in one's moral life. He makes a distinction between pleasures of the mind and those associated with the body. The former are altogether true and pure; however, the latter are deceptive, a kind of scene-painting (*Rep.* 583b). The deceptive pleasures are deceptive because they arise in the soul when the release from pain, which leads to a neutral state, is wrongly taken to be pleasure (584a). Socrates amplifies this distinction between true and deceptive pleasures by arguing for the relative reality of the parts of the soul involved and the relative reality of their objects (585a–e). We will not review the details of the argument here; what is important for our purposes is that the deceptive pleasures give rise to illusion in one's life. These deceptive pleasures

> engender raging loves for themselves among those without judgment and are fought over, just as Stesichorus says that the mere image of Helen was fought over by those at Troy through ignorance of the truth. (586c)

If the poetic images were watering and nurturing the parts of the soul that give rise to these pleasures, then they would be contributing to illusion in one's moral life.

Indeed, illusion is an important moral category. The prospect of a love affair, for instance, presents a vivid image, with its joys, heights and depths. The prospect that one will not fulfill one's love is painful and desolate. However, if the love affair is not pursued because, say, it is at odds with the contours of one's moral life, the subsequent experience can have an uncanny resemblance to awaking from a dream. One can look back at what was a tempting image and wonder what was so attractive. Comparing it to one's life of continued virtue, one can actually feel the whole prospect—the would-be love object and the entire situation—as a kind of illusion; for a while one's vision was distorted by something that is now seen to be wholly superficial. Now, at last, however, reality has reasserted itself. Of course, it is well known that illusion is generated by one's desires. For instance, it is notorious that the erotic drive makes one overlook vital facts about the character of one's love object and concentrate on sexual characteristics. The concentration on these characteristics becomes a fixation; as such it substitutes for the reality upon which, for example, a lasting relationship must be based. As well, the fixation can obscure one's own motives. Such is the stuff of comedy. It is likely enough part of the meaning of Oscar Wilde's aphorism that the only way to overcome a temptation is to give in to it; giving in to the temptation—satisfying the desire—is the best means of getting rid of it, and even of dispelling its illusory power. Portraying this pull between one's sense of right, or simply one's sense of sound policy, and one's erotic desire as a contest between reality and desire-generated illusion corresponds with our experience, then.

To see the relevance of knowledge of Forms to this issue, imagine a philosopher who is taking stock of his soul; he thinks about the possibilities presented by his sexual passion, *erōs*. He recognizes that it is possible to fall in love with any number of partners, that each of them could be an excellent lover—not just in the sense that each could be sexually adept but in the sense that each could be loving, considerate, compassionate, and exciting to be with, giving him new vistas, perspectives and insights. So this philosopher is not thinking about brief sexual encounters; rather he is talking about complete affairs—each with a beginning, a middle, and an end. If we assume that his partner is also an erotic adept, as well as a philosopher, each will recognize that the affair is not meant to last forever but to have its own natural rhythm of life and death. Each of these affairs promises to open up a different aspect of his, and his partner's, personality; there is an erotic exploration that both seek, coming to know each other so intimately. While mulling over all of these possibilities, the philosopher begins to notice that there is a great variety of interesting partners, promising many sorts of erotic adventure. His whole erotic life stretches before him, like an Odyssey.

Of course, in Plato's account, the philosopher must exercise the craft of justice in his own soul, see to it that each part of the soul is allowed to perform its peculiar function. In the first place, he would want to know how balanced such an erotic life would be, how just it would be to the other parts of his soul. In this account he would see that what he really proposes is a life devoted to arranging, having, and managing these love affairs. We can imagine the philosopher would suspect that such a life, while it has much to recommend it, is not particularly well balanced. *Erōs* must be brought into balance with other parts of the soul—first of all with the other appetites, then with the spirited part, and with reason. Erotic pursuits cannot crowd out the exercise of the spirited part and of the reason. But the philosopher might well wonder whether a life given over to erotic pursuits would leave enough time to the life of reason, with its rigorous demands of study and thought, or to the cultivation of the spirited part, which makes one bold enough to embody what one's reason discovers.

In this scenario, then, the philosopher is proposing to sacrifice a life of erotic adventure for the life of psychic justice. He ought to be sure that the sacrifice is required; he should have determining evidence in the contest between these two prospective lives. We can contrast his decision with that of the nonphilosopher who might be weighing the two lives. If the nonphilosopher feels pulled toward justice, he probably feels pulled more toward *erōs*. If we follow the account in Book IX, the vision of justice in the soul of the nonphilosopher will be clouded by passions, which will give rise to illusions. It will seem to him—like the theater-goer in Book X—that the life of erotic adventure is real good and the loss of erotic adventure real evil; the value of balance and harmony in the soul will appear pale in comparison to the other life. Indeed, passionate love—its exhilarations and its depths, its sighs and its joys—may seem more real than virtue itself. Finally, he may substitute the erotic life for real virtue and come to believe that the erotic life is the virtuous life. Now, suppose, *per impossibile*, that this nonphilosopher could have the vision of justice—a clear intuition of balance, proportion and harmony. Moreover, this intuition, let us suppose, is so clear that, in comparison, the life of erotic adventure will appear to be unbalanced, disproportionate, and disharmonious. Finally, because balance, proportion, and harmony are so attractive, the attraction of the erotic life will dissipate; it will now seem illusory. Now we can see that the philosopher must have just such a clear intuition of the importance of justice in his soul. His vision should be so strong that it makes clear what he is trying to establish in his soul and why he must do so. He must cherish justice in his soul more than he cherishes the monomaniacal claims of *erōs*. Given the strong attraction of the erotic life, this ideal must be a stronger and more attractive countervailing force—so strong that it will show the erotic life to be illusory.

At this point in our interpretation, we can perhaps see what Plato meant for the role of the Form as paradigm to be. The naive view suggests that the philosopher has something like an intellectual vision of an ideal for justice. This ideal is an independent Form that exhibits justice. As such it reinforces reason's rule because reason is inspired by what it sees. While the notion of a soul in which each part fulfills its function presents a strong case for acquiring justice, the Form of justice engages reason at a deeper level. The Form of justice—a paradigm that exhibits justice in its purity and clarity—is the stronger and more attractive countervailing force. In Book X the soul of the educated man can correctly measure and weigh the vicissitudes of life; both of the latter activities typically use a standard against which to measure or weigh. The standard tells us the true height or the true weight, which differ from what the appearances seem to tell us. While Socrates does not mention in Book X the role of Forms in this calculating, now we can see that the Form is the standard by which to measure and weigh one's life. When the philosopher wins the struggle with passions in his own soul, in this story, it will be because his vision of justice is strong enough. Now it is notorious that such a strong enough vision of justice is elusive, that people are frequently dazzled by the vision of pleasure that actually masks injustice—both to oneself and to others. However, the resolution of such bedazzlement would occur if a standard were to show that the vision of pleasure is an illusion. The very recognition of the distinction between reality and illusion settles the issue.

Finally, this account just given is not the whole story about the importance of appearance and reality in Plato's account of Forms as paradigms. We will fully address the issue in the next chapter, where we will talk about the highest Forms—goodness and beauty. For the present we can note that Plato develops most fully the motif of reality and appearance when he introduces the Form of the good. Forms thus represent not only a movement away from obscure appearance toward clear reality but also away from the appearance of goodness to the reality of goodness. The Form of justice—which the ruler uses as a paradigm—is also the reality of which the city and the soul are copies because the Form is real goodness (or—as we shall see—a "species" of real goodness); the city and the soul are appearances of goodness. To the contemporary mind, this ontology is at best cumbersome. Leaving aside all the other metaphysical questions about, for example, the reality of the perceptual world, we might simply ask what advantage Plato might think he can get from conceiving, in this way, of the relation between the Form of justice and justice in the city. The answer to this question must await our treatment of the Form of the good in the next chapter. However, the preliminary answer can be sketched. The Form paradigms are not in themselves paradigms for the perceptual world. They are primarily exemplars of varieties of goodness; they are intrinsically good, without reference to the perceptual world. They, as it were, define goodness in themselves. On the other hand, the perceptual world is innocent of true intrinsic goodness and gets the intrinsic goodness it has by imitating the goodness in the Forms. The perceptual world is as incapable of being intrinsically good as the painting is incapable of being the real Simmias. However, the perceptual world, by being an image of the good, can afford us access to the intrinsically good. To afford this access is the best that imitation of the perceptual world can offer. However, it would be a misconception to think that its best is something mean—as we shall see.

IV

Let us end this chapter by seeing how the notion of imitation addresses the problems encountered at the end of the last chapter. In the craft of justice from Book IV, we found a fuller account of what "consistency in the soul" meant. When Plato has given the complete moral psychology of Book IV, we can see that consistency is harmony of the three functions of the soul: the reason, the spirited part, and the appetites. However, the problem we encountered there was that it is not so clear, even with this complete moral psychology, that there is only one way to achieve harmony among the functions. After all, subordinating reason to insatiable desire also would achieve a type of harmony. Then, it is no longer clear that a life with justice in the soul—one in which reason rules—is obviously more valuable than a life in which insatiable desires are allowed to rule the rest. Callicles might still dismiss the happiness associated with the craft of justice as too pale when compared to the life of enormous pleasure promised by becoming a tyrant.

It is part of the aim of the present interpretation to have shown that the account of Forms as paradigms is an attempt to offer a higher order justification for justice in the soul. In Book IV we learn that justice in the soul is a harmony of the parts that respects the function of reason to rule. By implication, with this order in one's soul, insatiable desires must be subordinate to the rule of reason. In Book VI we learn that this type of harmony among the parts of the soul is really imitation of that divine order and harmony found in the Forms. When the harmony of parts of the soul is seen to be an image of the order and harmony of the Form of justice then there is an added argument for the position that the life of justice is more valuable than the life of enormous pleasure. The former is orderly and proportionate, like the Form, while the latter is disorderly and disproportionate.

Thus, the Forms tell us how to arrange our souls not only in the sense that they are a set of instructions we can follow if we so choose; they also have a certain compelling quality. In this passage Socrates asks, rhetorically, with respect to the way that the philosopher imitates the Forms of justice and temperance, is there any way for someone who associates with what he admires not to imitate that thing (500c)? The philosophers thus imitate the Forms because they love them. However, when Socrates talks about the features of the Forms that are imitated, he seems to shift from talking about justice and temperance to talking about order and proportion. What the philosopher admires and loves in the Forms is their order and proportion. In this way, the philosopher imitates them and thus becomes himself orderly and divine. When imitation becomes part of the craft of justice in Book VI there is also a curious addition to the list of Forms that are imitated by the ruler; Socrates includes the Form of beauty along with the Forms of justice and temperance (501b). In one way, it is natural to include beauty. The philosophical ruler is being compared to a painter. It is the beauty of his model that the painter admires and that he wishes to imitate. Thus, if the ruler is like a painter, then what he looks to as a paradigm must have beauty. Adding beauty is Plato's way of referring to the determining factor that the philosophical ruler finds in the Forms. So it is little wonder that the Forms of justice and temperance and the other common virtues are completed by the Form of beauty. Their real value is grounded in the Form of beauty.

We can now see, perhaps, how this account of paradigms counts against Callicles. Callicles' notion of the life of enormous pleasure must subordinate the functions of reason and the spirited part to that of the desires. Our imaginary Callicles at the end of the last chapter admitted as much. In the Calliclean ideal, reason does not rule because reason does not determine the goal of life; rather desire has this function. Although reason is able to calculate the long-term benefits and disadvantages, when desire rules reason can only calculate such benefits in terms of the pleasures of replenishment. Reason would have to calculate which course of action would provide the most pleasure, in intensity and in quantity. If such a course required reason to give up the pursuit of truth or the spirited part to give up adventure—as it frequently does—then reason, as desire's subordinate, would show the way (cf. *Rep.* 553d). Moreover, Callicles could dismiss the counterargument whose conclusion is that reason should rule. He could say that it is based on the assumption that it is the function of reason to rule. The latter seems little more than the question begging claim that reason should rule. Socrates' reply, of course, is that reason should rule because it knows what is good for the soul and its parts. However, by the end of Book IV this reply is little more than an assertion. If reason knows what is good for the soul and its parts because of its wisdom, we do not know what wisdom is. Thus, even to the sympathetic reader, reason's claim to rule is unsubstantiated.

In view of Books V and VI, the answer to this latter objection invokes the role of Forms. It is analogous to the answer to the objection brought against the notion of philosopher kings. The answer to the objection about philosopher kings is that their knowledge of the Forms makes them able and worthy to rule; presumably, knowledge of the Forms will bestow the knowledge of the way the city may maintain the best relations within itself and with other cities (*Rep.* 428d). So too, knowledge of the Forms will bestow the knowledge of what is advantageous for each part of the soul and for the whole (*Rep.* 442c). Presumably, this knowledge does not tell the philosopher such things as that reason calculates and exercises forethought for the soul; these characteristics of reason are already established (*Rep.* 439d and 441e). What the Form of justice would show is that the arrangement in the soul in which reason rules—that is, in which the calculating function makes the final decisions according to what it thinks best—is the just arrangement. It is the arrangement that most closely conforms to the paradigm for justice. In this arrangement, each part gets to fulfill its function, and fulfilling its function seems to be what is good for each and what is good for the whole. Thus, if Callicles could know the Form of justice, his initial objections could be overcome. Presumably the knowledge of the Form of justice would give him a deeper insight into the requirements of justice. He would see that when reason does not rule—but is subordinated to the passions, for example—its peculiar function of calculating and exercising forethought is not being treated fairly, is being foreshortened or stunted. In order to be treated fairly, the function of calculating and exercising forethought must rule; it—and not appetite—must decide the direction for one's life. As well, his increased sensitivity to the issue of justice would help him see that the indulgence of the appetites, in the life of enormous pleasure, is not actually treating the appetites fairly, is not giving them what is good for their own best functioning. Once Callicles' focus is shifted from bodily pleasure as the criterion of judgment to justice, presumably his assessment of the life of enormous pleasure would change.

This kind of determination is almost aesthetic. What is missing in the Calliclean soul is a certain type of order among the functions. It is as though one could look at the soul the way one looks at a painting, or a sculpture, or even a flower arrangement. The relation of reason to desire in the Calliclean soul is not an order that is proportionate, *kata logon*, to the functions of the different parts, whereas in the Platonic soul the order is proportionate. To some it may seem too ethereal to assess a life from the point of view of order and harmony within the functions of the soul. The real business of life would seem to be more concrete—to involve the immediate realities of satisfying desires. Of course, both Socrates and Callicles believe in the importance of satisfying desires; the difference between the two of them is that Socrates' version of that project entails the value of proportion and harmony within the soul. Finally, Plato seems to say that what is real seems ethereal to most people—proportion and harmony. This reality may be obscured by the prospect of enormous pleasure; the appetites may give rise to an illusory image of the good—one that substitutes for the real good. It would thus obscure what is really proportionate to reason—and just for reason—that is, ruling. Thus it would obscure what is really good for the parts and for the whole. If one's vision were clarified, however, one would understand what proportion and harmony among the functions of one's soul really are. In turn, the value of proportion and harmony would outweigh the value of the life of enormous pleasure, with its disproportion and disharmony.

Now we can see the importance of the motif that the life of virtue is one of image making, in which the images are appearances of the Form for justice. If we use this motif, the answer to Callicles takes on another dimension. The life of enormous pleasure is an image but it is a deceptive image; it substitutes for real justice—real virtue and goodness. Callicles even says that the life of enormous pleasure is virtue and happiness (492c). This deceptive image, like the poetic image, gains its ability to deceive from the appetites. On the other hand, the life of balance and proportion is an image as well; it, however, is not deceptive. The latter image does not substitute for real justice; rather it faithfully reflects real justice. Thus, even Callicles, if he could know the Form for justice, would see the life of enormous pleasure as an illusion. Its illusory quality would be evident, its force dissipated, in comparison with the Form. This result would not come from a proof or an argument; it would be something like an insight in which the value of the life of balance and proportion over the life of disproportionate pleasure would become so evident that the former would seem to be grounded in a more fundamental reality and the latter would seem to lack such grounding—that is, to be an illusion.

To the question, then, how does reason know what is best for the parts of the soul and for the whole, the first answer is that reason knows the Form of justice. The latter is the paradigm of proportion and harmony. Having this knowledge, reason can recognize that the arrangement of the soul in which reason rules is the one that allows each part—including reason—to fulfill its function and is the authentic image of the Form of justice. Until one sees the arrangement in the light of this paradigm of proportion and harmony one has not seen what finally makes it just for the soul and for its parts. If one stayed at the level of Book IV, one would have seen the appearance of justice without seeing its relation to the reality. At this level, the economy of functions appears to be just for the soul; however, only when one sees the arrangement of the soul in relation to the Form can one see the way this arrangement corresponds to the reality. What we have yet to see is why Plato thinks that the paradigm for justice is also good, necessarily good. In short, we have yet to see the relation between this Form and the Form of goodness. Plato's account of the knowledge of what is best for the soul and its parts is not finished, then. Until the Form of goodness is introduced, one cannot see that the proportion and harmony of the Form of justice is also good, is necessarily good. We turn to that issue in the next chapter where we deal with the Form of the good in Book VI.

NOTES

1. At 472a in Book V, Socrates slowly leads up to his suggestion about philosopher kings by reflecting on the problem of realizing the account of virtue in the individual. He says that, in devising their account of justice in the soul, he and his interlocutors were seeking a paradigm of the Form of justice (*paradeigmatos ara heneka, ēn d'ego, ezētoumen auto te dikaiosunēn hoion esti* [472c4–5]). They wished to look toward that paradigm in order to be able to discern whether the just person is happy or not. Here, it is important to note, the Form of justice is not called a "paradigm"—as it is in other places. Rather, the account of the just man is a paradigm of the Form of justice—not that the Form of justice is fashioned on the account of the just man. Rather, the account is a representation of the Form of justice; it is this representation that, in turn, is looked toward as a paradigm in judging about happiness and its opposite. Socrates then compares the interlocutors to a painter who paints, in loving detail, a paradigm of the most handsome man. Such a painter would not be thought a lesser painter because he could not show that such a man is possible. Presumably, what the painter cannot do is to show how such a man is possible in the perceptual world even though, in some sense, such a man is possible in the ideal world. Socrates now turns to their discourse about the ideal city. Just so, in that endeavor,

they were trying to make the paradigm, in words, of a good city (*paradeigma epoioumen logōi agathēs poleōs* [472d9–10]). They should not be faulted because they cannot show whether this city is possible. This passage is the first place in which the analogy with the painter is introduced. As we shall see, it will be used again in Book VI but in a different sense. However, already it should be suspected that the analogy between craft and justice is taking on an added dimension—viz., the way that imitation of a paradigm is an important aspect of craft.

2. For example, two such different interpreters as Vlastos and Allen adopt this reading of 'is': Gregory Vlastos, *Platonic Studies,* chap. 2 (Princeton: Princeton University Press, 1973); R. E. Allen, "Predication and Participation in Plato's Middle Dialogues," *Studies in Plato's Metaphysics,* R. E. Allen, ed. (London: Routledge and Kegan Paul, 1965), 54. The two disagree fundamentally about the consequences of this reading of 'is', of course. The latter holds that 'F' has primary and derivative application; in the primary designation 'F' belongs to the Form properly and is something like a name (46). See also Nicholas P. White, *Companion,* 160. For an excellent summary of the discussion on this topic see Julia Annas, *Introduction,* 195–200.

3. For instance, some disagree about what the objects of knowledge are. Against the traditional interpretation that holds that the objects of knowledge are exclusively Forms, Gail Fine, in "Knowledge and Belief in *Republic* V," *Archiv für Geschichte der Philosophie* 60(1978):121–139, argues that the objects of knowledge are truths rather than objects. One can know truths about, for example, perceptual objects, although these truths are dependent on Forms. See also Julia Annas, *Introduction, 210.* Fine's account makes knowledge in this passage seem more theoretical than practical. Annas moderates this reading with what she says about understanding, but neither exploits the way in which knowledge in this passage is still craft knowledge, that is, knowledge is directed toward a paradigm. Another traditional interpretation holds that the objects of opinion are particulars. J. Gosling has argued, however, that the objects of opinion are particulars taken to be types whose tokens are sometimes F and sometimes not F. See J. Gosling, "Ta Polla Kala" *Phronesis* 5(1960):116–128: "What, then, is Plato's point at 476a? Surely this: if we concentrate on objects we shall find, not that there are a good many beautiful ones, but that a good variety of them is beautiful, that objects of very varied descriptions are beautiful. Consequently when we try to give some account of what makes objects beautiful we shall find that we have to give a variety of different accounts; and though we may be sure that what we point to in this case is what accounts for the beauty of *this,* it is undeniably not what accounts for the beauty of this other thing. . . . *Ta polla kala esti kai ouk esti,* then in the sense that the many 'things' given in answer to '*ti esti kalon;*' fail as much as they succeed; and unless

'*kalos*' is to be said to be hopelessly ambiguous, or merely subjective, there must be some further account of an all-embracing kind" (122–23). See also F. C. White's objection in "The 'Many' in Republic 475a–480a," *Canadian Journal of Philosophy* 7(1977):291–306, and Gosling, "Reply to White" in the same volume, 307–314.

4. Cf. W. J. Verdenius, *Mimesis* (Leiden: E. J. Brill, 1972), 21: "It may be concluded that there are two points differentiating good art from mere trickery: its truthfulness and its modesty. The artist should not content himself with a superficial glance at his object, but he must try to penetrate its inner structure. His task is faithful interpretation, not slavish imitation. Secondly, he should have the honesty to admit the poorness of his means and not try to overstep the limitations they lay upon him. His work should clearly show that its representation of reality, in spite of, or rather, on account of, its very faithfulness, is fundamentally different from the reality itself. It should present itself, not as a copy, but as a transposition on a different level and as obedient to the laws of this medium."

5. Richard Patterson, in *Image and Reality in Plato's Metaphysics* (Indianapolis: Hackett, 1985), gives one type of sophisticated reading of the relation between Forms and particulars. He exploits the notion that a particular is an image of a Form. Thus, he assimilates the paradigm-copy relation to the original-image relation. For Patterson, the essence of the latter relation is that the image of a bed, for example, is not another real bed. Thus, the mirror image of a bed is not a real bed because it does not fulfill the function fulfilled by the bed produced by the carpenter (20–21, 61). In another passage, Patterson says that the dream image of Napoleon "will not be colored or shaped at all in the same sense as the portrait" of Napoleon (51). Indeed, he denies that any resemblance between original and image is required for the latter to be an image of the former. Other than the difference between original and image, Patterson does not seem to offer any other features of the relation; the notion 'image of' seems primitive (42). Patterson's reason for emphasizing this difference between image and original becomes clear when we understand his positive account of the nature of a Form. He holds that a Form for F is the abstract nature or essence of F (67–68). What he means by 'abstract nature' or 'essence' is not altogether clear. He does seem to think that abstract natures are comparable in one way to "a fixed abstract pattern or structure which does not exemplify itself" (18). A blueprint would be an example of such a pattern or structure. In any event, the notion clearly separates Fs from the Form for F; the Fs are not other real Forms of F because they are not abstract natures of F. This reading of paradigm avoids the naive view, then, because such paradigms do not have to have the characteristic for which they are paradigms. For example, a blueprint does not have any of the characteristics for which

it is a blueprint. However, the reading runs into difficulty with at least one aspect of Plato's way of expressing the paradigm-copy relation. Plato seems to apply the term F both to the paradigm of F and to Fs. Patterson says that 'F' is a name (*onoma*) that primarily designates the Form (71). But if there is no resemblance between the F itself and Fs, it sounds odd to say 'F' primarily designates the Form. Compare: one might call a blueprint of a house "a house" (in the architect's office one might say, "Look at this house."). But it would be odd to say that the name 'house' primarily designates the blueprint. Surely it designates houses; and, when it is used of blueprints, 'house' really means "blueprint of a house." Somewhat the same thing could be said for his other example of an abstract nature—political offices as defined by a charter, for example, dog catcher. Surely the name (*onoma*) of 'dog catcher' belongs to the dog catcher and not to the office of dog catcher.

6. Cf. Charles Kahn, "The Meaning of 'Justice' and the Theory of Forms," *The Journal of Philosophy* 69(1972):571: "From the philosophical point of view, however, there is no doubt that Plato does envisage the justice of man and city as derived from the more abstract or intelligible pattern of the Form. Let us, *exempli gratia*, generalize the definitions Plato does give in order to see what formula he might have given for the Form itself. We may suppose that it runs as follows.

(J) Justice is a well-ordered whole.

Or, more fully:

(J') Justice is a unity of differentiated parts, each with its own nature, and these parts are so interrelated that each one performs the task for which it is best fitted.

See also John Cooper, "The Psychology of Justice in Plato," *American Philosophical Quarterly* 14(1977):155: "So much for what one might call the 'functional properties' of the good-itself. How about its substance or nature? Here Socrates is deliberately least informative. One may, however, render this curious entity more concrete by thinking of it somehow or other as a perfect example of rational order, conceived in explicitly mathematical terms: a complex, ordered whole, whose orderliness is due to the mathematical relationships holding among its parts." Although this quotation deals with the Form of good, later we shall make the connection between the Form of good and the Form of justice. See also F. C. White, "Justice and the Good of Others in Plato's *Republic*," *History of Philosophy Quarterly* 5(1988):395–410: "The principle of 'doing one's own' not only at bottom constitutes justice in the individual and in society, but is responsible for the worthwhileness of these. *Pari passu*, in forming the basis of ordinary justice, the principle of 'doing one's own' will engender worthwhileness in this too. In their essence the three sorts of justice are the same: each is a kind of fittingness, balance, proper distribution and harmony. And it is this in the end, their *kosmos*, which makes them worthwhile" (404). Again, we see that, abstracted, justice is a kind of order; of course, White does not say that the Form of justice is abstracted order, even if his account of it is compatible with the Form's being such.

7. The relation between the order and harmony of justice in the city and the order and harmony of the Form is not one of analogy. The former is not analogous to the latter. The same characteristic is found in both; in one it is obscure and in the other it is clear. Similarly, the perceptual triangle is not analogous to the mathematical triangle.

8. 'Proportion' translates *kata logon*. The latter can also mean "according to reason"—the usual translation. However, "proportionate" is a possible translation; moreover, anything ordered according to reason would be proportionate.

9. White, *Companion*, in his commentary on 500c, takes the same approach to imitation: "In 500c it is said that a person observing the orderliness of the Forms will wish to make both himself and the city orderly in a like manner. This statement reveals an important aspect of Plato's views about the motives of his rulers, and indeed of anyone who is able to apprehend the Forms" (173, n.D). Reeve gives a very good description of this psychic order and harmony in his account of Plato's psychology. Cf. *Philosopher Kings*, 140–144.

10. Cf. Annas, *Introduction*, 236–239.

11. An obvious consequence of this account is that only the philosopher can practice the craft of justice. Only the philosopher has knowledge of the Forms necessary for imitating justice in her own soul. Thus, auxiliaries and artisans cannot practice the craft of justice. Of course, what sorts of virtue are possible for auxiliaries and artisans is a notorious problem in the *Republic*. If there is to be an answer, it has to be that their virtue is parasitic on the virtue of the rulers. For instance, auxiliaries are brave because they preserve the teaching of the rulers about what is to be feared and not feared (*Rep.* 429c). But rulers know what is to be feared and not feared because of their wisdom. Thus, the bravery of the auxiliaries is parasitic on the wisdom of the rulers. The temperance of the artisans is their deference to the rule of the guardian rulers; and the guardians regulate the appetites of the artisans (*Rep.* 431b–e). Thus their temperance depends on the wisdom of the rulers. The chief difference between auxiliaries and artisans in this regard is that auxiliaries (or some of them, anyway) will ultimately gain the knowledge necessary for the craft of justice. The artisans must always remain dependent on the rulers.

12. Substituting clear intuition of a paradigm for knowledge of general principles casts the issue of objectivity in moral judgment into an entirely different light, of course. One of the obvious consequences of

seeing the moral life in this way is that intuition of a paradigm allows for approximation to that paradigm. If justice is not a principle but a paradigm, then we can understand the phenomenon of shadings between the paradigm and those instances that are not fully just. Thus, one can have the objectivity of the Form without the consequence that many people fear—the overwhelming of the particularity of the individual case. Although Plato's moral theory is being increasingly represented as hostile to the details that are the substance of human morality, the naive interpretation of the Forms as paradigms points in the opposite direction.

13. Cf. Alexander Nehamas, "Plato on the Imperfection of the Sensible World," *American Philosophical Quarterly* 12(1975):105–117: "Thus the properties that particulars possess are perfect copies of the Forms in which these particulars participate. The imperfection of the sensible world does not consist in those very properties that it shares with the world of Forms. It consists, rather, in that sensible objects possess their perfect (that is, exact) properties imperfectly" (109). Nehamas seems to assume that particulars are substances with properties; they different from Forms in that the latter have the relevant properties by necessity. See Richard Patterson, *Image and Reality*, 16. One could interpret this passage in a way similar to Nehamas' interpretation without assuming that Fs are substances; if Fs are appearances of the Form of F, then they would be F and not F, while the Form is only F.

14. R. E. Allen has pointed out the importance of the reality-appearance metaphysics for deflecting the Third Man Argument in his article, "Participation and Predication in Plato's Middle Dialogues," in *Studies in Plato's Metaphysics*, Allen, ed. According to Allen, the infinite regress of the arguments at *Parmenides* 132a–b and 132d–133a is a problem only for those who take the meaning of 'F' to be univocal. If F things and the Form of F are F in the same sense, then the TMA works. However, if F things are F in a sense that is different from the way that the Form of F is F, then the TMA does not work. Of course, it will not do for Allen to say that 'F' is just equivocal, meaning something totally different when used of F things and of the Form. He wants 'F' to mark a community of character between F things and the Form of F (59). This peculiar kind of equivocity he finds in the appearance-reality distinction. The reflection of a scarf is not a scarf in the way in which the scarf is a scarf; the reflection is not even red in the way in which the scarf is red. (50) However, the reflections are resemblances of the original, even though they do not resemble the original (49–51). Clearly, reflections are appearances of a more fundamental reality; indeed, all appearances—including appearances of Forms—lack substantiality, are relational entities (57 and 60). The moral of the story, according to this interpretation, is that understanding the relation between appearance and reality is the key to seeing why self-exemplifying Forms are not liable to the TMA. Whether Allen's

argument is a successful defense of the notion of Forms as exemplars will have to be left aside; however, it is worth noting that if Allen's—or an Allen-like—defense is right, it would lend support to the present interpretation of the craft of justice as making images that are appearances of the Form of justice.

15. Gregory Vlastos, in *Platonic Studies,* says that Plato does not need a distinction among degrees of reality but only a distinction between kinds of reality. "To see that he got these results from a degrees-of-reality theory, while all he needed as a kinds-of-reality theory, will help us to recognize the ways, good and bad, in which his theory served him. Certainly a kinds-of-reality theory would have served him much better as an instrument of categorial inquiry. One has a better chance to see and state correctly the differences between particulars and universals, if one expects in advance the both will be equally "real" in their different ways. For then one will not be tempted to misconstrue universals as a higher grade of particulars, or think of sensible particulars as inferior "imitations" or "copies" of Ideal Forms" (75). R. E. Allen, on the other hand, takes the distinction between reality and appearance very seriously and thinks that degrees of reality is essential to Plato's metaphysics. "Particulars and Forms are not merely different types of things; they are types of things that differ in degree of reality, for the one is wholly dependent upon the other. Particulars have no independent ontological status; they are purely relational entities, entities that derive their whole character and existence from Forms" (57 in *Studies in Plato's Metaphysics,* Allen, ed.).

16. Cf. R. E. Allen, "Argument from Opposites from *Republic* V," in *Essays in Ancient Greek Philosophy,* John P. Anton and George L. Kustas, eds. (Albany: State University of New York Press, 1972), 168; Annas *Introduction,* 219 ff.; Sharvy, "Plato's Causal Logic and the Third Man Argument," *Nous* 20(1986):507–530. As well, in Book VII, Socrates talks about objects that summon the soul to dialectic. Substances like finger do not while comparatives like large and small do (*Rep.* 523a ff.).

17. Even Socrates is so mixed with injustice that, from some point of view, he is unjust. It is not possible to disambiguate Socrates' justice from its context. Take for instance Socrates' treatment of Alcibiades, recounted by Alcibiades at the end of the *Symposium.* The story of his attempted seduction of Socrates is replete with irony. Even Plato's representation of Socrates is ironic. Alcibiades' view of Socrates' refusal to be seduced by his considerable beauty is that it was a vision of beautiful courage—of authentic virtue. And yet, as we reread the account, we might see something else, something less attractive. Did Socrates lead Alcibiades on? Did he have to deal so harshly with the young man, even if he was absorbed in his own beauty? Was Socrates fair to Alcibiades? Even supposing the answers to these questions are all positive, it is hardly obvious that they are positive. There is still something ambiguous about

Socrates' behavior here, something even dark. At the very least, one would be ill advised to attempt to replicate Socrates' behavior in another context, with another self-absorbed young man. Even the best intentioned moral teacher might find himself embroiled in a disaster if he let one of his students, for example, carry out a plan of seduction, in order to rebuff the beauty proffered as some sort of moral lesson. Such behavior would show far too great a confidence in the justice of Socrates' treatment of Alcibiades.

18. Cf. Alexander Nehamas, "Plato on Imitation and Poetry in *Republic* 10," *Plato on Beauty, Wisdom, and the Arts*, Julius Moravcsik and Philip Temko, eds. (Totowa: Rowman and Littlefield, 1982), 67: "Poetry, therefore, tends to appeal to the irrational aspect of the soul much more than painting, since the domination of reason is what gives most poets their object of imitation. Moreover, in this passage Plato seems to oppose reason both to spirit (*thumos*) and the appetite (*epithumētikon*). It has been claimed that this is evidence that he was never serious about the existence of spirit or emotion as a part of the soul in the first place. But emotion is in fact a source of motivation, and Plato thought so for good reasons. The explanation of why he opposes reason to spirit and appetite together, it seems to me, is simply that he does not need to distinguish these two for his present purposes."

19. For an illuminating discussion of this section of Book X see Elizabeth Belfiore, "Plato's Greatest Accusation Against Poetry," *New Essays on Plato,* Francis Jeffrey Pelletier and Johyn King-Farlow, eds. (Guelph: Canadian Association for Publishing in Philosophy, 1983), 39–62.

CHAPTER 4

Imitation and Inspiration in the Republic *and the* Symposium

At this point in our exposition we can read the *Republic* as an extended argument about the value of justice in the soul. More, of course, is going on in the dialogue than an argument for the value of justice in the soul; but at least that much is there. Moreover, the argument for justice in the soul has three tiers. The first tier of the argument—Book II–IV—could be called "naturalist"; it argues that justice in the soul is perfection of its underlying nature. Thus, according to this tier of the argument, justice in the soul is good because it perfects the soul's natural function. The argument may not be explicitly so stated; but these books are clearly urging the value of this arrangement in the soul because of the perfection of its underlying function. The second tier of the argument—the first part of Book VI—could be called "idealist"; it starts by arguing that justice in the soul is achieved by imitating the Form of justice. But this argument, too, implies a claim about value; justice in the soul is valuable because it is an embodiment of the ideal of justice. These first two tiers present justice as a craft, both a ruling craft that perfects the soul at the same time that it is an instance of that perfection and a ruling craft imitative of the Forms.

The third tier of the argument—the last part of Book VI and Book VII—is the last and highest justification for justice in the soul. In this tier, Plato shows the relation between imitating the Form justice in the soul and the Form of good; in this tier the value of justice in the soul is finally grounded in the Form of good. It tells us why imitating the ideal of justice is valuable. Thus, when we reach this Form we have reached the apex of Plato's argument for the value of justice in the soul. It is this tier that Socrates gives over to the greatest learning (*megiston mathēma*), the knowledge of the other Forms by means of knowledge of the good itself. In this chapter we will elaborate on Plato's account of the relation between the good itself and the craft of imitating justice in the soul.

In the first tier, Plato's account of virtue is psychological. In this way, it differs in a subtle but important way from most modern accounts of virtue. Modern philosophy attempts to define the acts that are morally correct, by specifying either the rule such acts should follow or the consequences such acts should provide. Plato, by contrast, identifies virtue with having a certain disposition. Disposition is distinguished from action in that the former is the capacity and the proclivity to act, that is, it is the source of action. The virtue of courage, for example, is the capacity and proclivity to act in certain ways—ways not always foreseeable, not always specifiable by a rule. What medieval thinkers called "*habitus*," dispositions are what we moderns might call "qualities of character." Of course, since these dispositions naturally give rise to certain kinds of actions, if one never performed virtuous acts, one could not be said to have the disposition of virtue. Still Plato identifies virtue with the deeper source of the actions; virtue is a way of being—morally speaking, a style of life. Dispositions as inner sources of action are attributed by Plato to the soul. As a consequence, Plato's account of virtue tells us what the soul of the just person will be like. It is an account of the character of the just person seen from his interior life. As Glaucon says, "For what I want to hear is what each (justice and injustice) is and what power each has, itself by itself, dwelling in the soul, the rewards and consequences that follow from them being left aside" (358b). As we have seen, this account is also an account of happiness. The person who has in his soul the virtues of justice, wisdom, courage, and self-control is also and always the person who is happy in a sense that includes but is not exhausted by our notion of pleasure.

Before Plato can give an account of virtue as dispositions he must first have a theory about the soul, its parts and its structure. This kind of theory is sometimes called a "moral psychology" and tells about those assumptions that a moralist is making when she recommends one way of life over another. Generally, a moral psychology tells us something about reason and its functions, about the role of the will, and about that recalcitrant source of most moral conflict, the passions. Plato has something to say on all of these subjects with his tripartite division of the soul.

After giving us this inventory of psychological functions, Plato quickly turns to his account of virtue in the soul (*Rep.* 441d–

448e). Virtue is that set of dispositions that perfect these psychological functions. These functions become virtuous by acquiring the capacity and proclivity to function well or correctly. Thus, wisdom is reason's ruling in the soul with knowledge of what is good for the three parts and for the whole formed by the three parts. Wisdom is the disposition for reason to make long-term policy for one's life and short-term decisions within it, armed with insight into what is truly beneficial for reason, *thymos*, and the passions—as well as for the polity formed by the three. This sort of disposition is best appreciated when it is contrasted with, say, the disposition to give over policy and decisions to the passions. Heedless of the others, none with any sense of the good of the whole, the passions as rulers are the very picture of folly. There may be more to wisdom than rule by informed reason—but not much more. Our greatest hesitancy may be that no place is arranged for experience of life. But then if one really *knew* what was for the good of the parts and the good of the whole, experience might not seem so greatly needed. Courage is the quality of the spirited part. When *thymos* follows the lead of reason about what is to be feared and what is not to be feared, a person is courageous. *Thymos* becomes virtuous when it habitually points its aggressive and adventurous energies towards the goals reason sanctions. Presumably reason guides the *thymos* so that it is aggressive against the passions—and against other people—only when one's real interest is threatened. Since one's real interest is one's stable disposition to act wisely, courageously, temperately, justly, a courageous person has the disposition to fend off those influences that would undermine these dispositions. Real courage is the courage to preserve virtue, the courage to persevere in a way of life. Temperance is that condition of soul that results when the extravagant appetites and the ebullient *thymos* are controlled by the wise and naturally moderate reason. But Plato has a more profound notion of this virtue as well. One is temperate when all parts of her soul agree to reason's rule. One is temperate, then, when the appetites, for example, are accustomed to recognize that reason knows best what are the limits to each drive and the proper balance among them. Striving each for its own fulfillment, each passion has the disposition to defer to the deeper insight of reason.

Finally, justice is the state of soul achieved when each part of the soul has the disposition to perform its proper function and not to interfere with the functions of the other parts. In the first

instance, this virtue means that the appetites seek their own satisfactions without attempting to rule in the place of reason. One
seeks, for example, such food as the appetite for food wants—in
whatever variety and quantity—as long as doing so does not keep
reason from exercising its benevolent rule over the psychic commonwealth. Reason must control these satisfactions so that the
good of other appetites, of the *thymos*, and of reason itself is
achieved. However, it should not be overlooked that justice
works—by implication—in another direction. It would be equally
unjust for reason to constrain the appetites in favor of its own narrow interests. Reason rules to achieve the good of all, not just its
peculiar good. Thus, an ascetic repression of the appetites is not
at all just, even if one achieved thereby the superficial peace
needed by reason to read, study, puzzle, or contemplate. This
implication is rendered less secure by what Plato says about sublimation. But even at that, there must be a difference between sublimation and repression. The latter is clearly unjust usage of an
appetite. Such a life would show a deftness at being human that
would clearly be a kind of natural perfection. Plato calls this life
"happy"—*eudaimōn*; literally put, it is well geniused. A lifelong
performance of this sort would be as graceful, adroit, and fitting
as that of the gymnast. It would be the spiritual equivalent of the
Olympic athlete. At this level of understanding of Plato's account
of virtue in the soul, we might think that we have all the recommendation necessary. A life built of dispositions to perform at this
level—a life based upon the ability and proclivity to be an Olympic hero of the spirit—such a life seems to have the highest possible recommendation. Not only is it the most satisfying life, it is the
most fitting, graceful, and well done. But there is another level of
understanding of virtue in the soul.

   This second level is the subject of the second tier of his argument. In the latter, he explains how one establishes virtue in the
soul. The process is portrayed as one of imitation. Most of the
passages show the philosophical ruler looking to the Forms as paradigms to be copied in some way. When the virtuous person gazes
upon the Forms, he sees ideal exemplars of justice, temperance,
and beauty. They are used as models—the way a painter uses a
model—to bring order and harmony into the soul. Becoming and
remaining an Olympic hero of the spirit is finally based upon imitation of the order and harmony of these ideal Forms. In this tier
of the argument, the reason for having justice in the soul would

seem to be that such an arrangement—besides providing satisfaction to all parts of the soul, besides being the perfection of all the functions of the soul—is an imitation of an order found among these ideals. We would strive to establish this order in the soul because we are inspired by its perfect embodiment in these Forms. At this level, the way Plato describes justice in the soul begins to emphasize the beauty of this arrangement in the soul. Indeed, justice in the soul can be seen as valuable from this point of view as well. If the just person is the Olympic athlete of the spirit, we all know that sport has its beautiful aspects and can be appreciated purely from that point of view. If the life of the just person could be frozen into one moment—rendered in sculpture rather than in drama—it would have all of the spiritual balance and harmony, energy and ease to which the fifth-century athletic statues are the physically ideal equivalent.

As we have seen, at this level of the account, in Books V and VI, the motif is the painter and the paradigm. Thus, it is natural to introduce the notion of beauty into the account. If we take this motif as more than metaphor, we would seem to have ample justification for seeing the value of a virtuous life in terms of those values we call "aesthetic" (although we must be careful to understand the terms as more than aesthetic). Finally, however, even this level of commendation is not enough in Plato's account. While the *Republic* introduces the idea that the Forms are both patterns and motivation for embodying those patterns, as we noted in the last chapter it is the Form of the good, in the final analysis, that is the ultimate motivation for imitating these Forms. If we use terms borrowed from Aristotle we can now say that Forms have two functions in this account. The first function is to be a kind of formal cause. The Form of justice, for instance, is the formal cause of justice in the soul and in the city because the philosophical ruler uses it as the form or pattern that she tries to replicate in her soul and in the city. However, Forms are the final cause for imitation. Thus, these exemplars constitute both a set of directions and a motivation. Although motivation is not the central theme of these passages, it is nevertheless present. Not only does the exemplar act as a model of what is to be imitated but it shows what is to be imitated as more attractive than any alternative. In the *Republic*, Plato's exemplars for virtue are the Forms of justice, temperance, and beauty:

> . . . looking to those things which are well ordered and remain
> the same always and seeing that neither do they transgress upon,
> nor suffer transgression by, one another—they are orderly and
> proportionate—he imitates them and makes himself as like them
> as possible. Or do you think that there is any way for someone
> who associates with what he admires not to imitate that thing?
> (500b–c)

Plato's introduction of the good itself emphasizes and develops the
notion that Forms inspire imitation. The philosophical ruler
wants to imitate the Forms because of their goodness. As we shall
see, there is a sense in which the good itself is that for the sake of
which the philosophical rulers imitate the Form of justice, for
example. Thus, Plato intends to develop a more profound argument as to why justice, order, and harmony are good in order to
explain why these ideals inspire the philosopher to imitate them.
So, it is now time for us to look at imitation and the Form of good.
Here we take up the third tier of the argument: the final reason for
imitating the Forms.

I

After elaborating the analogy between the ruler and painter in
Book VI, Plato is ready to introduce the greatest learning—the discipline of dialectic that leads up to the Form of the good, that
Form that completes the learning of the ruler. After explaining
why in Athens philosophic natures are corrupted, Socrates discon-
certs his interlocutors by saying that, in the ideal city, philosopher
kings will be tested finally by means of this greatest learning.
When he is questioned about the greatest learning, Socrates says
that it is about the Form of the good. Then he delivers an explanation of why learning about the Form of the good is important.
Since this explanation forms something of an introduction to the
passages about the analogy of the Sun, the Divided Line, and the
simile of the Cave, the tendency is to overlook it in order to concentrate on the latter passage. However, it will repay us to concentrate instead on the explanation itself as an introduction to what
we have called the "third level" of this account.

In general, we can say that the Form of the good is important
because, without it, we cannot realize any benefit from trying to

be just. Thus, as soon as he introduces the notion that the highest learning is the Form (*idea*) of the good, Socrates adds,

> by which (that is, the Form of the Good) just things, and all the other things undertaken become useful and beneficial. And now surely you know that I am going to talk about this [learning] and [say] that, when it comes to it, we do not have sufficient knowledge of this [Form]. Further, if we do not know [it] then, even if we fully knew the other things (*scil.* just things) without this [Form], you realize that it will benefit us nothing, just as if we possessed something without its goodness. (505a)

The context makes clear that the "just things" are the account of justice in Book IV. Socrates is saying that the account of justice in the city and in the soul may seem impressive to his hearers. However, without knowledge of the Form of good, this knowledge of the accounts of justice—and the other virtues—will not be beneficial. In short, Socrates is warning his hearers that the account in Book IV is not complete.

Moreover, we have just seen in the immediately preceding paragraphs of Book VI that establishing true justice in the soul and in the city is accomplished by imitating the Form of justice. Indeed, almost all commentaries fail to note sufficiently that the highest learning is introduced to complete the account of the knowledge of Forms that themselves have been introduced as paradigms for imitation. We should conclude that the highest learning is introduced in order to round out what the philosopher needs to know to be successful in imitating the Form of justice. Indeed, the subsequent passages—the Sun and Divided Line—tell us that knowledge of all other Forms, presumably including the Form of justice, depends on knowledge of the Form of good. Since it seems safe to assume that imitation of the Form of justice depends on knowledge of the Form of justice, imitating the Form of justice would then depend on knowledge of the Form of good.[1] Moreover, this implication is one that Plato would have expected his readers to make, given that imitation is the immediate concern before the introduction of the Form of the good.

In what follows, then, we shall treat the Form of the good as having a role to play in the philosopher's task of imitating the Forms, both in her own soul and in the city. As we shall see, however, there are two aspects to the role of the Form of good in imitating the Form of justice. The first aspect is epistemological and the second is causal. Besides being necessary for understanding and thus imitating justice, the Form of good is also the source of goodness. This latter claim is different from the epistemological one. It is not just the claim that one must know the Form of good in order to imitate justice, it is the claim that the goodness of imitating justice depends not only on the knowledge of the one who imitates it but, apart from that knowledge, it depends on the existence of the Form of goodness. Whatever good comes from imitating the Form of justice depends not just epistemologically but ontologically on the Form of good. The Form of goodness is an epistemological paradigm of goodness for the philosopher to imitate; the Form of goodness is at the same time the continuing cause of goodness in that which the philosopher produces. In what follows we shall see that both of these aspects are important for understanding the role of the Form of goodness in imitation.

First of all, we will trace the epistemological role of the Form of the good. Then we will turn to its causal role. The latter, as we shall see, is the same as the theory of participation, the most important implication of Plato's theory of Forms. As might be expected, these two aspects have implications for one another. The chief implication for our purposes is what these two aspects can tell us about the motivation of the philosophical ruler. As we shall see, the two aspects give us an important insight into why the philosophical ruler imitates the Forms both in her soul and in the city. In fact, this insight will help us address that nagging problem, the reluctant philosopher of Book VII—that is, the philosopher who is reluctant to return to the "cave," to take up the task of ruling in the city.

We can begin with the epistemological aspect. It is, in some ways, the most obvious to us; it is the one outlined in those famous passages from Book VI, the analogy of the Sun and the Divided Line. In the Sun passage, the Form of good is compared to the sun. Just as the sun sheds light on visible objects to make the eyes to see them, so the Form of good makes the other Forms to be known by reason. As the images of light and shadow indicate, the emphasis is on epistemological aspects of this chief Form. In looking at visible objects illuminated by the sun, we see clearly. Just so when we look on intelligible objects where truth and being shine forth (*hou katalampei alētheia te kai to on* [508d5]), we grasp, know, and have understanding. In the Divided Line, Socrates outlines divisions of epistemically graspable objects, from the dimmest to the clearest—from images and reflections to visible objects, to mathematical truths, finally to the Forms themselves. However, knowledge of these latter is conditioned on attaining knowledge of the good itself. In this last section of the Divided Line, reason itself grasps, by means of dialectic, what were up to this point ungrounded assumptions, treating them now as stepping stones

> and going right up to the beginning point of all, which is not itself an assumption. There reason grasps this beginning point, and laying hold of those things that pertain to it, reason proceeds down to its conclusion, not by way of visible objects, but by way of Forms, and through Forms, to Forms, concluding in Forms. (511b–c)

The notoriously difficult passages in which Socrates sets forth the Sun and Divided Line cannot be adequately dealt with in short compass, of course. However, if we stay on a certain level of generality, one thing seems obvious. At this level of generality, the Sun and Divided Line passages seem to say that one cannot grasp what Forms are unless one first grasps the central Form, the good itself. This general claim, however, must not be read as one simply about propositions. Admittedly, Plato's language in the Divided Line tempts us to think that the good itself is a mathematical axiom from which the existence and nature of the rest of the Forms could be derived by a logically deductive method—as though the good were a particularly rich proposition. The Sun passage reinforces that temptation. The reason that we are so tempted is that Plato seems to be talking about necessary relations between the good and the other Forms. To the contemporary philosophical understanding, necessary relations exist only between propositions. However, the good itself is not a proposition; it is an entity in its own right that has, nevertheless, what seem to be certain necessary relations to other entities—that is, the other Forms—relations implied by the upward movement of dialectic and the downward movement through Forms. Moreover, that necessary relationship is in the order of value. The good itself stands in some sort of necessary relation to the other Forms because each of them is necessarily good and the good itself defines goodness.

So there are two aspects to the relation between the good itself and the other Forms. First, it is a necessary relation; second, it is a relation that defines the value of the other Forms. The two aspects of the relation are themselves interrelated. First of all, we can see that the necessity of the relation is bound up with the goodness of the Forms. If Socrates had said that we could not understand the goodness of the just itself without understanding the good itself, the relation between the two might not be thought to be necessary. Suppose, for instance, that goodness is not a necessary property of justice; then its relation to the good would not be a necessary one. The dialectician could understand the just itself without understanding its goodness. But Plato said that we cannot understand the just itself without understanding the good itself—as though goodness were an essential property of the just itself, but one that cannot be grasped until we had grasped the good itself. Given this role of the good itself in understanding an essential property of the just itself, we say that the relation between the two is a necessary one; but it is a necessary one because it is a relationship in the order of value. It is as though Plato wanted to say that the other Forms participate in the good itself but he did not want to imply that the other Forms participate in the good itself in the way in which perceptual particulars participate in Forms. Perceptual particulars are, of course, only contingently good. However, the other Forms are necessarily good. Thus, the relation of the other Forms to the good itself is not contingent but necessary. While it is never easy to say what Plato means here, of course, there is a certain sense of it that is suggestive for the naive view. Fundamentally, it comes to this: (1) the good itself is intrinsically good in such a way that it defines intrinsic goodness for the other Forms; (2) when we come to grasp this intrinsic goodness, we understand that or how the other Forms—for example, justice—are, by necessity, intrinsically good and thus understand them fully.

It is a view like this that Gerasimos Santas sets forth in his book, *Plato and Freud*. Claiming that Plato conceived of Forms as "ideal exemplars or paradigms, self-exemplifying or self-predicating," Santas distinguishes between the proper and ideal attributes of a Form. For example, the proper attribute of the beautiful is beauty; its ideal attributes are those shared by all Forms. In turn, he says that the Form of the good "is the formal cause of all the other Forms having their ideal attributes. . . ." In turn,

> The ideal attributes of all the other Forms are proper attributes of the Form of the Good; or, the Form of the Good consists in the ideality of the Forms. So conceived, each Form other than

> the Form of the Good is the best object of its kind, and it is such
> by virtue of participating (fully) in the Form of the Good.[2]

By contrast, the goodness of perceptual particulars is caused by a lesser participation, or resemblance to some degree, in the good.

On the naive view being defended in our interpretation, if the just itself is an abstract, but real, proportionate order, then, once we understand the good itself, we understand that this proportionate order is by necessity intrinsically good. It is not the intrinsic good but it is a type of intrinsic good. In saying that it is a type of intrinsic good, we should not think that the just itself and the other Forms together constitute the good itself or that the good itself is a genus of which the other Forms are species. The good itself is still a Form in its own right, beside these other Forms.

Given this account of the relation between the Form of good and the Form of justice, we might be tempted to conclude that the role of the Form of good in imitation is confined to being something like a higher set of instructions. Both Forms are integrally related as patterns for imitation. The Form of justice tells the philosopher what justice is; the Form of good tells the philosopher how the Form of justice is good. Thus, the imitation is good—and thus is a faithful imitation of justice. Presumably, the Form of good does have this epistemological role. However, it has another distinctive role; it is also the cause of goodness. At first one might be tempted to think that its epistemological role is the same as its causal. After all, if one depends on the Form of good for instructions about imitation, in some sense this Form is causal. It is causal in the sense that it causes the good of just things by mediation through the agency of the one who imitates the Form. However, the sense in which the Form of good is causal is distinct from this epistemological causal role.

In the quotation from 505a we can see a reference to this distinct causal role. At first, the passage seems to imply that the only role for the Form of good is epistemological since the passage emphasizes the need for knowledge of the Form. However, the passage says more than that. The opening sentence does not say that it is by the knowledge of the idea of the good that just things become useful and beneficial—as though knowledge of the idea of the good is only a set of instructions for the one who imitates the Form. It says that it is by the idea of the good that just things become useful and beneficial (*epei hoti ge hē tou agathou idea megiston mathēma . . . hēi dē dikaia kai talla proschrēsamena chrēsima kai ōphelima gignetai* [505a2–4]). In the Greek, the grammar of the sentence makes clear that there is a direct causality between the idea of the good and the just things. Again, at the end of the passage, we have a reference to the causal role of the idea of good. If the role of the idea of good were only epistemological then we would expect the sentence to say that knowledge of the idea of the good provides us with the knowledge of just things so that we will know how to use them so that they will be beneficial. Instead the sentence says that knowledge of the just things without this Form—that is, idea of the good—would be like having the just things without their goodness. While the sentence is consistent with an epistemological reading, it is also consistent with a causal reading. In this reading the Form of good is the cause of goodness in the just things; thus, to know the just things without this Form is to fail to obtain the goodness of these things—as though knowing the cause of goodness is a part of having the goodness of just things. This kind of claim is different from saying that knowing the cause of goodness is necessary for producing goodness; rather this kind of claim makes the cause of goodness more integral to the goodness of just things. The Form of good is like a continuing source of goodness in the just things. Knowing this continuing source is integral to having the goodness of these just things.

There is, obviously, a special sense of the notion of cause at work in these passages. Since this sense of cause is essential to understanding the role of the Form of goodness in imitation, we will spend some time in, first, explicating it and, then, showing that it occurs in *Republic* VI and VII. The causal role of the Form can be summed up in this way; the Form of good, by itself being good, causes whatever goodness there is. Indeed, this type of causality is Plato's famous doctrine of participation. This fundamental principle of participation is found in the *Phaedo* (100c): "If anything is beautiful besides the Beautiful itself, it is beautiful only through participation in the Beautiful itself." This familiar statement implies (1) that the beautiful itself is beautiful—indeed, perhaps the only authentically beautiful thing—and (2) that all other beautiful things are derivatively beautiful—are beautiful only by participation. Thus, only the beautiful itself is not derivatively beautiful; moreover, without the beautiful itself there simply would not be anything that is beautiful.[3]

    In order to understand fully the dependence of all other beautiful things on the beautiful itself we must understand the context in which the doctrine of participation is introduced. This passage in the *Phaedo* begins with a methodological reflection in which Socrates has said that his investigation into the causes of coming-to-be led him to the method of hypothesis. According to this method, first of all he would posit as true, or hypothesize, a proposition he judged to be "the strongest." Then he would "accept as true whatever agrees with (*symphōnein*)" the hypothesis (100a). Richard Robinson argues convincingly that Plato meant "accept as true what agrees with" as a way of referring to deducing the logical consequences of the hypothesis.[4] After this methodological reflection, Socrates states his hypothesis that Forms exist, "There exists the beautiful itself by itself, the good, the great, and all the others"(100b). Then the first consequence of the hypothesis is the doctrine of participation. What is peculiar about this progression of thought is the notion that participation is a consequence of the existence of Forms. At first glance, it is not obvious that participation should be a consequence. After all, even if we suppose that the beautiful itself exists, even if we suppose that the beautiful itself is perfectly and unqualifiedly beautiful, it does not follow that every other beautiful thing must participate in the beautiful itself. It would seem possible that there could be imperfectly beautiful objects not related to the beautiful itself by participation; there could be imperfectly, and independently, beautiful things. The difference in the way in which the beautiful itself is beautiful and the other beautiful things are beautiful does not by itself seem to imply participation. However, Socrates talks as though participation is a necessary consequence of the notion of Form. It is as though the Form of beauty is beautiful in such a way that it would be impossible to think of it without realizing that all other beautiful things are beautiful only by participation. If the Form is unqualifiedly and perfectly beautiful, then we would say that it is impossible to think of the Form as unqualifiedly and perfectly beautiful without realizing that all other beautiful things are derivatively beautiful, or beautiful by participation. So the Form of beauty is not just instrumentally valuable, as a means for identifying the beautiful things or as a means for making beautiful things. It is intrinsically valuable; but, more to the point, it is intrinsically valuable in such a way as to be also the source of value. The beautiful itself is intrinsically beautiful; it does not depend on anything else for its beauty. It is also the source of beauty because it is beautiful in such a way as to be the cause of beauty in all other beautiful things.

If we return to the *Republic* we can see that the causal role of the good itself fits this doctrine of participation. If we apply participation to the good itself, we see that there are two corollaries to this application: (1) the good itself is the only authentic goodness and (2) all other good things are good only in a derivative way. They derive their goodness from the good itself. What follows from this claim is a view of value that is strange to our ears and sometimes hard to understand.

Let us begin the account of causality with the first part of the claim—only the good itself is authentic goodness. In a subsequent passage, Socrates says that when it comes to just things, many people will choose what seems just.

> However, when it is a question of good things, no one is satisfied to possess what seems to be good, but everyone seeks to have what is really good, shunning the seeming good immediately. . . . Indeed, each soul seeks this good and does all that it does for its sake, divining that it is real, but actually being at a loss and not having an adequate grasp of what it is, nor does the soul have a stable belief about it, as it does with the others (*scil.* the just things), and because of this situation it fails to get (*apotugchanei*) whatever benefit there may be from these others. . . . (505d–e)

There are two ways to read this passage. One is to read the project of finding the good itself as a project of finding the concept or definition by which we can identify those things in our perceptual world that count as authentic good. The other is to read the project of finding the good itself as a project of finding a thing that is authentically good, and thus outside our perceptual world. As we shall see, Socrates presents the good itself not as a means to this real authentic good but as identical with it.[5] Those who seek authentic goodness, not seeming goodness, are actually seeking the good itself. The good itself is at one end of the continuum from appearance to reality. The good itself, thus, will satisfy a longing that the appearances of good will not. The longing is not simply an epistemological longing for a true account of goodness, nor a longing for authentic goodness in this world made possible by knowing the Form of goodness, but a longing for the good itself.

That the Form of good—and not a perceptual good—is what everyone seeks when they seek goodness is shown by the intervening passage where Socrates assesses two views of the good (505b–c). While he says that these views are mistaken, it is instructive to see how these views are mistaken. First of all, Socrates says that most people think pleasure (*hēdonē*) is the good. There is in this admittedly mistaken opinion at least the suggestion that the many see the good as something good. Since, however, some pleasures are good and some are bad, this opinion of the many is wrong. The second opinion given by Socrates is that of the better people, who say that knowledge (*phronēsis*) is the good. While Socrates does not say that these people are wrong in this opinion, he does say that the opinion is not very illuminating because, when elaborated, it turns out to be the opinion that knowledge of the good is the good. What we need to know, however, is this good of which the knowledge is the good. The problem here is not just one of begging the question. Rather, the problem could be stated in this way: if knowledge of the good is the good, then it is parasitic on the good for being the good. Thus, the value of the knowledge of the good is not fundamental; as such it cannot be the good.[6]

In referring to these two candidates for the good, Socrates recalls for us the earlier discussion in Book II of that which is good in itself and that which is good in itself and in its consequences. The many identify the good with pleasure; in Book II, simple pleasure was an example of something good in itself. The better people are identifying the good with knowledge, which in Book II was among those things that are good in themselves or good in themselves and in their consequences. The mistake of these people in Book VI is not in thinking of the good as good in itself or as good in itself and in its consequences; their mistake is that they have identified the good with the wrong item. While the good is good in itself or good in itself and in its consequences, it is not either pleasure, which is good in itself, nor knowledge, which is good in itself and in its consequences. The introduction of the Forms into the dialogue has intervened since the discussion of Book II. So, the reason that pleasure and knowledge will not do as candidates for the good is that neither is good in itself and in its consequences in the way in which the Form of good is good in itself and in its consequences.

In these mistaken opinions we can see a common assumption. The good itself is something that is good. Moreover, in comparing it to two items that are themselves good, Plato is implying that the good itself is a good thing like these—only better. As a Form, it is something that is perfectly and unqualifiedly good in itself—unlike pleasure, for example, which is sometimes good and sometimes bad. Further, unlike the knowledge of the good, the good itself will be perfectly and unqualifiedly good in itself and good in its consequences. Thus, the good itself is the true object of people who are seeking the good. We also find the second aspect of participation in the *Republic*. The good itself also has a causal role. Of course, in the Sun passage, there is the mysterious reference to the good itself being the cause of the existence and being of the other objects of knowledge. Less mysterious, but perhaps more significant, is the summation of the three passages in Book VII. Here Socrates quickly says that the Cave passage is to be compared to the Sun passage, the realm of sight being the situation of those in the cave and the realm of intelligence being the upper world. Summing all of this imagery up, he says

> . . . having been seen, the Form of the Good requires the conclusion that it is itself the cause (*aitia*) for all things of all that is right and beautiful. (517c)

Thus, the relation of all other good things—including justice in the soul and in the city—to the good itself must be one of effects to cause, as the unique source of goodness.[7]

This kind of causality is a strange type of causality—indeed, a strange type of effect. Usually, we think of cause and effect as being ontologically independent of one another. A causes B; but after causing B, A can cease to exist without jeopardizing the existence of B. For instance, the carpenter causes the table to exist; when the carpenter dies the table does not cease to exist. However, in the type of causality that Plato is talking about, cause and effect are not ontologically independent. A is the cause of B in such a fashion that if A did not exist, B would not exist—but more to the point if A ceased to exist, B would cease to exist. It is in order to portray this kind of causality that Socrates uses the language of appearance and reality. In fact, the language of appearance and reality becomes prominent in the *Republic* at the point where he introduces the Form of the good. At that point, the good becomes the reality behind the appearances. The reason is not difficult to see. If we are talking about a continuing cause, one whose disappearance would mean the disappearance of the effect, a good way of expressing such a cause is by the notion of appearance and reality. For instance, the real scarf, if it were to disappear, would mean that the reflection of the scarf would disappear. So the use of the language of appearance and reality is another indication of the kind of causality Socrates is attributing to the Form of the good.

Perhaps we can understand this dependence between the Form of goodness and all other goods in another way. We can use the notion of the gold standard. Under the gold standard, gold is the standard of value for all paper currency. To understand the value of a dollar, or a pound, or a drachma one has to translate the value of each of these currencies into a certain weight of gold. Of course, an American could sell her dollars to a British subject in exchange for pounds without first buying gold and then using the gold to buy pounds; however, it would be understood that what gave each of the currencies value at all was the possibility that each partner in the exchange could exchange the currency for gold. There is a sense, then, in which the value of the other currencies is dependent on the value of gold. Without gold these currencies would be valueless. In turn, on this theory, gold is not dependent in this way on any other currency.

Of course, many people would attribute this function of gold to convention. We just decide to use gold as the standard of value for other currencies. However, if one is completely in the grip of the gold standard theory, he would deny that the gold standard is just a convention, that we have just decided to use gold as the standard for all other currencies. Rather, such a person might argue, gold in fact is the only value that stays constant; over the years, people who hold dollars, or pounds, or drachmas find that these currencies lose value. But people who keep their assets in gold find that they never lose any value. The value of all other currencies fluctuates; the value of gold does not fluctuate. Such a person might conclude that, when it comes to currencies, gold is intrinsically valuable because it is the only thing whose value remains constant. In turn, one might go on to say that, without gold, the value of the other currencies would collapse. They would lose their value, would become "worthless paper." One might even say that without gold there would be no standard of value of currencies in the market place. Without the gold standard, the value of other currencies would vanish. I might agree, for example, to exchange my dollars for your tomatoes at a certain rate of exchange; but—without the gold standard—you have no guarantee that the next person will exchange her okra for your just acquired dollars. Thus, ascending to the level of theory again, one might conclude that, by being intrinsically valuable, gold defines value. Without it, there would be no value to currency. Thus, because gold is the only thing with intrinsic value, all other currencies derive their value from gold.

Reasoning analogous to that of the gold standard theory can explain Plato's notion that the good itself is the source of value. Of course, its value is not that of the marketplace. Indeed, the analogy will seriously mislead unless we purge it of one important feature of the marketplace—the way in which gold can be exchanged for other goods; we must confine our attention to the relation between gold and paper currencies. If we do so, the good itself is like the gold standard for every thing of value. The value of all other goods fluctuates; the value of the good itself is constant. The good itself is constant because it is perfectly and unqualifiedly good in itself. Nothing is more valuable. Under the gold standard, there is also a dependency between gold and the other currencies because the other currencies can be exchanged for gold. Of course, no such exchange takes place in the case of the good itself. However, something analogous happens with the good itself and other goods. In Plato's account, when one knows about the good itself, one necessarily compares the other goods to the good itself.[8] In our experience, goodness is so unstable that without the comparison to the good itself we cannot grasp whether it is present or not. We need the good itself to be able reliably to identify good in our experience. But the obscurity here is not just epistemological. The problem is not just that there is authentic intrinsic goodness in our experience that is obscured in some way—for example, by some intervening medium. The goodness of our experience is itself ontologically obscured, so to speak, because nothing in our experience is authentic intrinsic goodness. It is all unstable and incomplete. Like the paper currencies, the good things in our experience have no authentic intrinsic goodness. What goodness they have is there only because of its relation to the good itself. As with paper currency, we see that all other goodness must be seen as dependent on the intrinsic goodness of the good itself.

To see what is at stake here we might ask why Plato might have thought that there is no authentic intrinsic goodness in our world. When something is intrinsically good, its goodness is not due to another; one could say that it is unconditionally good.[9] It is good no matter what is added or subtracted—good no-matter-what. However, there do not seem to be any candidates for the title of unconditioned good among those things we find in the perceptual world. Some things, in some aspects, for some periods of time, seem to qualify—for example, love. But love is not an unmixed good—indeed, that may be its secret attraction. Another candidate for intrinsic good, pleasure is, of course, notoriously unreliable. We know, for instance, that its goodness is not durable. Moreover, its constant repetition will pall. Nothing in our experience is unconditionally good—good always, from all aspects. So that which is completely and fully good in itself has to be an improvement over all those things in our world that count in their qualified way as good; it will be something outside our experience of the good things of our world. Plato is claiming that besides the goods of our experience, which are ambiguous and transitory, there must be a good that is unconditionally good. As he says in Book VI, apart from the appearances of good there is the real good—we might say the good no-matter-what, the always good. Like the Form of beauty in the *Symposium*, the Form of good does not come to be or pass away, does not grow or diminish; it is not good from one point of view and bad from another, good to one person and bad to another, good at one time and bad at another.

This understanding of the relation between the good itself and the good things of our perceptual experience is somewhat disconcerting. Just how disconcerting can be seen if we inspect one of its important implications. If the good itself is the source of goodness, the knowledge of the Form does not just allow us to discern better among images. The knowledge of the good itself not only shows philosophers which image is closer to the ideal and, thus, how better to imitate the Forms. It also shows that the good itself is more valuable than any image.[10] The good itself, as the source of goodness in the image, is necessarily more valuable than the image. In an analogous way, gold is necessarily more valuable than the paper currency. What would follow from this relation between source and image is that, if one has to choose between image and original, one would choose the original, that is, the good itself. One might hesitate to read into the central books of the *Republic* this understanding of the relation between the good itself and good things, with its implication about the relative value of the good itself and good things. Nevertheless, this very relative valuation is found in *Republic* VII, in the famous Cave passage. In this allegory, the philosopher, of course, ascends to the vision of the good itself. Rather than immediately returning to the cave—that is, the actual city—and the images of reality, the philosopher wants to contemplate the Forms themselves (519d). The philosopher does not want to rule at all; he must be made to do so. We must be careful not to make too much out of this passage. Plato's main interest is to show a contrast between those rulers who want to rule and those who do not. The latter, according to Plato, are the ones who should rule because their motivations are pure. Still, as the contrast shows, the philosopher understands that ultimately the true value of good things is found in the good itself. That he has this understanding is shown by the fact that, left to himself, the philosopher would naturally choose to contemplate the good itself rather than look at images of the good itself.

Incidentally, if the good itself were just the concept of goodness, something that helps us to understand the goodness of our perceptual world, the reluctance of the philosophers would be a foible instead of a real temptation. If the good itself were only a concept, then the philosopher would be one who just likes the world of theory, of concepts and their connections, instead of practical application. He would be like the mathematician or theoretical physicist; he would prefer the activity of theorizing to that of application. However, Socrates presents the philosopher not as one who loves the activity of theorizing over the activity of practice but as one who loves the object of his philosophy over the objects in the perceptual world because the former is real goodness and the latter image.

Plato shows us that the philosopher understands this feature of his situation. Returning to the cave, the philosopher's eyes are dim because of the darkness; but once his eyes have grown used to the darkness he will have an advantage (520c). The philosopher would be a better ruler because he would have a better insight into the day-to-day issues; he can see more clearly when justice is at issue. However, even at this juncture in the argument, the ability of the rulers is not just epistemological; it is not just the ability to discern well among images. It also implies that the philosopher knows what is truly valuable. Socrates contrasts the philosophical with the nonphilosophical rulers:

In this fashion the city will be governed by us and by you, as waking, not as in a dream, as now many cities are governed by those who fight shadows and raise factions against one another in order to rule, as though this were in reality a great good. (520c–d)

The contrast between the nonphilosophical and the philosophical ruler is clearly that the nonphilosophical rulers, lost in a world of shadows, take ruling to be a great good in reality whereas the philosophical ruler knows what the great good in reality is. The philosophical ruler, not mystified by shadows, does not mistake ruling for the good itself. Presumably, the nonphilosophical ruler is not aware that the images are images—thus the reference to the dreaming state, first mentioned in Book V, where the one who mistakes the image for the reality is said to be in a dreaming state. On the other hand, the philosophical ruler would be immune to that kind of mistake. He would understand the images in their proper relation to the good itself. Understanding the proper relation, the philosophical ruler understands their relative worth.

If this passage confirms the account of the causal role of the good itself, it also implies disaster for Plato's whole program in the ideal city. If the good itself is more valuable than any of its images, the philosopher has great motivation to remain with the good itself and to avoid its images. If remaining with the good itself means contemplating the Form, then the philosophers would prefer a life of contemplation. But if they remain in contemplation of the Form, they cannot exercise rule in the city. Then the whole project of the ideal city falls to the ground.

II

We have reached an odd point in both the *Republic* and in our interpretation of the *Republic*. We introduced the case of the reluctant philosopher in order to substantiate our account of the causal role of the Form of the good. The latter is the cause of goodness because it is itself good, indeed the epitome of goodness. The text corroborates the last part of this claim by saying that the philosopher would prefer to remain contemplating the Form of good. However, the account of the causal role of the Form of good was also supposed to illuminate the way that the philosophical rulers imitated the Form in their ruling in the city. The prospects for illumination are suddenly dimmed by what was supposed to corroborate. The Form of the good is so good it appears to make ruling unattractive. Instead of having a causal role in imitation, the Form of the good seems to militate against imitation. Thus its explanatory power seems to point in the opposite direction. So the disaster for Plato's account of the ideal city has a parallel in the disaster for our account of the causal role of the Form of the good in the philosophical rulers' imitation of the Form. Fortunately, the parallel turns out to be helpful.

Indeed, recognizing the disastrous consequence for his account of the ideal city, Plato immediately launches into an argument to counteract it. Although Plato's argument is ultimately disappointing, exploring it will prove important for our account of the causal role of the Form of the good in Plato's moral theory. By looking closely at this argument, we will be able to develop our account of the way in which the Form of the good is the ultimate cause of the philosophical ruler's activity of ruling. What we will find is that the argument has attracted the attention of several commentators, some of whom have attempted to supplement it with other arguments, drawn from other parts of the dialogues. As we shall see, one type of these supplementary arguments—which we will call the "expressive" or "creative" argument—will prove valuable in explaining the causal role of the Form of the good in imitation. In effect, we will offer a new version of the expressive or creative argument—one that incorporates imitation and the causal role of the Form of the good.

We can begin with Plato's curiously disappointing argument. Socrates says that in actual cities philosophers are justified in avoiding the tasks of ruling. Such cities do not educate nor nurture the philosophers so that the latter do not owe any duty to the city. In the ideal city, however, the city has educated and nurtured the philosophers; thus—the argument seems to go—they are obligated to undertake the task of ruling (520b–c). The conclusion is that the philosopher will assume rule as a result of the argument because the argument will be proposing just things to just people (520e). Thus, the argument assumes that the countervailing motivation of the philosopher is to do what is just. The motivation is not explained further, although it is supposed to overcome the contrary motivation to spend one's life contemplating the Forms.

This problem of the reluctant philosopher forms something of a crux in interpretations of the *Republic*. Some believe that it shows Plato's account of the ideal city to be incoherent.[11] Philosophers can be either happy or just, but not both—contrary to the central claim that the just person, and only the just person, is happy. Even among those commentators who wish to defend Plato against the charge that his account of the ideal city falls apart at this crucial point, there are many who find Socrates' argument unconvincing. They try to supplement it in various ways. Some offer what we can call a "prudential defense"; in some sense of the term, it is prudential for the philosopher to assume rule, even though it is more attractive, in some other sense, for the philosopher to remain contemplating the Form of goodness.[12] For example, Socrates means for the philosopher to have an expanded sense of her own welfare that includes the welfare of those for whom she assumes rule in the city. However, others argue that the philosopher is motivated to rule by a creative or expressive urge.[13] In these accounts, the philosopher has a need to create virtue or justice. Thus, not only is the philosopher moved to create justice in her own soul, but in those of others and in the city in general. Obviously, if this creative, expressive urge is not only a motivation, but the leading motivation, of the philosopher, then she would have an excellent reason to return from contemplating the Form of goodness to the tasks of establishing virtue in the city.

So, having arrived at this interpretative crux, we are, oddly enough, now in the position to take up the discussion of the Form of goodness and imitation in the central books of the *Republic*. In particular we want to see how the philosopher comes to see this creative or expressive role to be so central as to require her to give up contemplation of the good itself in order to create goodness in the city. What we will see is that the creative or expressive urge in the philosophical ruler is best explained by the causal role of the Form of the good. In this explanation, the Form of the good causes the philosophical ruler to express or create goodness both in the city and in the soul. To begin with, the expressive or creative urge of the philosopher finds adequate grounding in Book VI, where the notion of imitation is introduced for the first time. Indeed, the problematic passage in Book VII is tied, by implication, to this passage. In the problematic passage we are told that the philosopher is already a just person. Presumably the philosopher would already be just—and thus liable to do the just thing— because he has already established justice in his soul by imitating the Form of justice (500d). However, if we can make this assumption we can also offer another argument to show that the philosophical ruler has good reason to assume rule in the city. In essence, the argument says that the philosopher has a strong motivation to establish justice in the city because doing so is an imitation of the Form of justice. Such an argument would be an extension of *Republic* VI where Socrates says that the Form is a pattern for imitation both in the soul and in the city (500d ff.). Not only are Forms patterns for imitation, they are also motivation. Talking about the impact of the knowledge of the Forms of justice, temperance, and beauty on the philosopher's soul, Socrates says that the philosopher must imitate what he admires. The necessity for such imitation is stated in a particularly emphatic way. While this inspiration is directed toward the soul, there is no reason to believe that it is not also directed to the city.[14] In the next sentence, Socrates says that the philosopher will be equally as effective as a craftsman of the city—presumably not only because he has the same knowledge but also because he has the same motivation to imitate the Forms.

Thus, the philosopher would have some motivation for taking up the task of ruling in the city. He cannot help but imitate what he admires; he admires the Form of justice; so he cannot help but imitate the Form of justice in his own soul and in the city. Of course, such an argument is somewhat formal since we do not yet understand why his motivation for imitating what he admires is so strong in the philosopher. We would like to know more about the philosopher and his motivations. Indeed, what has happened since this account in Book VI is the introduction of the good itself. One would expect that the introduction of the Form of the good would give us some further insight into the philosopher's reasons for imitating the Forms. If anything, the notion of the good itself ought to make clearer the role of Forms as motivation for imitation. If the philosopher cannot help but imitate what he admires, certainly he can admire nothing so much as the Form of the good. However, in the *Republic* Plato does not give us an account of the way in which the Form of the good motivates imitation. Yet it ought to round out the notion of the Form of justice as a motivation for imitation. It would seem reasonable to suppose that the philosophical ruler is ultimately motivated to imitate the Form of justice by the Form of good. Since the Form of justice is an ideal type of goodness, the philosophical ruler wishes to replicate that justice because it is an ideal type of goodness. This reference to goodness as the source of motivation is seen in the creation account of the *Timaeus* (29e). The Demiurgos wishes the Cosmos he is about to create to be as good as possible; thus he chooses to imitate the best possible Form. Desiring the good for her own soul and for the city, the philosophical ruler will be moved to imitate the Form of justice because of its relation to the Form of good. The Form of justice is the paradigm of goodness for the soul, both as pattern and as motivation.

In this way the Form of goodness would complete the claim made in Book VI that the philosopher must imitate what he admires. Indeed, those commentators who exploit the notion of the expressive or creative urge of the philosophical rulers agree that the final motivation for establishing justice in the soul or in the city is that doing so instantiates goodness and that the final motivation for the philosopher is to instantiate goodness.[15] However, with the notable exception of Richard Kraut, these commentators do not pay much attention to the notion of imitation. Kraut maintains that Plato meant for the philosophical rulers not only to know the Forms but to love and imitate them as well—a position that corroborates the interpretation offered here.[16] In what follows we will embellish these accounts by developing the notion of imitation and by looking at a dimension of that notion to which these commentators, including Kraut, do not pay attention. We wish to look at the way in which the Form of goodness inspires imitation through its causal role. In effect, we are offering a new version of the expressive or creative account of the philosophical rulers.

The new version is based on the claim that the Form of goodness is the final cause of imitation. However, it is important to appreciate the sense in which, in this account, the good itself is the final cause for the philosophical ruler. In the following we will construct an account of what it means when we say that the Form of goodness is the final cause for imitation. We can begin by noting that what the philosopher wants is that her soul and her city be as good as possible. In this desire, she is motivated by self-interest, presumably; she wants the best for her soul and her city because they are hers. However, in our account, beyond this sort of self-interest there is another motivation. Since the philosophical ruler has no independent knowledge of what the best is, she must look to the good itself. The good itself is the best *tout court*. Thus, it shows her what the best is. It is an important part of our account that—because the good itself is the best—it also inspires her in a certain way. We might say that the good itself—because it is the epitome of goodness—deserves or requires instantiation or dissemination. The philosopher now desires not only to know goodness but to propagate goodness. Thus she not only wants to understand the good itself—the epitome of goodness—for herself but she wants herself and other things to participate in it, to have a share in the good itself. If the philosopher's motivation is to embody justice in the city and her soul, this motivation has a peculiar dependency on the good itself, then. The good itself seems to be the ultimate justification for the project of bringing justice into the city and soul.

The good itself as final cause of imitation has two aspects then. The two aspects correspond roughly to the two senses of final cause in Aristotle's *Metaphysics*, Book XII, chapter 7 (1072b1–5). The context is the explanation of the way that the unmoved mover is the cause of motion. Aristotle reflects on the notion of final cause and how it might apply to unchanging things like the unmoved mover. However, final cause seems to have the sense of something to be achieved; this sense of final cause is found in *Physics* II (194b30) where the final cause of walking is to be healthy. This sense is not appropriate to unchanging things like the unmoved mover because nothing about them can be achieved. As though he were trying to address this problem, Aristotle claims in chapter 7 that 'final cause' has two meanings: the good for something and the good as object of desire. The former sense is the one exemplified by Physics II; health is the final cause because it is the good for the one who walks—the good to be achieved. However, no unchanging object—including the unmoved mover—can be final cause in this sense because nothing about it can be achieved. Thus, the unmoved mover can be final cause only in the sense of object of desire, where the desire can only admire and not change the object. These two senses of final cause do not seem unrelated. That the object of desire would inspire one to do something else besides simply admiring the object is a natural enough motif. Thus the object of desire as final cause might inspire one to pursue what can be achieved as final cause. Indeed, in the traditional reading of this passage, the unmoved mover causes motion in the outer sphere because it is final cause in the sense of object of desire—the desire of the outer sphere. The unmoved mover is pure contemplation. Unable to engage in that activity, the outer sphere does the next best thing; it imitates the object of its desire in eternal circular motion.[17] In this reading the two senses of final cause are linked; the desire for the unmoved mover—final cause as object of desire—gives rise to eternal motion—final cause as the good for something, as what is to be achieved.

While the details of Aristotle's physics are not relevant to Plato metaphysics, the two senses of final cause can be adapted to explicate the role of the good itself as motivation for the philosophical rulers. In our account, the good itself is final cause in the sense that it is the object of admiration. Imitating the Form of justice is final cause in the sense of the good to be achieved. The link between these two aspects requires two assumptions. First, her admiration for the good itself is an inspiration for the philosopher; in it she sees the necessity to disseminate goodness. Second, the philosopher comes to admire the Form of justice in the same way because of its necessary relation to the good itself. Once the necessary relation between the good itself and the Form of justice is recognized, the philosopher seeks to imitate the Form of justice out of admiration for the good itself and its necessary dependency, the Form of justice.

In what follows we will explicate both aspects of final cause and the relation between the two. In the first aspect, the good itself is an object of admiration. Its being such an object is an implication of the naive theory of Forms. In the naive view, the good itself is not just an instrumental value. It is not, for example, a formula that shows us qualities that we know otherwise to be good. Nor is its chief function as an aid in finding or producing goodness in other things. While it is, in fact, useful for producing goodness, its proper goodness is not instrumental; it is good in itself, unconditionally good. The philosopher admires the good itself because it is unconditionally good. Of course, this aspect is the root of the problem of the reluctant philosopher. However, the account being offered here is that this admiration gives rise to, even expresses itself as, the desire to disseminate goodness. This desire arises because the good itself shows the necessity to propagate goodness. If one understands the good itself, one understands the necessity to disseminate goodness; and, thus, one desires to disseminate goodness. In this way admiration for the good itself overcomes the reluctance of the philosopher. All talk to the contrary is Platonic rhetoric to show that the philosopher is a worthy ruler because she does not want to rule—as indeed she does not, in the sense that would make her an unworthy ruler, even in our account. This admiration that gives rise to the desire to disseminate is already found in Book VI when Socrates, talking about the Forms, asks whether it is possible to admire something without imitating it. If one takes this feature of the naive view seriously, one can see its affects on the second aspect of the good itself as final cause. We have said that because the good itself is unconditionally good, it requires dissemination or propagation; however, it is not disseminated as such. Rather it is disseminated in its various "types" and the Form of justice is one of its types. Thus, imitating justice is a way of instantiating or disseminating goodness. Finally one imitates the just itself because, in its integral relation to the good itself, the just itself requires dissemination. In this account, the just itself, because of its relation to the good itself, is suitable for copying because it is good; it is not good because it is suitable for copying. Now we can see the reason that the Form of justice must be self-exemplifying. In this account, the Form of justice, because of its necessary relation to the good itself, exemplifies goodness. If the Form of justice were a universal, a formula, or a blueprint for justice, it is hard to see how it could exemplify goodness. A universal tells us about goodness; a formula helps us to identify goodness; a blueprint tells us how to construct goodness. None of these exemplifies goodness, except perhaps in some nonrelevant way by being a good universal, good formula, or good blueprint. Rather, in the naive view, if the Form of justice exemplifies goodness, it does so by exemplifying justice.

This sense of the Form of goodness as final cause for imitation offers a way of understanding the causal role of the Form in imitation. The philosophical ruler is the agent who makes the city to be good by making it to be just. However, if the city or the soul is good, it is good only by participation in the good itself; the good itself is thus directly causal. The philosophical ruler, then, makes the city or the soul to be good in a way that is consistent with the fact that each participates in the good itself. Given the doctrine of participation, this account of imitation is not surprising. If everything that is good is good only by participation in the good itself, it would follow that if justice in the soul or in the city is good, it is good only by participation in the good itself. In turn, if justice comes about in the soul or in the city by way of imitation—by the philosophical ruler imitating the Form of justice in its necessary relation to the Form of goodness—the imitation would be a conscious participation, so to speak, in the good itself. Thus, the philosophical ruler would produce something that she understands is good only because it participates in the good itself. The goodness of justice in the soul or in the city would be that kind of goodness dependent on the good itself, as its source. This relation between perceptual goodness and the good itself is also expressed by saying that the perceptual goodness is the appearance of the good itself. Put this way, the relation clearly implies the dependence of perceptual goodness on the good itself. It also implies that correctly understanding perceptual goodness entails understanding its dependence on the good itself. Thus, the philosophical ruler would produce something she understands as an appearance of the good itself, something whose ultimate value derives from the good itself.

So much follows from the causal role of the Form, understood as participation. However, seeing imitation in the light of this causal role suggests another claim, one about the philosopher's motive in imitating the Form. So far we have said that the product of imitation will participate in the Form of goodness. If participation implies that the product of imitation will have this kind of dependence on the Form, it also suggests that the activity of imitation has an analogous dependence on the Form of goodness. The one who imitates the Form of justice sees that goodness of the product of imitation comes from the Form of goodness; in turn, the one who imitates sees that the activity has that dependency as well. That the activity is so dependent means that the motivation for imitating the Form of justice is dependent on the Form of goodness. So to speak, the value of the product of imitation flows from the good itself; thus, the value to the imitator of the activity of imitation flows from the good itself. The good itself is the cause of the goodness of the activity of imitation for the imitator. We can explain this causal role by casting it in terms of final causality—by saying that the Form of goodness is the final cause of imitation. That the Form is the final cause implies that one imitates the Form of justice because of its integral relation to the Form of goodness and one understands that the latter must be disseminated; one wants to disseminate goodness out of admiration for the good itself. If one imitates the Form of justice because of this relation to the Form of goodness—because one believes that the Form of goodness must be disseminated—then the Form of goodness is the final cause of the goodness of the activity of imitation for the imitator.

However, we must be careful in the way in which we understand the second aspect of final cause. In this aspect, the final cause of imitation is that imitating the Form of justice brings the city and in the soul to participation in the good itself. In one way of looking at it, imitating the Form of justice in these ways is just the particular means the philosopher adopts for disseminating the good itself because it is the good itself. However, in another way of looking at it, disseminating goodness is good for whatever receives the goodness, for whatever is made good. The philosopher is motivated by this aspect as well; the philosopher also seeks to disseminate goodness because doing so is good for whatever receives the goodness. Seeking to embody justice in the city and the soul means making the city and soul good. After all, the good itself is the paradigm of goodness; each thing has whatever goodness it has by participating in the good itself. The philosopher understands this relationship and consciously participates in it when she imitates the Form of justice. Such imitations are themselves good and the philosopher is moved by the prospect of achieving that goodness.

Christine Korsgaard makes a important point that can be used to illuminate the second aspect of our account. Although she is interpreting Kant, she has something relevant to say about the relation between unconditioned and conditioned goods. While conditioned goods depend on the unconditioned for their goodness, the former are not in themselves valueless; nor are they merely means to the unconditioned good. Since she is explicating Kant, Korsgaard holds that the unconditioned good is the good will; from it flows all the goodness in the world.[18] Thus, all other goods are conditioned on the good will. The other goods, however, are not therefore in themselves valueless nor merely means to the good will. Her reason for this position is that, once the conditioned goods are properly related to the unconditioned good, they are objective goods.[19] Their being objective goods seems to mean that, their condition for being good being met, they have some objective claim to be regarded as good. In some way, their goodness belongs to them and not just to the unconditioned good upon which their goodness depends. For this reason, conditioned good, whose condition for goodness has been met, are valuable in themselves.[20] For instance, once happiness—a conditioned good—is related to a good will, it becomes an objective good. Its condition for being good being met, happiness then has an objective claim to be regarded as good. In turn, it is then desirable in itself—not as a means to the good will, but as something properly related to the good will. So to speak, happiness "packaged" with a good will is something valuable in itself.

Although the good itself is an entirely different kind of thing from the good will, something analogous can be said about its relation to the other good things dependent on it—for instance, justice in the soul. Justice in the soul is a conditioned good in the sense that it depends on the good itself for its goodness. Without the good itself, justice in the soul would not be good; it would not even exist—at least in the sense in which Plato understands justice in the soul. However, once its relation to the Form of goodness is established, we can say that it is an objective good; its condition for goodness being met, it has an objective claim to be regarded as good. Since its condition for being good is met, justice in the soul is also valuable in itself. Although it is an appearance of the Form of goodness, it is not simply a means to the Form of goodness. Justice in the soul and in the city, seen in relation to the Form of goodness, are valuable in themselves. They have value in themselves as images of justice and goodness in a world in which there can never be unmixed justice and goodness. So we must not take the images produced by imitation to be mere images. They are true images whose relation to the Forms confers on them an inherent or objective value. To realize the relation does not rob the image of its value; rather it is to understand the proper (in both senses of 'proper') value of the image. The philosopher is moved to imitate the Form of justice because doing so is a way of getting goodness into circulation, so to speak. The images are like paper currency in a world in which gold cannot circulate. In this sense, justice in souls and justice in the city are tokens of the Forms. The philosopher wishes to produce these tokens because they have value for the project of leading one's life or for the project of ruling the city. This value comes from the Form; but it is not confined to the Form, so to speak. It has value for the soul and the city because it comes from the Form. In this way of interpreting the notion of Form as final cause, the Form is good in itself and good in its consequences, if we take the consequences to be, among other things, the images produced by philosophers and others. In fact, the Form is good in its consequences because it is good in itself.

This way of seeing the relation between image and original addresses the issue of egoism in Plato's thought—that is, the claim that virtue is justifiable in terms of one's own welfare always. Thus, Socrates goes to great lengths to show that these arrangements in the soul are productive or constitutive of happiness (*Rep.* 580b). Happiness is the ultimate motivation for pursuing a way of life.[21] Our account of imitation must be consistent with this basic tenet of Platonic thought. The answer is that, in this interpretation, happiness is not just a certain arrangement in the soul. It is a certain arrangement based upon imitating the Forms of justice and goodness. Moreover, the value of imitation comes from the value of what is imitated. Even though happiness is valuable in itself, it is valuable in itself because it is an imitation of the Forms. Thus, the ultimate justification the philosophical ruler can give for any law or decision, any institution or arrangement in ruling the city, or for establishing justice in the soul—for arranging the parts of the soul so that reason rules—is that such arrangements imitate the good itself. All of these perceptual goods are tokens or appearances of the good itself; that status is the reason that the philosopher wants them. Moreover, as tokens of the good itself, they are good for the soul and for the city.[22] The notion of perceptual goods as tokens of the good itself fits with Plato's distinction between good and bad images. A bad image is one that substitutes for the reality; it is the cause of, or the occasion for, deception. The one who is deceived takes the image of good to be the good, for example. The opposite attitude is to understand that the image is an image, to understand the relation between image and reality. However, to understand this relation is not to devalue the image. The deceptive image is devalued, of course, if one overcomes the deception. Its claim to be valuable collapses when it is seen in relation to reality. But the true image—the one whose relation to reality is clear—is not devalued through realizing this relation. Its value does not collapse into transparency before the good itself. If the true image had no inherent value, the philosophical ruler's ability to distinguish among images would be of no earthly use and the philosopher's ability to distinguish which images were faithful to the original would have no political significance. Still, the philosopher can only realize this usefulness by appreciating the relation between image and Form.

We are now able to return to the problem of the reluctant philosopher. If we accept that the motivation for imitating the Form of justice is found in its relation to the good itself, we can see a new argument for the philosopher to take up the job of ruling in the city. Imitating the Form of justice is a way of instantiating the Form of goodness; it is a way of bringing to the world of our everyday experience an image of intrinsic goodness. This image has value for undertakings within our everyday experience, of course. However, one imitates the just itself because of its relation to the good itself. Imitating the just itself is a way of instantiating the good itself and one understands the necessity for instantiating the good itself. This understanding means that the philosopher is motivated by the desire to disseminate goodness because of her admiration for the good itself. We could also say that one imitates the just itself because of what it is in itself, assuming its necessary relation to the good itself. If the good itself—and its dependencies such as the just itself—require instantiation, replication, dissemination, this requirement becomes the philosophical rulers' ultimate motivation. Imagine the young philosophers contemplating the just itself and the good itself without wishing to instantiate them in their own souls. Such an attitude seems impossible; one must imitate what one admires. However, in instantiating goodness in their own souls, the philosophers' motivation is not only that this goodness is their goodness. Their final motivation for instantiating goodness in their own souls is that it is an instantiation of the good itself; they understand the necessity for instantiating the good itself. Their admiration for the good itself moves them to disseminate goodness. Such a motivation means, in turn, that the philosophers will also seek to instantiate the just itself in the city. They seek to instantiate justice in the city because of its relation to the good itself. It is their consistent motivation not only in imitation but for imitation.

At the end of Book VII, in recapitulating the education of the guardians, Socrates attributes this motivation to the philosophical rulers. In this passage, the motivation of the philosophers is clearly different from the motivation Socrates gives at 520b–c where the philosophers should rule as a way of repaying obligations to the city; here philosophers are inspired by their vision of the good itself. Moreover, the good itself is more than the goal of dialectical investigation. Socrates says that it will be required that the philosophers raise the vision of the soul to fix its gaze on the source of all light, thus seeing the good itself, then using it as a paradigm (*paradeigma*) in bringing order into the city, its citizens and themselves (*Rep.* 540a). Thus, becoming true philosophers they will look down on the honors that now are considered such; rather, having esteemed the right (*to orthon*) to be of the greatest importance, and the honors that come from it, and the just (*to dikaion*) to be the best and the most necessary thing, serving that [the right and the just] and making it to increase, they would bring order into their own city. (540d–e)

It seems natural to suppose that "the right" and "the just" are ways of referring to the general existence of justice in our perceptual world—justice without reference to any particular instance. The philosophers esteem the existence of justice as such to be of supreme importance. We must understand this esteem in the light of the fact that the philosophers, because of their vision of the good itself, treat it as a paradigm for ordering the city; then they come to esteem the embodiment of justice as such. In turn, they serve this embodiment and increase it. As a way of serving and increasing justice as such, they pursue justice in this instance by bringing order into the city. This passage reflects our account of the good itself as final cause; in the first place, the philosophers esteem the right and just as of greatest importance, as the best and most necessary, because of their knowledge of the good itself. According to our account, knowledge of the good itself includes its necessary relation to the Form of justice; it is this knowledge of the relation between the good itself and the Form of justice that leads the philosophers to conclude that the right and the just are of supreme importance in our world. They transfer, so to speak, the value relations among the Forms to the perceptual world. In the second place, this good-itself-inspired knowledge of the importance of justice leads them to conceive of propagating justice as the final cause of their actions; they serve and increase the right and the just. In our account, the good itself, and its necessary dependencies such as the just itself, require dissemination. The Form of justice, as a logical dependency of the good itself, deserves propagation or dissemination. Again, transferring to the perceptual world, the philosophers come to conceive of serving and increasing the right and the just in a universal sense as the final cause of their actions; in turn, this conception takes the form of bringing order into the city. The passage reflects the central claims of our account, that the motivation for bringing order into the city comes from the desire to imitate justice. Imitating justice is necessary because it is a way of disseminating goodness. The necessity for disseminating goodness, and thus imitating justice, is inspired by knowledge of the good itself.

III

Like all of the other readings of the expressive or creative role of the philosophical rulers, our interpretation is a construct placed upon the *Republic* in order to understand the ultimate motivation of the rulers. Its plausibility depends on how well it illuminates that problem. In addressing that problem we have attributed to Plato a rather strong position. We have claimed that the ultimate motivation of the philosophical ruler is to disseminate goodness, that the Form requires dissemination. Ultimately, value for the philosophical ruler is found in producing images of the Form of justice because of its relation to the good itself. We have said that this strong position follows from what Plato says about imitation and participation. Whether Plato drew this implication in its full strength in the *Republic* is not altogether clear, although the implication does develop that strain of interpretation which holds that the philosophical ruler is motivated to express or create virtue. However, the best place to see what Plato thinks about the expressive or creative facet of the philosopher is in the *Symposium*. It is in the latter dialogue that we find the most complete account of the way in which one creates virtue in one's own or in another's soul. Socrates' famous speech, in fact, explores the intricate relation between virtue and the Form of beauty. Recent commentators have compared this motif with the project of the *Republic*; in ways not always clear, the two dialogues echo one another on these vital themes.[23] So we will turn to the *Symposium* to see what it has to say about the motivation for creating virtue. We want to see how far it offers backing for what we have called the "strong position."

The *Symposium* begins this account of acquiring virtue with Socrates' speech to the assembled celebrants. In fact, in an intriguing and dramatic move, Socrates quotes his teacher in these matters of love, Diotima, the Mantinean seeress. She began by saying that all love—even earthly love—is always love of something beautiful (204b). Leading her disciple, Socrates, through the steps of elementary learning about love, next, she asks Socrates what it is that the lover loves—presumably, what is his object in loving the beautiful (*ho erōn tōn kalōn ti erai* [204d5–6]). Socrates cannot answer, so Diotima changes the object of love from the beautiful to the good; she asks then, What does the lover desire in loving the good?[24] Socrates answers promptly that the lover desires that the good belong to him (204d). There follows Diotima's argument to the effect that all love the good (*hōs ouden ge allo estin ou erōsin anthropoi ē tou agathou* [205e7–n 206a1]). Finally, she says that they desire it not just to be theirs but to be theirs always. She sums up: love has as its aim that the good be one's always (*ho erōs tou to agathon autōi einai aei* [206a11–12]).

Now, however, her account takes an unexpected turn. she asks about the method that *erōs* pursues in its seeking to have the good always. At this point, without announcement, the beautiful makes its appearance again as the object of *erōs*.[25] There follows a passage remarkable—almost breathtaking—for its mixture of sexual and birthing images. The lover is pregnant with virtue in his soul; but this pregnancy is also an erotic tension that can only be relieved by spiritual discourse with a beautiful youth. This parturition, which is also a consummation, is completed in creating the beauty of virtue in the soul of the beloved (206c–d). After this revelation, Diotima changes one of the conclusions previously agreed to.

> For love is not [love] of the beautiful, as you thought, Socrates. . . . It is [love] of the generation and bringing forth in the beautiful (*tēs gennēseōs kai tou tokou en tōi kalōi*). (206e)

The strange mixture of sexual and birthing introduces the extremely important, and mysterious, notion of bringing forth in the beautiful. Diotima seems to be shifting the focus of *erōs*; she is attempting to show Socrates that it has a more fundamental goal than immediate pleasure. The point of *erōs* is not possession, much less consummation, but, rather its point is bringing forth in the beautiful. Thus, after having related that a person conceives and brings forth in the presence of beauty, Diotima turns to the distinction between physical and spiritual lovers (*Sym.* 206c–e). When the person is of the physical type, he marries a woman and brings forth children. When he is of the spiritual type he falls in love with a youth—especially if the youth has spiritual beauty—and brings forth, by speech and beautiful conversation, virtue in the soul of the beloved and ultimately in his own soul (*Sym.* 209b–c).

The thrust of the passage is significant for the whole project of the *Gorgias* and *Republic*. In this dialogue Plato is addressing the role of *erōs* positively. Instead of a force that must be disciplined and controlled because it too easily seeks only pleasure, Plato portrays *erōs* now as having a more useful role. Diotima is claiming that *erōs* does not seek only the pleasures of replenishment; in fact, it seeks the good to be one's forever. Putting the matter in this more general way allows Diotima to argue that *erōs* seeks a good that is much broader in content than the good of immediate pleasure. If *erōs* seeks to have the good, it might well seek to have something besides immediate pleasure. Indeed, as we have just seen, *erōs* becomes the chief driving force for acquiring virtue both in the city and in the soul. Describing it as "seeking to have the good always" lays the groundwork for this sort of role for *erōs*; once virtue is seen as constituting the good forever, *erōs* will naturally seek virtue. Obviously Plato is again dealing with the relation between desire and the good; but instead of making reason the ruler that establishes virtue in the soul by forcing or guiding desire, Plato has made desire the chief underlying force in the activity. This new role for *erōs* is astonishing in many ways. However, the transformation of *erōs* into the chief force for acquiring virtue depends on Diotima's further claim that *erōs* seeks really to bring forth in the beautiful. It is not a radical departure to claim that *erōs* really desires the good to be one's forever. Even Callicles would agree; defining pleasure as the good, he would say that *erōs* simply desires to have pleasure forever. However, saying that *erōs* seeks to bring forth in the beautiful is a radical departure because it would imply that *erōs* simply cannot have pleasure as its only goal. At first blush, moreover, the change in the function of desire seems gratuitous. It sounds more hopeful than realistic to say that *erōs* seeks to bring forth the beautiful rather than to possess the beautiful. After all, not everyone who has married, and even begotten children, would say that generation was the goal of their desire. And the previous speeches of the *Symposium* show that some lovers seek only sexual gratification. As though mindful of this lack of plausibility in the shift of the goal of *erōs*, Diotima launches into a fairly lengthy argument that seems designed to back up this shift; in this argument she explains the purpose of this love of generation.

She gives an argument to show that seeking to generate and bring forth is a way of achieving immortality. In the previous passage, they had agreed that the lover desires the good to be his always; so she concludes that the lover desires immortality (206e). The reasoning may be specious; however, the conclusion in itself holds some interest for anyone who is persuaded—or even intrigued—by the Calliclean hero of the appetites. For Callicles, *erōs* has as its aim possession and consummation as a means to pleasure. Diotima says that the point of *erōs* is begetting in the beautiful as a means to immortality. She doubtless would see Calliclean erotic behavior as a frantic attempt to attain immortality— an insight not unfamiliar to readers of John Updike. Thus, *erōs* will not be stilled until it reaches its goal, to bring forth something that can be seen as achieving immortality.

Of course, Diotima says that humans cannot truly become immortal. Only the gods are immortal. The most that humans can do is leave after them offspring or works. She seems to say that these satisfy the desire for immortality. Diotima's claim here is puzzling in view of Plato's view of immortality in other dialogues, for example, the *Phaedo* and the *Phaedrus*, in which he says that the soul is immortal. This difference between Diotima's speech and other Platonic writing has led some to hold that the speech does not represent Plato's thinking on this, or any other, topic.[26] A. W. Price offers one way to reconcile Diotima's views about immortality with other Platonic writing. Price makes a distinction between the soul, which is immortal, and the life led by the soul, which is mortal. Thus, the soul is like a bare particular, which might lead any number of lives, whereas an individual identifies herself with the life that the soul leads during a particular lifetime.[27] Thus, Diotima is not denying the immortality of the bare soul but only the immortality of the led life; so, if Plato, in the other dialogues, is talking about the immortality of the bare soul, Diotima is not denying that immortality. Thus, her speech does not contradict Platonic teaching. Such a position has, at least, one very attractive feature. It offers some plausibility to Diotima's claim that people would accept the substitute immortality of children and accomplishments. We are expected to believe, according to Diotima, that human beings, convinced of their own mortality, would accept substitutes for individual immortality—that is, children or accomplishments in public and political life. If children and accomplishments extended or replicated features of one's life, one might settle for such substitute immorality. A child would perpetuate, in its own life, some of the features of its parent's life; a treatise or a work of art would likewise perpetuate some feature of one's intellectual life.[28] Thus, even if one's bare soul were itself immortal, one might be more interested in perpetuating features of one's life, which otherwise are destined to perish when one dies.

However, even if we accept this rationale for substitute immortality, the force of Diotima's argument is still obscure at this point. Even if humans can be seen as satisfied with substitute immortality, the latter notion is problematic in its turn. It is hardly obvious that children and accomplishments achieve even substitute immortality. While it may be true that a child or a work will outlast one's own life span, such an object hardly confers immortality. Children, at most, confer a place in the memories of the next several generations. Even if parents do not seek the immortality conferred by memory, but only the immortality of having offspring who replicate one's physical or psychological characteristics, having children does not even guarantee the latter kind of immortality; one's physical progeny can easily peter out in several generations. In the case of accomplishments, the results are somewhat more durable. Constitutions and buildings can last centuries; the latter are usually more durable than the former—lasting sometimes millennia. Poetry seems to be the most durable, as the works of Homer and Hesiod attest; in turn, such heroic deeds as are recounted in Homer and Hesiod have their own immortality—but only because of the immortality of the poet. Finally, however, the immortality of the poets is not guaranteed; it is always possible that all the manuscripts of the *Iliad* and every memory trace will disappear.

Even if we put that possibility aside, we should note that the immortality desired by a poet can have two forms. The poet might desire to be immortal in the sense that she desires to have her name always associated with her work and her work to last forever. In another way, she might only wish for immortality in the sense that she wishes to have her poem read and recited as long as there are human beings, even if no one remembers her name. If we suppose the latter kind of desire, we can suppose a poet wishing to write for the ages; the object of her labor would be to write a poem that would be read, recited, and anthologized as long as there are humans to read, recite, and publish. However, it is hard to see how even such a modest desire could be satisfied. At the most, she could realize the satisfaction of having written a poem that received wide acclaim during her lifetime; from this acclaim she might hope that the poem would be read in the next generation and thereafter. But surely, any poet must realize the cruelty of public opinion, the ways in which some poems come to be ignored and finally lost to memory. At this point it is hard to take Diotima's argument literally, in spite of the amount of time she uses to develop it. If we suppose that there is a specific desire for immortality—even the attenuated desire for immortality that is satisfied by the creation of objects that last forever—it would be reasonable to suppose that such a desire would be satisfied only by the creation of an object one knew would last forever in the esteem of humanity. Otherwise, the desire would be doomed to frustration. In fact, we must wait for the next segment of her instruction in *erōs* before we can see the answers to this problem.

However, we should not leave this passage without making clear Plato's achievement in introducing the notion of bringing forth in the beautiful. In explicating the notion, David Halperin makes a useful distinction between the object of *erōs* and the aim of *erōs*. Its object is the beautiful (*to kalon*) and its aim is what *erōs* wants from its object—that is, good (*to agathon*). "But there is a difference between desiring something for the sake of a good and desiring it because it is good."[29] In fact, Halperin maintains that Plato distinguishes these two ways of desiring. "Plato differentiates these two aspects of erotic desire by distinguishing the lover's *boulēsis* from his *erōs* proper (*Symp.* 204d–205a)—by distinguishing, that is, what the lover wants (that is, his aim) from what he is attracted to or desires (that is, his object)."[30] The relation between the two is that the object inspires the lover to achieve the aim.

> What Diotima is trying to elucidate, then, is not only our motive for wanting the things that we value but also for valuing the things that we do. Beauty, she concludes, contributes an essential element to the way or activity (*tropos, praxis*) by which we set about to possess the good forever (206b), for it causes us to cherish . . . whatever enables us to give birth to *aretē*; it thereby motivates us to possess the good and so conduces to our *eudaimonia*.[31]

Halperin's distinction between desiring something because it is good and desiring something for the sake of a good seems to contain the two senses of final cause. The thing desired because it is good is final cause in the sense of object of desire and the good for the sake of which a thing is desired is final cause in the sense of what is to be achieved—the latter, according to Diotima, being immortality. However, the relation between these two senses of final cause is more complicated now. We cannot say that the desire for beauty gives rise to the lover's striving for immortality in the way in which the love for the unmoved mover gives rise to the outer sphere's undertaking perpetual circular motion. In Diotima's account the desire for immortality seems to be fundamental; still the desire for beauty and the desire for immortality become related when the latter gives rise to the desire to bring forth in the beautiful. The desire for immortality becomes the desire for bringing forth in the beautiful because of a kind of frustration. Unable to have immortality, properly speaking, the desire is satisfied by substitute immortality. It is as though the desire for beauty—were it capable of it—might try to possess the beautiful forever in its own right and, thus, come to enjoy immortality; in this way it is a desire for beauty and immortality. Unable to possess the beautiful forever, the desire, so to speak, bifurcates into the desire for beauty and the desire for immortality. By this transformation, Diotima in effect makes the object of *erōs* and the aim of *erōs* distinct. The beautiful becomes the object and substitute immortality the aim. In this way, begetting in the beautiful combines both substitute immortality—the good to be achieved—and beauty—the object of desire.

Diotima has saved the fullest account of immortality for the initiate into the highest mysteries of *erōs*. Now she tells Socrates that earthly love is really striving for contemplative union with the most authentic beauty, the Form of the beautiful. One may realize this striving through initiation in the mysteries of love. This initiation is the famous ascent passage of the *Symposium*.[32] First the lover, rightly initiated, learns to love more and more abstract things, moving from love of one beautiful body to many beautiful bodies to beautiful souls, thence to beautiful customs and laws, and thence to the beauty of knowledge. The penultimate step is a summary view of what Diotima calls the "sea of beauty." In this upward movement, the lover has been discovering more and more abstract beauty in preparation for a final vision of beauty.

> The one who has been taught up to this point in the affairs of love (*ta erōtika*), viewing the beautiful objects in right order, and now coming to the goal of the affairs of love, suddenly has revealed something amazing, beautiful in its nature, that thing,

> O Socrates, on account of which all previous labors have been suffered. (210e)

This beauty is the Form of beauty. It does not come to be nor pass away; nor does it suffer any of the other vicissitudes of the beauty that is seen with the eyes (*Sym.* 211a). Perhaps most remarkable of all, it is not a quality found in another substance. Nothing but undiluted, pure beauty, it is not even in anything else—not in face nor hands nor knowledge. It is hard to decide whether what makes this latter claim so remarkable is the metaphysical implication that there is a substanceless quality or the moral and psychological implication that supreme love has an object that is not personal in any way.

The effects of contemplating this unearthly beauty seem to be automatic and profound. At this point the soul experiences the most authentic genesis of virtue, quickened by the most authentic beauty. Diotima says

> Do you think contemptible . . . the life of the one who so gazes, looking upon that thing—by that means which he ought to use—and being with it? Or rather do you suppose . . . that there belongs to that one alone, who sees by the means by which he ought to see the beautiful, to bring forth (*tiktein*) not mere images (*eidōla*) of virtue, since he is not pursuing a mere image, but true virtue, because he is pursuing the truth? When he has brought forth and nurtured true virtue he will be beloved of the gods, and if any human is immortal this one is. (212a)

The talk of bringing forth (*tiktein*) true virtue is a signal that we are to import into this passage the previous discourse about bringing forth in the beautiful. In the earlier passage the beautiful was found in the beloved. Presumably, then the virtue brought forth would have been a mere image because it was inspired by an image of beauty—the image of beauty found in the beloved—not by the reality, the Form. In gazing upon the Form of beauty, the lover now brings forth true virtue. While it is not clear what Diotima is trying to indicate with this distinction between the mere images of virtue and true virtue, she is basing it on a distinction between the inspiration in the two cases. Diotima says that the nonphilosophical lover pursues an image; the nonphilosophical lover is inspired by a beautiful youth, who is an image of beauty (cf. *Phaedrus* 251a). An image is not the beautiful itself and is necessarily limited because there are ways in which it is not beautiful. One might expect the beauty produced under such a limited inspiration to be itself an image of beauty—the mere image (*eidōla*) of virtue, as Diotima says in her speech. The philosophical lover, however, is inspired by the beautiful itself; thus he would produce true virtue. The distinction between the inspiration of the philosophical lover and that of the nonphilosophical lover is reminiscent of the distinction in *Republic* X between the carpenter, who sees the Form of bed, and the painter, who sees only the image of the Form (597d–e). Thus, the difference between the image and true virtue is like the difference between the bed produced by the painter—thrice removed from reality—and the bed produced by the carpenter—twice removed from reality.

Moreover, the notion of true virtue, which is left unexplained, contains an answer to the problem of immortality. At least, Diotima ends the encomium to the lover of beauty with the promise of immortality. We might suppose that the true lover of beauty will bring forth virtue that will, in some way, partake of the eternality of the Form. Enlivened by beauty itself, this immortality seems to be a more authentic immortality than that conferred by children and by the works of poetry and philosophy inspired by one's beloved. We want to know why it is a more authentic immortality. While Diotima has told Socrates that the lover brings forth in the beautiful because he wants to be immortal, we should note the way in which these tokens of immortality also embody beauty.[33] Throughout these passages, bringing forth in the beautiful is said to produce something that is beautiful. At 210a8, on the ladder of *erōs*, the one who loves one body brings forth beautiful (*kalous*) speech—perhaps love poetry. When the lover has ascended to the sea of beauty, by his contemplation of it, he brings forth beautiful (*kalous*) philosophical treatises. At 209c6–7 the spiritual lovers are said to bring forth "children (that is, virtue) which are more beautiful and immortal (*kallionōn kai athanatōterōn*)" than those of physical lovers. From these examples we can conclude that bringing forth in the beautiful entails both being inspired by the beautiful and embodying the beautiful.

What this presence of beauty at these stages of the ascent suggests is that beauty has an integral role to play in the attempt to achieve immortality. Achieving immortality means transcending the limits of one's own life. According to Price, one way to transcend the temporal limits of one's life is to pass on one's own characteristics to another. Still, there are two approaches to such a project. One can pass on a characteristic because it is one's own or because it is a valuable characteristic to pass on. Similarly, one can pass on a memento whose only value is that it is one's own—a lock of hair, for example—or a memento that has some inherent value—a collection of books, for example. If we take seriously the way in which the results of bringing forth in the beautiful are themselves beautiful, then we can see that it is the latter kind of passing on that Diotima intends. The lover, inspired by his beloved's beauty, gives something valuable to the beloved, something beautiful in return. In this way the lover transcends the temporal limits of his life. His life is extended beyond his death because he passes on something of his own to his beloved. However, he transcends another kind of limit in his life. The beauty that he passes on is able to serve different and wider purposes than his own particular purposes.[34] This beauty transcends the peculiar limitations imposed by a particular life. The lover, for instance, passes on virtue to his beloved because it is valuable in itself, apart from the details of his own life. Thus, he transcends another limit and achieves another type of immortality.

We can, then, amend Price's account of substitute immortality. At first we said that one achieves immortality by perpetuating certain features of one's own life in children or in other kinds of accomplishments. However, once we see the role of beauty in immortality, we see a deeper motivation at work. One wishes to create something beautiful that will perpetuate one's own life by outlasting it. The beauty is a feature of one's own life in the creation of it but will outlast one's creation of it. First, an important part of the motivation for reproducing these features is their beauty. Bringing forth in beauty means bringing forth because of beauty, motivated by beauty to produce beauty. Second, it is in this way that the lover achieves a kind of immortality. Bringing forth in beauty takes on a new dimension of meaning that relates to the issue of immortality. In fact, such immortality can be found at all levels of Diotima's account. In the case of the lover, seeking immortality takes the form of the lover's promoting virtue in the beloved's soul. The virtue is immortal to the extent that, in begetting and bringing it forth, the lover is not simply producing something valuable for himself but something valuable to his beloved. Moreover, according to our interpretation, he is able to transcend the limits of his life because of the beauty of what he is creating. He is not replicating his own virtue just because it is his virtue; he is replicating virtue because it is beautiful—because it is an independent excellence. It is by conceiving of it as something beautiful that he wants to transfer it to the beloved; therefore, it does not die with the lover but lives with the beloved.[35] When the lovers promote virtue in the society, their virtue child is immortal because it does not serve only their particular goals but the good of the city. Moreover, they wish to bring forth the virtue child not just because it is their virtue child but because of its inherent beauty. Thus, it lives on in the city; these tokens might well be immortal in the memories of humankind just because they capture beauty in this selfless way.

If the role of beauty is thus integral to the achieving of immortality at this level of the scale of beauty, then it has an analogous role at the higher level. Beauty sheds light on the difference between the immortality of the image of virtue and that of true virtue—that is, between the immortality achieved by the nonphilosophical lovers and the immortality achieved by the one who sees the Form. Diotima makes a strong—but not very clear—distinction between the substitute immortality of those who do not know the Form of beauty and the lover who does come to know the Form. The immortality of the latter seems to be of a different sort—either true immortality or the best kind of substitute immortality. Relying on the role of beauty in achieving immortality, we can see the difference: As we have argued, the beauty achieved by the lovers who do not know the Form of beauty would be only images of beauty inspired by images of beauty. The beauty achieved by the lover of the Form, however, would be inspired by the beautiful itself. The latter image might well have more durability than the former. In the former case, the vision of beauty is clouded, so the image produced will be less sure. Inspired by a partial view of beauty, the image is necessarily limited. One might expect the mere image of virtue—for example, virtue in the soul of the beloved—to falter occasionally; the beloved may sometimes fail to act virtuously. As well, the image is limited to context. While the virtue of the beloved is an image of beauty that is independent of the aims of the lover, it is not independent of the beloved in whom it is embodied. His virtue is confined to the context of his life and will perish with him. Nor is it clear that the beloved can overcome his limitations enough to pass virtue onto another. And while the virtue of the city is independent of the aims of its makers, still it is inspired by an image of beauty. Thus, it too might well falter from time to time; it also is circumscribed by the context of the city and its continuity too is in doubt. By contrast, if any image would escape this fate it ought to be the image of the beautiful itself.

The inspiration of the lover who knows the Form is not limited in these ways. First of all, unlike the beautiful youth, the Form of beauty does not change; its inspiration is constant. The philosophical lover's vision of beauty is surer therefore; thus his activity of bringing forth in the beautiful is constant and sure. The virtue he brings forth in the souls of others, or in the city, would not falter because it would be based on the reality of the Form. Such virtue would partake in the changelessness of the Form and would be a token of immortality. Another dimension of this more authentic immortality also depends on the knowledge possessed by the lover of the Form of beauty. If the true lover knows the Form of beauty then he can teach it to others. Thus, the lover would perpetuate his own virtue by his ability to show others the same vision of beauty, which will, in turn, engender true virtue in others. Inspired by the vision of the Form, this virtue is not limited by the life of the lover or even of the beloved. It is a virtue based on the universal vision of the Form of beauty; in theory, at least, it can be replicated in each succeeding generation.[36] And the city that is founded on this knowledge in its guardians has the best promise for lasting stability.

However, there is another aspect to the inspiration that comes from the Form of beauty. As we have seen, there is a sense in which beauty is the final cause of bringing forth in the beautiful. It answers the question as to why one brings forth—that is, one brings forth in beauty because of beauty. Beauty is final cause in the sense of object of desire; it is the lover's inspiration. The nonphilosophical lover is inspired by a particular beauty; he brings forth in a particular beauty—because of a particular beauty. That particular beauty is the final cause of his actions because he does what he does in order to bring forth in that beauty. By contrast, the philosophical lover is inspired by the beautiful itself; then his purpose will be different. We can put this difference by saying that the philosophical lover's final cause—in the sense of object of desire—for bringing forth in the beautiful is the beautiful itself. Bringing forth in the beautiful itself means propagating beauty under the inspiration of the beautiful itself—bringing forth beauty because of love for the beautiful itself, motivated by the beautiful itself to produce beauty. Of course, the final cause in the sense of what is to be achieved is immortality—or substitute immortality. The two senses of final cause are related in that love for the beautiful itself inspires the achievement of a more durable substitute immortality. The beautiful itself—not the beauty of the beloved—is the value the lover is trying to propagate. It is a stronger inspiration that evokes a purer motivation. The latter is the key to a more durable substitute immortality. Love of the beautiful itself is a motivation that assures a substitute immortality that comes closer to real immortality. Once he conceives of the beautiful itself as object of desire, his desire for immortality can reach another level. At the level at which he produces beauty because of the beautiful itself, the lover's inspiration is not limited to particular contexts. The beauty produced at this level is a surer kind of substitute immortality because the lover, while serving, also transcends his own and others' mortality—their individual desires, aims, and goals—to serve a value greater than anyone could conceive or create on his own. He may have seen this value dimly in the beloved but could not fully appreciate it until he saw the Form. Indeed, his work is more authentically immortal not just because it is destined to outlast others' but because it serves a good that, to the philosopher, is immortal—the beautiful itself. We can illustrate this point by thinking of someone who spends her life promoting a cause whose continued existence she recognizes is contingent. She is aware that this value she is trying to propagate may disappear altogether in several generations. Contrast her with someone else who spends her life promoting a cause whose continued existence she knows to be necessary. Since her cause is immortal her work has a kind of immortality. In her own mind, she is immortal not so much because of what she achieves but because of what she serves. The latter person is like Plato's lover of the beautiful itself, who through this kind of love achieves a substitute immortality that is closer to true immortality. Thus, when the Form of beauty becomes the focus of *erōs*, we are better able to understand Diotima's claim that the lover of the Form has a more authentic kind of immortality. When the focus of *erōs* is the Form of beauty—and not, for example, the beauty of the beloved—the lover fashions virtue on, and because of, the highest ideal.

Perhaps we can express the relation between the lover and the Form by saying that the real issue becomes one of appropriation. Fundamentally *erōs* is an urge to appropriate its object—to have the good always. Consummation and possession are ways of appropriating the object of one's love; they are, of course, destructive. Thus, consummation and possession are not the way to appropriate the Form of the beautiful.[37] On the other hand, while gazing passively on the beautiful itself is not destructive, neither is it a way of appropriating it. In passive contemplation the beautiful itself remains external to the lover because the lover does not incorporate the beloved—does not possess the good. Bringing forth in the beautiful itself is the only way to appropriate the Form without destroying it. Bringing forth in the beautiful itself is a way of appropriating the Form that recognizes the independence and intrinsic value of the Form. At the same time bringing forth in the beautiful itself produces something that partakes of the immortality of the Form because it appropriates its object without destroying it through possession or consumption. Now we can understand the transformation of *erōs* in the *Symposium*. Perhaps we can say that *erōs*, in seeking immortality, really seeks a good that it cannot possess or consume—a good that will not perish in being possessed or consumed; it seeks a good that will be with it always. Such a good is the beautiful itself. However, the price to pay for appropriating such a good is giving up possession and consummation as the end of life. Finally we arrive at a paradox. The only way to appease immortality-seeking *erōs* is to find an eternal good; but the only way to appropriate that good is to propagate it. Thus, bringing forth in the beautiful itself means producing virtue in the soul and in the city. In this way is *erōs* transformed into the chief motivation for acquiring virtue in the soul.[38]

If this reading of the role of immortality in the argument of the *Symposium* is correct, it corroborates the account in the *Republic* of the good itself as final cause. The two accounts are parallel to one another even if they are not exactly similar. In the *Republic* we said the philosophical ruler disseminates goodness in the final analysis because of admiration for the good itself. Thus her final justification for imitating the Form of justice rests with the good itself because the Form of justice, in virtue of its relation to the good itself, deserves or even requires dissemination. In the *Symposium*, imitation is not explicitly an issue; however, something similar is an issue—bringing forth in the beautiful. In our reading, bringing forth in the beautiful means propagating beauty under the inspiration of beauty. For the philosophical lover bringing forth in the beautiful means propagating beauty under the inspiration of the beautiful itself. For the true lover the purest love is the love of the beautiful itself; the purest motivation is love of the beautiful itself. When the philosophical lover is inspired by the beautiful itself, he propagates beauty because of his love for the beautiful itself. He is like the philosophical ruler in the *Republic*, who disseminates goodness because of admiration for the good itself. Of course, in the *Symposium*, Diotima does not say that the link between inspiration by the beautiful itself and the creation of beauty is imitation—although the beauty created will necessarily reflect the beautiful itself. However, the role of the Form in the account of the final cause is similar in both cases. Thus, neither the Form of goodness nor the Form of beauty is appropriated by being possessed and consumed. Nor are they appropriated by a loving gaze or even worship; these essentially passive attitudes are not modes of appropriation at all. In the naive view, on the other hand, propagation or dissemination is the way to appropriate the Form. Finally, it is the Form that motivates the philosophical ruler and the true lover to establish virtue in the soul and in the city. The need to propagate or disseminate the Form is based on love and admiration for the Form. The Form, then, finally explains the value of propagation or dissemination not by being a means to what we otherwise value but by being that which is most valuable.[39] When one grasps this entity, one grasps not a means to goodness and beauty but something unconditionally good and beautiful. The value of propagating or disseminating this kind of entity lies finally with the entity itself. It is because of this dependency that the propagating or disseminating is also valuable for what receives it. At last we see the third level of understanding of Plato's account of imitation. One seeks the perfection of the soul's function as the natural outcome of seeing the ideal in the Form. The lifelong performance of the virtuous soul is indeed striking, valuable in itself apart from whatever satisfaction it affords—although the satisfactions are not negligible. But finally it is valuable in itself because it is an embodiment of, a reflection of, the Form. It is love of the Form that provides self-perfection, justice in the city, and durable substitute immortality; until one conceives this love the latter cannot be achieved.

IV

What answer, at last, do we have for Callicles? At the end of the second chapter, our imaginary Callicles' objected that all of the talk about order and harmony is just talk about what is good for reason but not about what is good for the appetites. At the end of the third chapter, we tried to answer the objection by explicating the claim that reason, endowed with wisdom, knows what is good for the parts of the soul, including the appetites. We argued that knowledge of the Form of justice gives reason a grasp of the true contours of justice in the soul so that it will have insight into what is good for each part of the soul—just as someone sensitive to justice will be more likely to be careful in the assessment of others' needs and requirements. Still, beyond this general claim about the affect of knowledge of the Forms on the soul, we had nothing very specific to say. Now, however, Diotima's account of *erōs* addresses that deficiency; she has given an account of what is good for appetite—or at least for appetite as *erōs*.

The answer to Callicles is that proportionate order in the soul is not just reason arrogantly imposing its view point on the rest of the soul. It is not the soul imitating the Form of justice simply because reason finds such proportion and order attractive. In the *Symposium*, Plato is now saying that proportionate order allows *erōs* to achieve its true goal—its good. Fundamentally, *erōs* is love of the beautiful itself and its true accomplishment is bringing forth in the beautiful itself. First of all, only by moderating *erōs* can one hope to wean it away from unrestrained indulgence in pleasure toward love for the beautiful itself. Finally, however, proportionate order is the form that this accomplishment takes; proportionate order in the soul is what happens when *erōs* is accomplished and brings forth in the beautiful. It is not that such a life will not have the pleasures of replenishment. Rather it is that the goal of such a life will not be the pleasures of replenishment. The goal will be to achieve the embodiment of an ideal. The means will be to bring a certain order and harmony into the appetites. Not only will bringing order and harmony into the appetites allow one to pursue the ideal; it will embody the ideal. Embodying the ideal will satisfy *erōs* at its most profound level because, according to Diotima, *erōs* wants to bring forth in the beautiful. However, satisfaction at this most profound level means *erōs* must leave behind unrestrained possession and consummation.

What are the chances that Callicles will be convinced by this account? The answer depends on the answer to two other questions: (1) Will Callicles be convinced that there is an unconditioned good? and (2) Will Callicles be convinced that the aim of *erōs* is to bring forth in the beautiful? The answer to the first question depends on the success of Plato's metaphysical project in the middle dialogues. If Plato can fulfill his promises about the highest learning, Callicles could be convinced—if, of course, he has the soul of a philosopher and his soul has not yet been corrupted. Likewise, if he has the soul of a philosopher he might be able to follow the lead of a Diotima in discovering the lesser and the greater mysteries of *erōs;* in particular, he might be able to follow the argument that *erōs* is fulfilled by bringing forth in the beautiful. Suppose there is a good itself, a Form that is good from every point of view, unconditionally good. It is the distilled essence (like the essence of a scent or perfume) of goodness, unmixed, whose mixed and diluted traces are found in all the other goods of one's life. It is the full strength of the goodness only partially grasped in the pleasures of replenishment. It is not itself pleasure but what makes pleasure good. If one values pleasure one would value the good even more. One might not have to give up pleasure to grasp this other, greater good. It would, however, be rational to lead a life in which one had the pleasures of replenishment and the good itself. Now suppose that the only way to have the good itself always is the same as the way to have the beautiful itself—to propagate or disseminate it. This supposition is the key to the success of Plato's program; it expresses what Diotima means by bringing forth in the beautiful. What *erōs*, the leading appetite, really wants is to propagate beauty—and by extension here, goodness. However, disseminating goodness implies bringing order and harmony into one's appetites—bringing justice into one's soul and giving up the life of unrestrained pleasure. If the good itself were the essence of goodness, and if one's deepest desire were to appropriate that goodness, and if the only way to appropriate the good itself is by imitating the Form of justice, and if imitating the Form of justice implied restraining one's appetites, the rational person—if she grasped all of these conditions—would restrain her appetites.

Would the rational hedonist follow the argument and restrain his appetites? The answer, in Plato's way of looking at it, depends on whether he is more of a rationalist or a hedonist. If a hedonist identifies the good with pleasure, he would not agree that the essence of goodness is the good itself. He would not agree that the good itself is the full strength of the goodness only partially grasped in the pleasure of replenishment; if he did agree, he would not be a hedonist in this sense. While if he did not agree, he would not be a rationalist in Plato's sense. On the other hand, a weaker form of hedonism might be compatible with pursuing the good itself. Imagine a moderate hedonist for whom there are other goods besides pleasure but who requires that other goods entail pleasure—indeed, the higher the good the greater the pleasure. Since Socrates maintains that the philosophical life is the most pleasant life, then he should be able to convince the moderate hedonist (*Rep.* 587e). Indeed, it would be the usual sort of paradoxical argument which says that, if you want pleasure, you should give up pleasure as your goal and aim at something else; then you will have pleasure. At this point, we can see the importance of the reality-appearance motif. To get the hedonist beyond the conception of pleasure as the fundamental reality, Socrates must represent unrestrained pleasure as an illusory image of the good—one that substitutes for the real good. Of course, it is not a question only of representation; Socrates must be able to show the rational hedonist that there is a real goodness beyond the apparent good of pleasure. Then the life of unrestrained pleasure will appear to the hedonist as an illusion—a deceptive image; the life of unrestrained pleasure will appear as an image of the good that has substituted for real good. Indeed, Socrates should also be able to show the rational hedonist that, if one understands the real good, one can make images of the good that are not deceptive images but faithful reflections—even in the matter of pleasures. Presumably a faithful reflection of the good itself would be a life of moderate pleasures—balanced, proportionate, and harmonious.

Absent the completion of the project of Platonic metaphysics the prospects of convincing Callicles are, of course, somewhat dimmer. That is to say, without the knowledge needed to differentiate between appearance and reality, a completely convincing argument is not available. What we have in actuality are incomplete arguments and partial, fleeting insights. We have an extended argument, for instance, about the parts of the soul and their perfection in virtue; Socrates himself says that the account is incomplete (*Rep.* 504a–b). It needs completion in the highest learning about the Form of the good. It may, nevertheless, have some force in its incompleteness; it certainly gives a direction for the rest of the argument. In a similar fashion, Diotima's teaching about *erōs*—that it seeks completion in bringing forth in the beautiful, especially the beautiful itself—is a partial insight. Callicles could have that partial insight if he were to experience the incompleteness of *erōs* as consummation, if he were to see *erōs* as striving for something more than pleasure. Such an insight would take reflection and an adept guide but it seems possible even for Callicles. If he did get the point, he would not be the first nor the last to see the limitation of the life of *erōs* as consummation. Will the incomplete arguments and partial insights be enough to recruit Callicles to the craft of justice? The effects of incomplete arguments and partial insights are contingent, of course, on other matters less rational. Alcibiades, for instance, could escape Socrates' arguments by avoiding Socrates (*Sym.* 216b). However, we should not conclude that the fault lies with the incomplete arguments and partial insights. Alcibiades does not reject the arguments as fallacious or dismiss the insights as delusion. He feels the force of the life of virtue—especially in its appearance in the image of Socrates. His reaction to what Socrates says is well represented in his reaction to Socrates the person. Alcibiades feels the attraction of the life of virtue in the person of Socrates, whom he sees as a kind of image, even as he feels repelled by that life.

Lives whose goals are hidden and lofty ideals are always fascinating because they are both attractive and repellent. One is attracted by a life that has such a strong center, by a life lived with such clear and certain devotion. On the other hand, such a life is repellent because it seems to require the loss of so much that most of us associate with life. Fundamentally, such a life gives up pleasure—and ambition, for that matter—as goals. Of course, the life of devotion to a goal may also be pleasurable; but its pleasure is secondary and almost unintended. These idealists are happy but not because they seek pleasure as life's goal. Socrates is, of course, Plato's portrait of such a person. Nowhere is the portrait clearer than in the *Symposium*. Alcibiades, his beloved, paints it with inspired skill. By an ironic reversal, the physically beautiful Alcibiades came to see the beauty of the ugly Socrates' soul. Comparing him to one of the statues of the ugly satyr Marsyas, in which are concealed beautiful images of gods, Alcibiades delivers one of the most haunting eulogies of our tradition:

> I do not know if anyone has seen—when he is being earnest and open—those figures within him; but I did see them once and they seemed to me to be simply godlike and golden, altogether beau-

tiful and amazing; so that I had to do straightaway what
Socrates required. (216e–217a)

The beautiful images that Alcibiades saw were revealed to him
when he, the beloved, tried to become the lover. His ill-fated
attempt to seduce Socrates to physical consummation of *erōs*
failed, of course, because Socrates resisted his advances. Alcibiades himself, though abashed, admired Socrates' nature for its temperance and courage (*agamenon de tēn toutou physin te kai
sōphrosunēn kai andreian* [219d4–5]).

People like Socrates are not always sympathetic. In fact, much
about Socrates' portrait in the dialogues presents him as a difficult
and dangerous person just because he is so single minded. His
treatment of Alcibiades' attempt at seduction, for instance, is—as
Alcibiades says—arrogant. It is not clear how much he cares for
Alcibiades. However, there is also something attractive about
him—and it is his devotion to an ideal of life that makes him so.
Socrates is both attractive and repellent for the same reason, the
ideal that he pursues. These contradictory aspects of his life make
him fascinating. If he were always good or if he were always bad,
he would not be fascinating. It is the ingenious way in which Plato
has put the contradictory aspects together that makes the portrait
of Socrates itself so seductive. There is in the portrait something
that promises the contradiction will be resolved. If we study, read,
and imagine hard enough, we will at last see how the attractive
and the repellent are reconciled in some synthesis within Socrates'
personality. At this point we might suspect that, if there is to be a
reconciliation of the contradictory aspects, it is because the contradiction points beyond itself—just as Socrates' life, as portrayed
in the dialogues, points beyond itself. Socrates' life can be seen as
an image of the good itself; its value is in the fact that it is an imitation of the good itself. Like other images, it has conflicting
aspects; these aspects are reconciled when one sees that behind the
aspects there is a reality, the reality of the good itself. The philosophers who participate in the dialogues—both the characters in
the dialogues and the fascinated readers of the dialogues—are on
this side of the image. We are not yet true philosophers—those
who have grasped the Form of the good; we are at best those who
have hypothesized that there must be such an intrinsic good. Plato
has devised for us an image that is a most potent trace of evidence
for there being such a thing; the image of the good itself that Plato

creates in Socrates gives us an imaginative grasp of the reality that makes such a life possible.

V

Plato's craft of justice has two sources. One is the analogy between craft and virtue found in the early dialogues. In its fullest form in the *Euthydemus*, the analogy compares a craft like carpentry to the virtue of wisdom. Just as a carpenter both possesses tools and materials and knows how to use them, so the wise person knows how to use his physical and spiritual assets. The former produces, for example, a table; the latter achieves happiness. Of course, Socrates cannot tell his interlocutors what this knowledge of right use of assets is. The second source is the craft of ruling, which is presented in it fullest form in the *Gorgias* as a therapeutic craft—one that looks out after the soul in a way that is analogous to the way that medicine looks out after the body. The goal of the craft of ruling is to bring virtue into the souls of those it cares for—the souls of others. Virtue is identified with a harmony and balance of certain parts of the soul; while Socrates does not elaborate on the notion of parts of the soul, the usual bodily desires—such as those for food, drink, and sex—are the focus of his account of harmony in the soul. Socrates identifies unrestrained bodily desires as the source of disharmony and imbalance. Thus, the craft of ruling would have to restrain these desires in order to return harmony and balance to the soul. Judging is the craft that restrains the desires and it does so by punishment. Socrates does not go into much detail about the way punishment achieves restraint but he seems to present his own elenchus as a way of restraining desires by means of uncovering contradictions in beliefs.

The craft of justice combines these two crafts. Like ruling in the *Gorgias*, it is a therapeutic craft that cares for the soul by bringing balance and harmony—now of the soul's functions: reason, spirited part, and appetites; this harmony is the same as the arch virtue of justice. Moreover, it incorporates the virtue of wisdom from the *Euthydemus* because it is directed at one's self—one's own soul—not those of others; it also is the knowledge of the right use of one's assets, if assets are now taken to be the soul's functions. The craft of justice solves the problem of the *Euthyde-*

mus because it shows the happiness, which was the elusive goal of the craft of wisdom in that dialogue, to be—or to be largely—balance, proportion, and harmony in the soul. It solves the problem of the craft analogy, which we have called its "instrumentality": virtue cannot be a craft because craft is always instrumental to some other end and is not valuable in itself; but virtue is valuable in itself and is not instrumental to some other end. The answer is that the craft of justice not only brings balance and harmony into the soul—thus bringing happiness—it also is balance and harmony of functions. The craft of justice is not instrumental to happiness; it is—or is largely—happiness. Plato has accomplished this much by the end of *Republic* IV. At this point his focus shifts to justice in the city and the way to establish it there. The answer is to make philosophers rulers; philosophers are those who have the knowledge needed to establish and preserve justice because they know the Forms of justice, temperance, and beauty. In *Republic* VI, Socrates presents these Forms as paradigms that the philosopher, like a painter, copies. The philosopher imitates these paradigms in his own soul and in the city—bringing justice, temperance, and beauty into his soul and into the city because he must imitate what he admires. The Forms, then, fulfill two functions: they show what real justice, temperance, and beauty are and they inspire the philosopher to imitate them. In *Republic* VI, then, the craft of justice becomes an imitative craft, one informed by knowledge of the Forms.

If the craft of justice imitates the Forms, then what it produces will be images of justice, temperance, and beauty. What we learn in the *Republic* is that these images are also appearances of which the Forms of justice, temperance, and beauty are the reality. This association of image and appearance gives an important emphasis to the job of the philosophers. At the place in *Republic* V where Socrates introduces Forms, he does so by contrasting Forms with deceptive images. The latter are images of beauty that have come to substitute for the Form of beauty; the lovers of sights and sounds mistakenly think these images are real beauty. The philosopher can distinguish between the image and the reality. The philosophical ruler also can distinguish between images of justice and real justice; thus, the philosophical ruler can guard against the illusion that comes from identifying justice in the perceptual world with real justice. The philosophical ruler is aware of the dependent status of justice in the perceptual world—that our justice is a token of real justice but is not the real thing. This awareness gives him a surer grasp of the situation than that of someone who thinks that justice in the perceptual world is the same as real justice. Presumably, in creating images of justice, the philosophical ruler is also aware of the difference between even a good image of justice and real justice. This distinction between reality and appearance is important within one's own soul, as well, where illusion—what we have called "substitute deception"—is caused by the appetites when they are not disciplined. The Forms are a valuable guide in the moral life because they can expose the illusions generated by appetites and show them to be deceptive. Presumably, knowledge of the Forms of justice, temperance, and beauty can also guide the philosopher in making an image in her soul that is a faithful reflection of the balance and harmony found in the Forms.

So far our account is an elaboration of the notion of the craft of justice as imitative of Forms and what Socrates says about appearance, imitation, and illusion in the second half of the *Republic*. The account, thus far, has not addressed a fundamental issue: why do Forms have this authority in the life and practice of philosophers? Even if there is such a thing as the Form of justice, why should philosophers treat this Form as a paradigm for imitation? To find the answer to these questions we must leave Socrates' discussion of imitation and images in order to explore the subject of the greatest learning (*megiston mathēma*). The answer is that, in the *Republic*, the inspiration for imitating the Form of justice comes from knowledge of the Form of goodness, the subject of the greatest learning. Socrates introduces the Form of justice as a paradigm for imitation; he also introduces the Form of goodness as epistemically and ontologically prior to the other Forms, including justice. The implication for the craft of justice is that the Form of goodness is the final cause for imitation. It should follow that, once the philosopher grasps the Form of goodness, she realizes why she must imitate the Form of justice. The notion of the Form of goodness as final cause finds an analogue in the Form of beauty in the *Symposium*. In that dialogue, the account begins with Diotima's striking claim that the aim of *erōs* is to bring forth in the beautiful. Bringing forth in the beautiful makes propagation—and not mere possession—the aim of *erōs*; and in the case of the spiritual lovers it means propagating the beauty of virtue in the soul. Moreover, beauty is the final cause of bringing forth in the beautiful; it answers the question as to why they bring forth in beauty. Once the philosopher discovers the Form of beauty, bringing forth in the beautiful becomes bringing forth in the beautiful itself. The latter means propagating the beauty of virtue under the inspiration of the beautiful itself. The beautiful itself becomes the final cause for the philosophical lover's acquiring and instilling virtue. A similar motivation is at work in the craft of justice when it imitates the Form of justice. In the case of the city and the soul, the philosopher's producing images of justice—imitating the Form of justice—is the way of disseminating goodness. Finally, Plato's craft of justice is an imitative craft whose paradigm is the Form of justice and whose final cause is the Form of goodness. The philosopher who pursues this craft produces images of justice in her soul and in the city; these images are tokens of intrinsic goodness in a world that is innocent of authentic intrinsic goodness. Although these images are good for her soul and for the city, they are good because they are tokens of intrinsic goodness. The reason the philosopher imitates the Form of justice is to propagate these tokens both because they are valuable in themselves and because they are images of goodness, which is unconditionally good.

NOTES

1. See, for instance, J. Cooper, "Psychology of Justice," 153–154. J. C. B. Gosling, *Plato*, 55: "He [Plato] is liable to say first that a person only has knowledge if he can distinguish between good and bad; second, that if one can talk of a good (or bad) X, then X is something of which we can have knowledge; third, an ideal analogue of the first, real knowledge is of the good; fourth, an ideal analogue of the second, the good is responsible for knowledge."

2. Gerasimos Santas, *Plato and Freud: Two Theories of Love* (Oxford: Basil Blackwell, 1988), 45–46. C. D. C. Reeve (*Philosopher Kings*) also presents the Form of good as a system of Forms. Cf. 84–85. See also Nicholas P. White (*Companion*, 40–43), where the author presents an account of the relation between the good and the other Forms in which the good is responsible for the goodness of the other Forms. See also 175–181.

3. For a similar reading of the (unpromising candidate) Form of bed, cf. my "The Uniqueness Proof for Forms in Republic X," 140–141.

4. Richard Robinson, *Plato's Earlier Dialectic*, 2d ed. (Oxford: Clarendon Press, 1953), 126–133.

5. Cf. Cooper, "Psychology of Justice," 154: "First, pending a qualification to be entered directly, the good-itself is a good thing, over and above the good things of this world: over and above, that is both individual good things like particular persons and events, and such things as a quiet, studious life or a cool drink on a hot day which one might speak of as good things, though they are not individuals but classes of individuals. Unlike these other good things, however, it is not merely a good something-or-other, or good as such and such, or good for so and so or from such and such a point of view. To use Aristotelian language, one could say its essence is to be good; it is not, like every other good thing, essentially something else (a meal, a person) that, for one reason or another, happens to be good (is accidentally good). Its goodness is not, therefore diluted and compromised by being mingled with and made dependent on other features of things as is true of every other good. Thus its goodness is pure, as that of no other good is. Furthermore, it is the only perfect good."

6. Cf. H. W. B. Joseph, *Knowledge and the Good in Plato's Republic* (Oxford: Oxford University Press, 1948), 10: "That the good is knowledge, or *phronēsis*, Plato regarded also as an unsatisfactory doctrine; to know, or think, is good, but only if the object of your thought or knowledge is so."

7. Cf. David Hitchcock, "The Good in Plato's *Republic*," *Apeiron* 19 (1985), 71–72: "Likewise, the Form of the good will be a substantive determining criterion—pleasure, or wisdom, or some other property—such that by 'gazing at' it one can say that some particular thing is intrinsically good for a soul which possesses it because its possession by a soul is 'like' that property—that is, because the soul which possesses it will to that extent acquire the property in question. We should therefore take Plato's claims about the relation between the good and the being and truth of things known to be intended as holding true in virtue of what the Form of good is. If the good is pleasure, for example, then the claim that the good is the cause of the being of things known (including the Forms) would mean that pleasure is the cause of their being, that is, that, for a thing known (including any Form), to be is to be pleasant."

8. Cf. Cooper, "Psychology of Justice," 155: "He [the just person] knows the good-itself and therefore whatever he values he values strictly in the light of a comparison between that thing and the good. Whatever exhibits more fully and perfectly the sort of rational order that the form of the good possesses as its essence he values more highly than other things."

9. What Christine Korsgaard says in "Two Distinctions in Goodness" (*Philosophical Review* 92[1983]:169–195) illuminates this distinction between the goods of our experience and authentic intrinsic good. She points out that the distinction between intrinsic and extrinsic goods

is different from the distinction between things valued as ends and things valued in themselves. The former is the difference between things that have goodness in themselves and things that derive their goodness from something else. The latter is a difference between the ways in which things can be desired. The two distinctions are not the same and differentiating them allows us to see some important differences in moral theories. Claiming that Kant observes the difference between the two distinctions, she says that he allows there to be only one intrinsic good, the good will. Moreover, the good will is unconditioned good because it is good in all circumstances. "A thing is unconditionally good if it is good under any and all conditions, if it is good no matter what the context" (178). It is unconditional goodness that we were ascribing to the good itself when we called it "authentic intrinsic goodness"—being good no-matter-what. There are other good things that are not unconditioned goods; their goodness depends on other factors. Thus, in some circumstances they are good and in other circumstances they are not good.

10. Cf. Cooper, "Psychology of Justice," 157: "This is, I think, the direct consequence of the role played in Plato's theory by the form of the good. It is the ultimate object of pursuit, yet lies outside the world. Hence no worldly thing or activity can, because of its own properties, because of what it is, interest the just man; anything interests him only as a means of coming nearer to the good-itself."

11. See, for instance, S. H. Aronson, "The Happy Philosopher: a Counter-Example to Plato's Proof," *Journal of the History of Philosophy* 10(1973):383–398.

12. Cf. Joseph Beatty, "Why Should Plato's Philosopher Be Moral And, Hence, Rule?" *The Personalist* 57(1976):132–144; Thomas Brickhouse, "More on the Paradox of the Philosopher's Rule," *The Personalist* 59(1978):304–306, and "The Paradox of the Philosopher's Rule," *Apeiron* 15(1981):6–8.

13. Cf. R. Kraut, "Egoism, Love and Political Office in Plato," *Philosophical Review* 82(1973):330–344. "The philosopher, on his [Plato's] view not only wants the citizens of the polis to be virtuous, he also wants to help *create* virtue in those he loves. And if he receives no political assignment, this desire to create must remain unsatisfied" (339); R. Demos, "A Fallacy in Plato's Republic," in *Plato*, vol. 2, Vlastos, ed.: "To aim at the good is also to aim at the production of good things; thus for an individual to aim at justice means that he cares not only for justice in the abstract, but also that justice should be embodied in human beings in general. . . . The health of the soul includes, above all, the fulfillment of its reason: and the concern of reason is that the good should be exemplified everywhere" (55). Timothy Mahoney, "Do Plato's philosopher-rulers sacrifice self-interest to justice?" *Phronesis* 37(1992):265–282. "Thus, the preeminent aim of the ideal human life is to satisfy reason's

desire for the actualization of the good of everything and anything" (280).

14. Cf. D. Hall, "The *Republic* and the 'Limits of Politics'" *Political Theory* 5(1977):307: "Now, because theoretical and practical reason are the two aspects of the same power or faculty, we can generalize from reason's procedure in the theoretical mode to its operation in the practical. Because in the practical mode reason functions in the same way, it seeks naturally to reproduce platonic justice equally in any of the particular psychai that fall within the scope of its action. Just as in the theoretical mode reason's purpose of apprehending the forms is identical in relation to all the particulars of the sensible world, so, in the practical mode, its purpose of recreating the order of the forms is the same in all similar cases."

15. Cf. Nicholas P. White (*Companion*, 49). "I am inclined to believe, in fact, that Plato thought that the mere apprehension of the Good could move a person to action without any further step of any kind, and that, for him, to apprehend the Good fully along with a situation in which it might be exemplified simply is to have a desire overwhelming all others to see that instantiation take place" (cf. 53–54). Also "The desire to imitate the Forms, both in conducting oneself and in acting on other things, is not presented as derivative from some other desire, but seems to be regarded by Plato as itself basic . . ." (173), n.D. See also J. Cooper, "Psychology of Justice," 156: "But there is no cause for alarm, since the purer principles Plato himself has been espousing lead to the same conclusion. That these philosophers are just means, on Plato's account, that they know the good-itself and act always with a view to advancing rational order in the whole world." Cf. J. Cooper, "Plato's Theory of Human Motivation," *History of Philosophy Quarterly* 1(1984):8: "So what is inherent in reason is the desire for good, as such—not the desire for any particular good." G. Klosko, "The 'Rule' of Reason in Plato's Psychology," *History of Philosophy Quarterly* 5(1988):341–356, agrees with part of what Cooper says about the relation between reason and the good. What is significant for our account is his claim that in the souls of philosophers reason, in part at least, rules for the good. "According to Cooper's stronger view [one Klosko finds in Plato's psychology], health is desired, not because it satisfies other desires, but because it is perceived by reason to be good. Health is a condition in which the body fulfills its natural function, and Plato believes that such conditions are good. Thus the desire for health, as a particular manifestation of the desire for the good, is an inherent desire of reason (like cognitive desires)" (350–351). T. Irwin, *Plato's Moral Theory*, 237, 242, and 255–257, is also an advocate of the expressive thesis. Cf. Charles Kahn, "Plato's Theory of Desire," *Review of Metaphysics* 41(1987):84: "This is the second controversial thesis I shall defend here:

that reason in the *Republic* is not only essentially desire but essentially desire for the good. . . . Hence the goal of rational desire, of reason as such, is neither the good of the individual alone (as it is sometimes said to be, on egoistic readings of Plato) nor the good of the community alone, but the good in every case, the good in general or the Good as such." Finally, Gregory Zeigler, "Plato's *Gorgias* and Psychological Hedonism," *Personalist* 60(1979):123–133, makes an important distinction between egoism and altruism; Socrates' theory is neither. "Socrates' theory may best be captured by reference to the Greek word for good, agathos. He claims that all men have as their object of wish, when they act, the good, impersonally conceived. Thus, I wish to call him a psychological agathist" (125).

16. Richard Kraut maintains a thesis close to the one we maintain. "Return to the Cave: *Republic* 519–521," *Proceedings of the Boston Area Colloquium in Ancient Philosophy* 7(1991); "The Defense of Justice in Plato's *Republic*," *The Cambridge Companion to Plato* (Richard Kraut, ed. Cambridge: Cambridge University Press, 1992). To Kraut, love of the Form of good and imitating the Form go together. "The crux of my view is that the Forms constitute the supreme good because they exhibit the highest kind of order, and that human beings can possess this supreme good by entering into a certain kind of relationship with the Forms, a relationship that involves not merely understanding these abstract objects but loving and imitating them as well" ("Return to the Cave," 51–52, n.15). This view is more fully developed in "The Defense of Justice in Plato's Republic." "What he [Plato] must hold is that one's highest good is not always served by purely contemplating the Forms; rather, one's highest good is to establish and maintain a certain imitative relationship with Forms, a relationship that is strained or ruptured when one fails to do one's fair share in a just community" (328–329). Kraut differs from the commentators mentioned in the previous note in the emphasis he puts on imitation of Forms.

17. Ross says that the outer sphere's love of god implies the outer sphere "desires a life as like as possible to that of its moving principle." See W.D. Ross, *Aristotle* (London: Methuen, 1949), 181–182; see also J. L. Ackrill, *Aristotle the Philosopher* (Oxford: The Clarendon Press, 1981), 129 and 133. Its moving principle is god, who eternally contemplates thought. Unable to reproduce the eternal activity of contemplation, the sphere does the next best physical thing—eternal motion in a circle. Recently, in "Que Fait Le Premier Moteur D'Aristote" (*Revue Philosophique de France et de l'Etranger* 183 [1993]), Sarah Broadie objected to this interpretation; she says that the traditional interpretation multiplies entities not mentioned in the text. These are: a soul for the outer sphere, two objects of desire, two noetic activities for the soul, and two senses of final cause (385). It is not necessary for our purposes to

decide whether the traditionalists or Broadie is right, of course, because our interpretation simply uses the distinction between senses of final cause—a distinction Aristotle clearly makes. Whether this distinction explains eternal motion in the outer sphere is not integral to using the distinction. However, one might argue that Broadie's objections could apply to our reading of the distinction, *mutatis mutandis*. Broadie construes the distinction between the two senses of final cause, in the traditional reading, to be *end of action* and *beneficiary of action*. She objects that the distinction between the two senses of final cause, when understood in the traditional reading, does violence to the usual meaning of 'end'. She says that 'end' (what we have called the "object of desire") usually means something to be achieved. However, the Prime Mover, as end of desire, is not achieved in any way. Thus, she says, final cause as end of desire, in this traditional reading, really means exemplary cause (382). It is hard to understand why Broadie is objecting to this reading of final cause as exemplary cause. It hardly seems unusual to think of love for something being expressed by imitation; nor is it strange to say that the object of love is that for the sake of which one imitates. 'End', in this context, would refer to something whose value is not confered by being desired; one does not achieve such a value but merely recogizes it. Like an act of homage, imitation is a way of recognizing the value. This act of recognizing the value can be expressed by saying that this value is that for the sake of which one undertakes imitation.

18. Korsgaard, "Two Distinctions," 181.

19. Korsgaard, "Two Distinctions," 179.

20. Korsgaard, "Two Distinctions," 184.

21. This position touches on the issue of egoism in Plato's moral philosophy. Plato is an egoist in some sense because he holds that one's own happiness is the goal of life (*Sym.* 205a). However, if happiness is imitating the good itself because it is the good itself, then the egoism of happiness is somewhat complicated. Happiness takes on the paradoxical aspect of all idealist undertakings. Happiness is the result, but not the goal, of idealist lives. If one wants to be happy one should not aim at happiness. In "Two Conceptions of Happiness," *Philosophical Review* 88(1979):167–197), Richard Kraut distinguishes our contemporary notion of happiness—which he calls "subjective"—with Aristotle's—which he calls "objective." The former is subjective because it depends on the achievement (and awareness of achievement) of goals that an individual sets for himself (173 and 180). The latter is objectivist because it depends on the achievement (and awareness of achievement) of an ideal standard (181). In Aristotle's case the ideal would be specified by "certain deep seated facts of human nature and social organization . . ." (190). (It is the inability of objectivism to make such a specification that makes it impractical, according to Kraut [190–191].) We might adapt

Kraut's distinction in explicating Plato's idealism. Plato too would say that happiness is the achievement of an ideal. However, happiness is not the ideal; it is what happens when one achieves the ideal—for example, by successfully imitating the good itself—and is aware of doing so. Thus, the goal of life is to achieve the ideal.

22. As well, if the Form of goodness is the final cause of imitation, we can understand the full answer to the problem of the craft analogy. In chapter 2, we said that crafts could be used to do harm because, although crafts seek the welfare of their objects, craftsmen can misuse the crafts. There is a sense in which crafts are instrumental; they can be misused to seek some other end than the end of the craft. However, we said that the craft analogy was defensible if there is at least one craft that is not instrumental, cannot be misused. This was the ruling craft, which used what it produced. Because the ruling craft was the knowledge of good and evil the implication seemed to be that it would always pursue the good and use what it produced so that it would serve the good. Now we can see that the craft of imitating the just itself because of its relation to the good itself is this ruling craft. Imitating the just itself because of its relation to the good itself is not instrumental; it pursues the highest good as an end in itself. It seeks to disseminate the good itself because it is the good itself and because doing so is good for what receives the goodness.

23. Although the following discussion rests on the assumption that the *Symposium* has a fuller treatment of the expressive facet of the philosopher, it makes no assumption about the relative dates of the *Republic* and the *Symposium*.

24. A. W. Price, *Love and Friendship in Plato and Aristotle* (Oxford: Clarendon Press, 1989), 16, uses Kenneth Dover's distinction here. "The kalon is what presents itself appealingly (though not only to the senses); the agathon is good for someone in some way (though not only instrumentally); the kalon draws us and the agathon helps us. To spell out their equivalence: whatever attracts us also benefits us (if only in its contemplation); while, so long as our judgment colours the way things strike us, whatever serves us well is likely to create in us a favourable impression." Santas holds that this shift is actually a change of focus from a specific account of *erōs* to a general account of love for anything; such love is always for the good. The specific account applies to sexual love, where beauty is the specific kind of good object. Gerasimos Santas, *Plato and Freud: Two Theories of Love* (Oxford: Basil Blackwell, 1988), 32–33. David Halperin, "Platonic Eros and What Men Call Love," *Ancient Philosophy* 5(1985):180, sees in this move a distinction between what he calls the "object of erotic desires"—that is, the beautiful—and the aim of erotic desire—that is, possession of the good; we exploit this distinction subsequently.

25. Santas holds that this shift is a shift back to specific account of *erōs*, that is, sexual love (34). Of course, according to Halperin, the shift in the conversation would simply be a way of developing the aim of *erōs*—that is, how the lover can come to possess the good always. This ingenious suggestion, however, makes the reintroduction of beauty into the conversation a little puzzling since, according to Halperin, the aim of *erōs* is the good. Cf. R. G. Bury, *The Symposium of Plato*, 2d ed. (Cambridge: Cambridge University Press, 1969), 109.

26. Cf. William S. Cobb, translated with introduction and commentaries, *The Symposium and the Phaedrus* (Albany: State University of New York Press, 1993), 76.

27. This distinction, or its forerunner, was introduced by Martin Warner, "Love, Self and Plato's *Symposium*," *Philosophical Quarterly* 29(1979):337–338. However, Price, *Love and Friendship*, exploits the distinction in the way represented in this paragraph. Cf. 25 and 30–31: "The immortality that Plato proves elsewhere is a property of the soul as subject; the quasi-immortality that Diotima offers attaches to lives individuated independently of subjects."

28. Cf. Price, *Love and Friendship*, 34.

29. Halperin, "Platonic Eros," 179.

30. Halperin, "Platonic Eros," 179.

31. Halperin, "Platonic Eros,"181.

32. For two thorough analyses of this ascent of the ladder of love, see: J. M. E. Moravcsik, "Reason and Eros in the 'Ascent'-Passage of the *Symposium*," in *Essays in Ancient Greek Philosophy*, John P. Anton and George L. Kustas, eds. (Albany: State University of New York Press, 1972), 285–302, and Price, *Love and Friendship*, 38–42.

33. Cf. Cobb, *Symposium and Phaedrus*, 75. Talking about the concept of bringing forth in beauty, he says, "The basic metaphor, then, is that of giving birth in a beautiful manner, which can imply that the surroundings and product of the birth, as well as the event itself, are beautiful." Also Price, *Love and Friendship*, 52. "Yet there is a great difference between the role of the boy's beauty in 209c, and that of the sequence of beauties in 210: at each stage of the ascent the lover owes to the beauty in which he generates not only release from pregnancy, but the very character of his offspring; beauty has become less midwife than only begetter." G. R. F. Ferrari, "Platonic Love," *The Cambridge Companion to Plato* (Cambridge: Cambridge University Press, 1992), 255, referring to the passage at 209c: "This is the first time that what issues from the act of 'begetting in the beautiful' has itself been described as beautiful, and it reveals something that will be crucially important to love's Greater Mysteries: namely, that beauty can belong to the product as well as to the instrument of specific love."

34. An analogous position is found in Iris Murdoch's *The Sovereignty of Good* (London: Routledge and Kegan Paul, 1985). To Murdoch, the moral life is a struggle to overcome one's own selfishness and self-serving illusions. The aim of the moral life, then, is to see the other not as an instrument of one's own selfish aims but to achieve what she calls "a just and loving gaze directed upon an individual reality" (34). She sees the idea of the good in Book VII of the Republic as vital in this moral struggle. "Good is the focus of attention when an intent to be virtuous co-exists (as perhaps it almost always does) with some unclarity of vision" (70).

What is suggestive in this account is what she says about the roles of goodness and beauty in the struggle to break through one's selfish illusion. Goodness and beauty both resist the selfish urge to possess and destroy. Instead of the modern notion that will creates goodness, she says that we must retain Plato's idea of the good

> as a central point of reflection . . . Good, *not will, is transcendent*. Will is the natural energy of the psyche that is sometimes employable for a worthy purpose. Good seems to us something necessary because the realism (ability to perceive reality) required for goodness is a kind of intellectual ability to perceive what is true, which is automatically at the same time a suppression of self (66).

Thus goodness has a role in resisting selfishness. Murdoch seems to be hinting at an explanation for this resistance when she says that "The Good has nothing to do with purpose, indeed it excludes the idea of purpose. . . . The only genuine way to be good is to be good 'for nothing' . . ." (71 and 92). If the good excludes purpose, then to the selfish it is good for nothing. Paradoxically, it is this feature of goodness that can draw one out of selfish illusion. Although the good is the center of reflection in the moral life, "it cannot be experienced or represented or defined." Rather, it is beauty that is the "visible and accessible aspect of the Good" (70). Murdoch presents a striking case for the claim that beauty, fully understood, is fully capable of resisting selfishness.

> Art, and by "art" from now on I mean good art, not fantasy art, affords us a pure delight in the independent existence of what is excellent. Both in its genesis and its enjoyment it is a thing totally opposed to selfish obsession (85–86).

What she means by "enjoyment" is presumably a familiar experience. One's perception of beauty in the performance of a dancer, for instance, has the quality of unselfishness. Without reference to one's own interests or needs, one can simply rejoice in the performance of the other for what it is, for the way that it exhibits an ideal too little seen in our everyday world. There is an undeniable transcendence of self in the recognition of something that we all love and admire; part of this experience is the sense of leaving ourselves behind in this recognition. As for the genesis of art, the artist delights in the independent existence of what is excellent in a somewhat different way. In the case of the artist, presumably the independent existence is what she produces. In making it independent, the artist transcends her own selfish aims. In making it excellent, she is aiming at an ideal outside of herself. She is aiming towards that same ideal perceived by the one who enjoys the dance performance. This aim is also experienced in what we sometimes call "love of one's craft"—the carpenter who admires the excellence of the cabinet, whether he made it or not.

35. Cf. Peter Vernezze, "The Philosopher's Interest," *Ancient Philosophy* 12(1992):342. "Just as a parent leaves behind a child who instantiates his physical traits and will pass these on through time, we should think of the propagators at the level of the soul as leaving behind them a product that will pass on the virtue of the agent through time: by inspiring great and noble deeds, the poems of Homer and the laws of Solon will be responsible for bringing forth acts of virtue long after the death of their creators. Similarly, the pedagogical lover instantiates virtue in his beloved, who will in turn educate another, and so on down the line, thus assuring that his virtue survives death."

36. Martha Nussbaum, *Fragility of Goodness*, claims that the lover of the Form leaves human love behind. "Instead of flesh and all that mortal rubbish, an immortal object must, and therefore can, be found. Instead of painful yearning for a single body and spirit, a blissful contemplative completeness" (183). This severe assessment of Diotima's speech leaves out of consideration the way in which bringing forth in beauty is pervasive to the account of *erōs*—and thus the way the lover seeks to instill virtue in the soul of the beloved. In reality, *erōs* begins to look like benevolence, as the lover, eschewing sexual intercourse, seeks the spiritual improvement of his beloved. Inspired by the Form of beauty, the lover wishes to replicate the Form in the soul of the beloved. In this way, the lover achieves a kind of passionate detachment not unlike the passionate detachment of the artist. The lover who wishes nothing more for the beloved than the most beautiful of souls may not be Nussbaum's passionate lover, who aims "to achieve a more complete understanding of this particular complex portion of the world" (190), but neither does such a lover seem inhuman.

37. Cf. Kraut, "The Defense of Justice in Plato's *Republic*," *The Cambridge Companion to Plato*, Richard Kraut, ed. (Cambridge: Cambridge University Press, 1992), 321: "And so the mere fact that a Form cannot be possessed (that is, owned) gives us no reason to reject Plato's idea that if one bears a certain relationship to Forms—a relationship that involves both emotional attachment and intellectual understanding—then one's life becomes more worthwhile precisely because one is connected in this way with such valuable objects. In fact, there are similari-

ties between the way in which persons can enter our lives and improve them and the way in which Plato thinks we should be related to the Forms. We can easily understand someone who says that one of the great privileges of his life is to have known a certain eminent and inspiring person."

38. Indeed, in the *Phaedrus* the virtue of the immortal lovers is again associated with harmony and orderliness, a kind of beauty of the soul that is familiar to us from the *Republic*. However, while these lovers recollect the Form of beauty and while they acquire virtue by imitation, the imitation is of the gods. Lover and beloved have natures like the god they followed in the procession in the upper world; for example, those who followed Zeus have Zeus-like natures, philosophical and lordly (252c–e). The lover honors and imitates (*timōn te kai mimoumenos* [252d2]) that god. Somehow, in associating with the beloved, the lover gazes upon his god, grasps it by way of memory, and takes on the god's character and ways of acting (253a). Finally, by imitating his god, the lover helps the beloved to take on the ways of acting and form of the god (253b).

39. This interpretation of the role of the good contrasts instructively with the interpretation of C. D. C. Reeve (*Philosopher King*.) For him the good is pleasure; reason is instrumental. While Reeve denies both of these claims his denials really amount only to qualifications of them. "The good is the structure . . . within which the pleasure of knowing the truth is reliably made available to those who find it most pleasant . . ." (154). However, Reeve never tells us how the structure is good in itself; it is clearly an instrumental good—good as a means to rational pleasure. Again, comparing Hume favorably with Plato, Reeve says that Plato is, nevertheless, different in that he includes in reason "conative and cognitive elements" (168). That is, reason has its own desire; satisfying rational desire by discovering the truth provides the pleasure of discovering the truth. So the cognitive part of reason serves this conative part— finally, reason—or its cognitive part—is instrumental.

BIBLIOGRAPY

Ackrill, J. L. *Aristotle the Philosopher.* Oxford: Clarendon, 1981.

Allen, R. E. "The Argument from Opposites from *Republic* V." In *Essays in Ancient Greek Philosophy.* John P. Anton and George L. Kustas, eds. Albany: State University of New York Press, 1972.

———. "Participation and Predication in Plato's Middle Dialogues." In *Studies in Plato's Metaphysics.* R. E. Allen, ed. London: Routledge and Kegan Paul, 1965.

Annas, Julia. *An Introduction to Plato's Republic.* Oxford: Clarendon, 1981.

Anton, John. "Dialectic and Health in Plato's *Gorgias*: Presuppositions and Implications." *Ancient Philosophy* 1(1980):49–60.

Aronson, S. H. "The Happy Philosopher: a Counter-Example to Plato's Proof." *Journal of the History of Philosophy* 10(1973):383–398.

Bambrough, J. R. "Plato's Political Analogies." In *Plato: A Collection of Critical Essays,* vol. 2. Gregory Vlastos, ed. Garden City: Anchor, 1971.

Beatty, Joseph. "Why Should Plato's Philosopher Be Moral and, Hence, Rule?" *The Personalist* 57(1976):132–144.

Belfiore, Elizabeth. "Plato's Greatest Accusation Against Poetry." In *New Essays on Plato.* Francis Jeffry Pelletier and John King-Farlow, eds. Guelph: Canadian Association for Publishing in Philosophy, 1983.

Benson, Hugh. "The Problem of Elenchus Reconsidered." *Ancient Philosophy* 7(1987):67–85.

Brickhouse, Thomas. "More on the Paradox of the Philosopher's Rule." *The Personalist* 59(1978):304–306.

———. "The Paradox of the Philosopher's Rule." *Apeiron* 15(1981):1–9.

Brickhouse, Thomas and Nicholas D. Smith. *Socrates On Trial.* Princeton: Princeton Unversity Press, 1989.

———."Vlastos on the Elenchus." *Oxford Studies in Ancient Philosophy,* vol. 2. Julias Annas, ed. Oxford: Clarendon, 1984.

Broadie, Sarah. "Que Fait Le Premier Moteur D'Aristote." *Revue Philosophique de France et de l'Etranger* 183 (1993): 375–411.

Broadie, Sarah Waterlow. "The Good of Others in Plato's *Republic.*" *Proceedings of the Aristotelian Society* 73(1972–73):19–36.

Bury, R. G. *The Symposium of Plato.* 2d ed. Cambridge: Cambridge University Press, 1969.

Chance, Thomas H. *Plato's Euthydemus.* Berkeley: University of California Press, 1992.

Cobb, William. S., ed. and trans. *The Symposium and the Phaedrus.* Albany: State University of New York Press, 1993.

Cooper, J. "Plato's Theory of Human Motivation." *History of Philosophy Quarterly* 1(1984):3–22.

————."The Psychology of Justice in Plato." *American Philosophical Quarterly* 14(1977):151–157.

Crombie, I. M. *An Examination of Plato's Doctrines,* vol. 1. London: Routledge and Kegan Paul, 1962.

Cross, R. C., and A. D. Woozley. *Plato's Republic.* London: Macmillan, 1964.

Demos, R. "A Fallacy in Plato's *Republic.*" In *Plato,* vol. 2. Gregory Vlastos, ed.

Dodds, E. R. *Plato: Gorgias.* Oxford: Clarendon, 1959.

Ferrari, G. R. F. "Platonic Love." In *The Cambridge Companion to Plato.* Richard Kraut, ed. Cambridge: Cambridge University Press, 1992.

Fine, Gail. "Knowledge and Belief in *Republic* V." *Archiv für Geschichte der Philosophie.* 60(1978):121–139.

Foster, M. B. "A Mistake of Plato's in the *Republic.*" *Mind* 46(1937):386–393.

————. "A Mistake of Plato's in the *Republic*: A Rejoinder to Mr. Mabbott." *Mind* 47(1938):226–232.

Gifford, E. H., ed. *Plato's Euthydemus.* New York: Arno Press, 1973.

Gosling, J. C. B. *Plato.* London: Routledge and Kegan Paul, 1973.

————. "Reply to White." *Canadian Journal of Philosophy* 7(1977):307–314.

————. "Ta Polla Kala." *Phronesis* 5(1960):116–128.

Gosling, J. C. B., and C. C. W. Taylor. *The Greeks on Pleasure.* London: Clarendon, 1982.

Gould, J. *The Development of Plato's Ethics.* Cambridge: Cambridge University Press, 1955.

Gulley, Norman. *The Philosophy of Socrates.* London: Macmillan, 1968.

Hall, D. "The *Republic* and the 'Limits of Politics.'" *Political Theory* 5(1977):293–313.

Halperin, David. "Platonic Eros and What Men Call Love." *Ancient Philosophy* 5(1985):161–204.

Hawtrey, R. S. W. *Commentary on Plato's Euthydemus.* Philadelphia: American Philosophical Society, 1981.

Hitchcock, David. "The Good in Plato's *Republic.*" *Apeiron* 19(1985):65–92.

Hutchinson, D. S. "Doctrines of the Mean and the Debate Concerning Skills in Fourth-Century Medicine, Rhetoric and Ethics." *Apeiron* 21(1988): 7–52.

Irwin, T. *Plato's Moral Theory.* Oxford: Clarendon, 1977.

———. *Plato: Gorgias.* Oxford: Clarendon, 1979.

Joseph, H. W. B. *Knowledge and the Good in Plato's Republic.* Oxford: Oxford University Press, 1948.

Kahn, Charles. "Drama and Dialectic in Plato's *Gorgias.*" *Oxford Studies in Ancient Philosophy*, vol. 1. Julia Annas, ed. Oxford: Clarendon, 1983. 75–121.

———. "The Meaning of 'Justice' and the Theory of Forms." *Journal of Philosophy* 69(1972):567–579.

———. "Plato's Theory of Desire." *Review of Metaphysics* 41(1987):77–103.

Kelly, Jack. "Virtue and Pleasure." *Mind* 82(1973):401–408.

Kenny, Anthony. "Mental Health in Plato's *Republic.*" *Proceedings of the British Academy* 55(1969):229–253.

Klosko, George. "The 'Rule' of Reason in Plato's Psychology." *History of Philosophy Quarterly* 5(1988):341–356.

———. "The Technical Conception of Virtue." *Journal of the History of Philosophy* 19(1981):95–102.

Korsgaard, Christine. "Two Distinctions in Goodness." *Philosophical Review* 92(1983):169–195.

Kraut, Richard J. R. "Comments on Gregory Vlastos 'The Socratic Elenchus.'" In *Oxford Studies in Ancient Philosophy,* vol. 1. Julia Annas, ed. Oxford: Clarendon, 1983.

———. "The Defense of Justice in Plato's *Republic.*" *The Cambridge Companion to Plato.* Richard Kraut, ed. Cambridge: Cambridge University Press, 1992.

———. Egoism , Love and Political Office in Plato." *Philosophical Review* 82(1973):330–344.

——— "Reason and Justice in Plato's Republic." *Exegesis and Argument.* Lee, Mourelatos and Rorty, eds. Assen: Van Gorcum, 1973.

———. "Return to the Cave: *Republic* 519–521." *Proceedings of the Boston Area Colloqium in Ancient Philosophy* 7(1991): 43–61

———. "Two Conceptions of Happiness." *Philosophical Review* 88(1979):167–197.

Lesses, Glenn. "Weakness, Reasons, and the Divided Soul in Plato's *Republic.*" *History of Philosophy Quarterly* 4(1987):147–161.

Lycos, Kimon. *Plato on Justice and Power.* Albany: State University of New York Press, 1987.

Lyons, J. *Structural Semantics.* Oxford: Basil Blackwell, 1963.

Mabbott, J. D. "Is Plato's *Republic* Utilitarian?" *Mind* 46(1937):468–474.

———. " Is Plato's *Republic* Utilitarian?" In *Plato: A Collection of Critical Essays,* vol. 2. G. Vlastos, ed.

Mackenzie, Mary Margaret. *Plato on Punishment.* Berkeley: University of California Press, 1981.

Mahoney, Timothy. "Do Plato's philosopher-rulers sacrifice self-interest to justice?" *Phronesis* 37(1992):265–282.

McKim, Richard. "Shame and Truth in Plato's *Gorgias.*" In *Platonic Writings/Platonic Readings.* Charles L. Griswold, ed. London: Routledge, 1988.

McPherran, Mark. "Socratic Reason and Socratic Revelation." *Journal of the History of Philosophy* 29(1991):345–373.

McTighe, Kevin. "Socrates on Desire for the Good and the Involuntariness of Wrongdoing: *Gorgias* 466a–468e." *Phronesis* 29(1984):193–236.

Moravcsik, J. M. E. "Reason and Eros in the 'Ascent' Passage of the *Symposium.*" In *Essays in Ancient Greek Philosophy.* John P. Anton and George L. Kustas, eds. Albany: State University of New York Press, 1972.

Murdoch, Iris. *The Sovereignty of Good.* London: Routledge and Kegan Paul, 1985.

Nehamas, Alexander. "Plato on Imitation and Poetry in *Republic* X." In *Plato on Beauty, Wisdom, and the Arts.* Julius Moravcsik and Philip Temko, eds. Totawa: Rowan and Littlefield, 1982.

———, "Plato on the Imperfection of the Sensible World." *American Philosophical Quarterly* 12(1975):105–117.

Nicholson, P. P. "Unraveling Thrasymachus' Argument in the *Republic.*" *Phronesis* 19:1974:210–232.

Nussbaum, Martha. *The Fragility of Goodness.* Cambridge: Cambridge University Press, 1986.

O'Brien, Michael J. *The Socratic Paradoxes and the Greek Mind.* Chapel Hill: University of North Carolina Press, 1967.

O'Neil, Basil. "The Struggle for the Soul of Thrasymachus." *Ancient Philosophy* 8(1988):167–185.

Parry, Richard. "The Agent's Knowledge of His Action." *The Personalist* 55(1974):44–52.

———. "The Uniqueness Proof for Forms in *Republic* X." *Journal of the History of Philosophy* 23(1985):133–150

Patterson, Richard. *Image and Reality in Plato's Metaphysics.* Indianapolis: Hackett, 1985.

———. "Plato on Philosophic Character." *Journal of the History of Philosophy* 25(1987):325–350.

Penner, T. "Plato and Davidson: Parts of the Soul and Weakness of the Will." *Canadian Journal of Philosophy* [Supplementary Volume] 16(1990):35–74.

———. "Thought and Desire in Plato." *Plato: A Collection of Critical Essays*, vol. 2. Gregory Vlastos, ed. Garden City: Anchor, 1971.

———. "Socrates on Virtue and Motivation." In *Argument and Exegesis*. Lee, Mourelatos, and Rorty, eds. Assen: Van Gorcum, 1973.

Preus, Anthony. "Socratic Psychotherapy." *University of Dayton Review* 16.1(1982–83):15–23.

Price, A. W. *Love and Friendship in Plato and Aristotle*. Oxford: Clarendon, 1989.

Reeve, C. D. C. *Philosopher Kings*. Princeton: Princeton University Press, 1979.

———. *Socrates in the Apology*. Indianapolis: Hackett, 1989.

Reshotko, Naomi. "The Socratic Theory of Motivation." *Apeiron* 25(1992):145–170.

Robinson, Richard. *Plato's Earlier Dialectic*. 2d ed. Oxford: Clarendon, 1953.

———."Plato's Separation of Reason and Desire." *Phronesis* 16(1971):38–48.

Roochnik, David L. "Socrates' Use of the Techne-Analogy." *Essays on the Philosophy of Socrates*. Hugh H. Benson, ed. New York: Oxford. 1992.

———. "The Serious Play of Plato's *Euthydemus*." *Interpretation* 18(1990–91):211–232.

Ross, W. D. *Aristotle*. London: Methuen, 1949.

Ryle, Gilbert. *Concept of Mind*. New York: Barnes and Noble, 1949.

Sachs, David. "A Fallacy in Plato's *Republic*." *Plato: A Collection of Critical Essays*, vol. 2. Gregory Vlastos, ed. Garden City: Doubleday, 1971.

Santas, Gerasimos. *Plato and Freud: Two Theories of Love*. Oxford: Basil Blackwell, 1988.

———. *Socrates: Philosophy in Plato's Early Dialogues*. London: Routledge and Kegan Paul, 1979.

Schaerer, René. *EPISTHMH et TEXNH*. Macon: Protat Frère, 1930.

Schiller, Jerome. "Just Men and Just Acts in Plato's *Republic*." *Journal of the History of Philosophy* 6(1968):6–10.

Sharvy, Richard. "Plato's Causal Logic and the Third Man Argument." *Nous* 20(1986):507–530.

Sparshott, F. "An Argument for Thrasymachus." *Apeiron* 21(1988):55–67.

Sprague, Rosamond Kent. *Plato's Philosopher-King*. Columbia: University of South Carolina Press, 1976.

———. *Plato's Use of Fallacy*. New York: Barnes and Noble, 1962.

Stalley, R. F. "Mental Health and Individual Responsiblity in Plato's *Republic.*" *Journal of Value Inquiry* 15(1981):109–124.

———. "Plato's Arguments for the Division of the Reasoning and Appetitive Elements Within the Soul." *Phronesis* 20(1975):110–128.

Stewart, M. A. "Plato's Desiring." *Aristotelian Society* [Supplementary Volume] 51(1977):21–44.

Tiles, J. E. "The Combat of Passion and Reason." *Philosophy* 52(1977):321–330.

———. "*Technē* and Moral Expertise." *Philosophy* 59(1984):321–330.

Urmson, J. O. "Aristotle on Pleasure." *Aristotle: A Collection of Critical Essays.* J. M. E. Moravcsik, ed. Garden City: Anchor, 1967.

Vlastos, Gregory. "Justice and Happiness in the *Republic.*" *Plato: A Collection of Critical Essays,* vol. 2. Gregory Vlastos, ed. Garden City: Doubleday, 1971.

———. *Platonic Studies.* Princeton: Princeton University Press, 1973.

———. *Socrates: Ironist and Moral Philosopher.* Ithaca: Cornell University Press, 1991.

———. "The Socratic Elenchus." In *Oxford Studies in Ancient Philosophy,* vol. 1. Julia Annas, ed. Oxford: Clarendon, 1983, 29–58.

Vlastos, Gregory, ed. *Plato's Protagoras.* New York: Bobbs Merrill, 1956.

Verdenius, W. J. *Mimesis.* Leiden: E. J. Brill, 1972.

Vernezze, Peter. "The Philosopher's Interest." *Ancient Philosophy* 12(1992):331–349.

Warner, Martin. "Love, Self and Plato's *Symposium.*" *Philosophical Quarterly* 29(1979):329–339.

White, F. C. "Justice and the Good of Others in Plato's *Republic.*" *History of Philosophy Quarterly* 5(1988):395–410.

———. "The 'Many' in *Republic* 475a–480a." *Canadian Journal of Philosophy* 7(1977):291–306.

White, Nicholas P. *A Companion to Plato's Republic.* Indianapolis: Hackett, 1979.

Woodruff, Paul. "Plato's Early Theory of Knowledge." *Essays on the Philosophy of Socrates.* Hugh H. Benson, ed. New York: Oxford University Press, 1992.

Zeigler, Gregory. "Plato's *Gorgias* and Psychological Hedonism." *The Personalist* 60(1979):123–133.

Zeyl, Donald."Socrates and Hedonism." *Phronesis* 25(1980):250–269.

———. "Socratic Virtue and Happiness." *Archiv für Geschichte der Philosophie* 64(1982):225–238.

INDEX OF
AUTHORS AND SUBJECTS

INDEX LOCORUM

DATE DUE

			Printed in USA